Start Your Own

TRAVEL BUSINESS AND MORE

Additional titles in *Entrepreneur's* Startup Series

Start Your Own

Arts and Crafts Business

Automobile Detailing Business

Bar and Club

Bed and Breakfast

Blogging Business

Business of eBay

Business Support Service

Car Wash

Child-Care Service

Cleaning Service

Clothing Store and More

Coaching Business

Coin-Operated Laundry

Construction and Contracting Business

Consulting Business

Crafts Business

Day Spa and More

e-Business

e-Learning Business

Event Planning Business

Executive Recruiting Business

Fashion Accessories Business

Florist Shop and Other Floral Businesses

Food Truck Business

Freelance Writing Business and More

Freight Brokerage Business

Gift Basket Service

Grant-Writing Business

Graphic Design Business

Green Business

Growing and Selling Herbs and Herbal
 Products

Hair Salon and Day Spa

Home Inspection Service

Import/Export Business

Information Consultant Business

Information Marketing Business

Kid-Focused Business

Mail Order Business

Medical Claims Billing Service

Net Services Business

Online Education Business

Personal Concierge Service

Personal Training Business

Pet Business and More

Pet-Sitting Business and More

Photography Business

Public Relations Business

Restaurant and More

Retail Business and More

Self-Publishing Business

Seminar Production Business

Senior Services Business

Specialty Travel and Tour Business

Staffing Service

Tutoring and Test Prep Business

Vending Business

Wedding Consultant Business

Wholesale Distribution Business

Start Your Own

2ND EDITION

TRAVEL BUSINESS AND MORE

*Cruises • Adventure Travel
Tours • Senior Travel*

Entrepreneur Press and Rich Mintzer

EP

Entrepreneur Press, Publisher
Cover Design: Beth Hansen-Winter
Production and Composition: Eliot House Productions

This publication is designed to provide accurate and authoritative information in regard to the subject matter covered. It is sold with the understanding that the publisher is not engaged in rendering legal, accounting or other professional services. If legal advice or other expert assistance is required, the services of a competent professional person should be sought.

Library of Congress Cataloging-in-Publication Data
　　Mintzer, Rich.
　　　Start your own travel business and more/by Entrepreneur Press and Rich Mintzer.
　　　　p.　　cm.
　　　Includes index.
　　　ISBN-13: 978-1-59918-111-0 (alk. paper)
　　　ISBN-10: 1-59918-111-8 (alk. paper)
　　　1. Travel agents. 2. New business enterprises. I. Mintzer, Richard. II. Entrepreneur Press.
　　G154.S787 2007
　　910.68'1—dc22　　　　　　　　　　　　　　　　2007021172

Printed in the United States of America

16 15 14 13 12　　　　　　　　　　　　　　　　　　　10 9 8 7 6 5 4 3 2 1

Contents

▲

Acknowledgments

First a big thank you and best regards to Jere Calmes for always thinking of me for projects. I'd also like to thank Karen Billipp for her patience and more patience.

Thank you so very much to travel writer Susan Decoteau-Ferrier for her assistance.

A big thank you to Tom Ogg and Joanie Ogg; you were both so very helpful—it was much appreciated. Big thank yous also go out to Geoff Millar, Ultimate All-Inclusive Vacations; Margie Jordan, JETS & ASAP Travel; and Jennifer Doncsecz, VIP Vacations Inc.

▲

I'd also like to thank Jeff Adam, AAT Kings North America; Dan Austin, Austin Lehman Adventures; Connie George, Connie George Travel Associates; Jim and Nancy Terracciano, Cruise and Land Affairs; Judy Ebrey, Cuisine International; Chuck Flagg, The Flagg Agency; Barry Simpson, Grand Prix Tours; Jesse M. MacKay, J&L Travel; Kerrie Strumolo, KS Travel and Tours LLC; Dr. Phil Schoenberg, New York Talks and Walks; Sue Bonchi, Odysseys Unlimited; Andy Crisconi, One World Trekking; Dale Williams, Rod and Reel Adventures; Terry S., Seattle Walking Tours & Events; Dr. Robert W. Joselyn, Bruce B. Tepper, and Maxi S. Joselyn, Joselyn Tepper & Associates Inc.; and Toni Lanotte-Day, Toni Tours Inc.

Also special thanks to Bob Sharak of CLIA, Peter Stilphen of Coral Sands, Terry Dale of USTOA, and my computer experts David and Jennifer Lipschitz.

Preface

The world today is focused on technology to help us in so many ways and to handle some of life's many chores without us having to exert ourselves. Thanks to technology we can explore the far corners of the earth without having to leave the comfort of our own homes. Yet we do leave all the time. Why? Because nothing can replace the excitement, the adventure, the learning opportunities, and the fun of travel.

Yes, there's a whole world of opportunities out there, with places to see and things to do. And you want to be a part of

▲

it, which is why you've picked up this book to read in its bound/printed form or via Kindle.

Starting your own business, of any kind, is one of the most exhilarating things you can do for yourself and for your family. It's also one of the scariest.

Owning a business means you are the boss, the big cheese, the head honcho. You make the rules. You lay down the law. It also means you can't call in sick (especially when you are the only employee) or let somebody else worry about making enough to cover payroll and expenses. Nor can you defer that cranky client or intimidating IRS letter to a higher authority: You're it.

We're assuming you've picked up this particular book on starting and running a travel business for one or more of the following reasons:

- You have a background in the travel field.
- You have wanderlust in your veins and a permanently packed suitcase in your hall closet, and you think the travel business would be fun and exciting.
- You have a background in sales, communications, or planning and/or you like helping people learn new things about new places.
- You have no particular experience in the field, but believe you can sell travel or help people experience travel in an entertaining, informative fashion.

Which did you choose? (Didn't know it was a quiz, did you?) Well, you can relax because there is no wrong answer. Any of these responses is entirely correct, so long as you realize that they all involve a lot of learning and a lot of hard work. They can also involve a heck of a lot of fun, as well as a tremendous amount of personal and professional satisfaction. Our goal here is to tell you everything you need to know to:

- Decide whether a travel business is the right business for you;
- Decide what area or areas in the travel business interest you;
- Get your business started successfully with the necessary tools and equipment;
- Keep your business running successfully; and
- Make contacts and market your business successfully.

We've interviewed lots of people out there on the front lines of the industry, from all over the country, to find out how the travel business really works and what makes it tick. We've set aside places for them to tell their own stories and give their advice and suggestions—a sort of round-table discussion group, with you placed right in the thick of things. (For a listing of these successful business owners, see the Appendix.)

We've attempted to make this book as user-friendly as possible. We've broken our chapters into manageable sections on every aspect of startup and operations, and we've left some space for your creativity to soar. Our pages are packed with helpful tips so you can get up and running on your new venture as quickly as possible. We've also provided an Appendix crammed with contacts and resources.

So sit back—don't spill your coffee.

1

Pack
Your Bags

Whether it's an exotic destination with scenic windswept beaches, an epic adventure at sea, a golfing getaway, an extreme activity on the slopes of a majestic mountain, a casino junket, or taking a bite out of the Big Apple, everyone seems to be going somewhere to get away. What they are getting away from differs and their destinations of choice will also vary, but there's no doubt that travelers, bad economy notwithstanding, are still traveling 12 months a year.

Sure, the modern traveler has access to the wide world at the click of a mouse, but for the discerning adventurer, budget websites are inadequate.

And that's where you come in.

Once upon a time, travel was primarily for the wealthy and/or the adventurous. It took a fair amount of capital, an inordinate amount of time, and—unless you were going the luxury trans-Atlantic liner route on a first-class ticket—a willingness to accept discomfort as your due. Today, however, almost everybody travels, which explains why travel is a trillion-dollar industry that has skyrocketed since the first trans-Atlantic commercial jet took to the air back in 1957.

Although we still tend to think of travel in terms of airline seats or trips in the family wagon, today's touring encompasses far more than coach class to St. Louis or an endless drive to Wally World spent squabbling in the back seat with your siblings. You can choose from among a staggering number of cruises and specialty tours featuring everything from a trip down the Amazon studying ethnobotany with local shamans or sports camps with your favorite athletes to walking, biking, hiking,

Angela Waye/www.shutterstock.com

or chocolate-bingeing tours. There are tours for gardeners, gourmet cooks, antiques lovers, and art history buffs, and tours based on auto racing, agriculture, rafting adventures, wine tasting, exploring the historic world of King Arthur, dog sledding, storm chasing, llama trekking, caving, cattle driving, and more—much more!

This opening chapter takes a broad look at the flourishing travel business. We will explore some of the industry numbers, dip into some of the secrets, and help you determine whether it is the business for you to pursue.

Travel Today: Industry Stats Galore!

According to the U.S Travel Association's Travel Answer Sheet, direct spending on leisure travel by domestic and international travelers totaled $489.7 billion in 2009, with 77 percent of domestic trips being for leisure purposes.

This does not mean business professionals aren't still traveling. After all, video conference calls and WebEx cannot provide the post meeting dinners, parties, and nightlife. As a result, direct spending on business travel by domestic and international travelers, including expenditures on meetings, events, and incentive programs (ME&I), totaled $214.7 billion in 2009.

And in case you think you're part of a shrinking industry, there are 7.4 million people whose jobs are directly related to travel expenditures with $186.3 billion in wages shared by American workers directly employed in the travel industry as of 2009.

Direct spending by resident and international travelers in the United States (in 2009) was just over $700 billion, or an average of $1.9 billion a day, $80 million an hour, $1.3 million a minute, and $22,300 a second to be precise.

It is also anticipated that travel will continue to thrive, but with new, less typical, tourist destinations, possibly more ground travel until the price of fuel drops, and more cruising as the oceans and seas are ripe with more and more exquisite boats than even before. There are also a rapidly increasing number of adventure tour activities that are generating more excitement.

But not all travel is recreation-oriented; business travel is also expected to increase.

Stat Fact

Thirty years ago, the average American went on vacation once a year and spent a leisurely two to three weeks off the job, says the United States Tour Operators Association (USTOA). Today, people take shorter but more frequent vacations that average seven to ten days each.

▲

Winds of Change:
A Bit of Travel History

In ancient times, leisure travel was reserved for nobility or for the wealthy who could afford to indulge in leisure activities. For the ancient Romans it could have been a visit to a lavish spa, while for esteemed Greeks it might have been a junket to talk with great philosophers in Athens. Egyptians enjoyed the leisure gardens as a place to relax.

In the summer of 1841, however, a Baptist missionary named Thomas Cook decided to send a group of people round-trip from Leicester to Loughborough in England for a temperance meeting. He got the Midland Counties Railway Company to take on these passengers at a group rate of one shilling per person—and thus was officially born the modern tour operator.

From that modest beginning, Thomas Cook went on to fame and fortune by developing the first packaged tours. By 1851, he was arranging tours to the Great Exhibit in London, and in 1856, he organized a European grand tour. By the end of the 19th century, Thomas Cook & Son had blossomed into a major travel and tour operation with a chain of agencies that sent travelers around the world.

Thomas Cook & Son had lots of emulators. According to the USTOA, other budding tour operators probably got a jump-start on the business while working as ticket agents for steamship lines and railways. Since the tour operators were already selling the journey itself in the form of tickets, it was only a small jump to the additional business of planning itineraries and booking hotels for their customers. Even today, many of the new independent travel agents were once sitting in a travel office cubicle working for an agency owner, before embarking on their own.

By the 1850s—courtesy of Thomas Cook and others—you could commonly buy a railway tour; and soon after World War I, you could also purchase a steamship tour package. By 1927, prior to the Great Depression, the tour industry was

> ### Fun Fact
> On August 25, 1919, Air Transport & Travel Ltd., the forerunner of British Overseas Airway Corporation, launched the world's first scheduled international airline with service between London and Paris. Its maiden flight boasted one passenger and a cargo of Devonshire cream, newspapers, and grouse. Air travel was definitely an adventure—according to the British Airways' website, one pilot took two days to make the two-hour flight, making 33 unscheduled stops along the way.

beginning to thrive. However, the industry didn't really soar until after World War II, when aviation technology made long-range commercial flights not only possible but also affordable. Since those heady days, the industry has continued to fly high. The USTOA estimates that, taken as a whole, its active members have logged more than 1,100 years in the travel business. If you imagine that number as a chronological dip backward in time, you can just make out, through the mists, an ancient tour operator booking his flock on a trip to Constantinople.

If It's Tuesday

Leisure travel has come a long way since the cattle-car version of packaged tours made famous—or maybe infamous—by the 1969 film *If It's Tuesday, This Must Be Belgium*. When the movie was first released, the USTOA says 95 percent of tour passengers were traveling on a passport for the very first time. Today, less than 5 percent of tour and vacation passengers are passport newbies.

If you haven't seen *If It's Tuesday*, you should. It's charming and funny; and it depicts the quintessential escorted tour of the mid-20th century, in which an eclectic assortment of passengers are herded onto a bus for a whirlwind tour of about 14 European countries in 10 hectic days. But lest you think packaged tours are still like that—they're not!

Thirty years ago, says the USTOA, Western Europe was the destination of choice for most Americans, with few brave souls venturing anywhere else. Today, people are eager to visit far-flung outposts from China to the Antarctic to the Amazon. While back in 1969, 80 percent of escorted tours were whirlwinds, featuring a dozen countries in as many days, 80 percent of escorted tours in the new millennium are going to be regional, concentrating on a single country or region, with many focusing on specific activities, from sports and cultural expeditions to ecological exploration in the rainforests.

Today's modern travelers are both more sophisticated and more adventurous. Many want to be active, rather than just viewing the sights. They want to experience everything from rappelling down cliff faces to participating in archaeological digs to joining the locals at a Scottish ceilidh (a Highland dance party, pronounced kay-lee). And while new-millennium travelers

Stat Fact
In 1969, only 2.3 million Americans traveled to Europe. Thirty years later, by 1999, that figure had swelled to 11.6 million and topped 13 million by 2006. That's a lot of tourists!

are eager for new experiences and more than willing to sample the unusual, they're also more discerning and demanding. Travelers today, thanks to internet research, know that all sorts of amenities are offered. Therefore, many are willing to pay more money to travel than ever before. However, travelers are looking for first-rate accommodations, whether it means a choice campsite or a suite at a five-star hotel. Today's travelers are savvy, well-educated, and have seen plenty of luxurious settings on TV and the internet.

The Travel Agent vs. the Internet Travel Websites

Before we progress too far, and even before you embark on your travel agent education, it's important that we address the giant elephant in the room—internet travel websites.

The internet has played a major factor in altering the manner by which many travelers now book their vacations.

It is also largely the reason why you see so few storefront travel agencies. Liberty Travel is one of a small few that, after some 60 years in business, is still around.

Travelers today can make reservations, book airfares, and rent cars from their home computers using one of several major discount websites. They can view itineraries and put together a trip from the comfort of their own homes. While this would seem like doom and gloom for the travel agent, it has resulted in many homebased travel agents giving clients something more than the agents' high-tech competitors.

Of course, to succeed against these low-cost web-based alternatives, you need to stay one step ahead of the curve. This means finding a niche such as providing tours for adventure travelers, college students, seniors, or disabled passengers. It means offering the special amenities that a website cannot offer, and more significantly, being able to provide the much-needed human touch.

What this means is it's time to join the rapidly growing world of independent travel agents working primarily from homebased offices, sending people around the world while enjoying the comforts of home . . . and making money to boot.

But if you're not convinced that there is a place for the travel agent, let's look more closely.

Clearly, anyone who is comfortable on the internet can book a vacation by following the relatively easy steps on the discount websites. So why should they pay you for the same services?

Well, for one thing, if you consider that most people book one or two vacations a year as downtime from their daily routines, you can understand the importance of having a trip that goes as planned, or better.

What happens when all that online clicking leaves someone without the room they thought was booked? What happens when the tour the online traveler booked has been changed or canceled or is not English speaking? How about when the hotel the person booked online turns out to be in a not-so-safe area or the room is not at all like the room in the online photo? This kind of stuff happens all the time.

Trying to make changes via a discount travel website is difficult and adds plenty of unnecessary stress that vacationers would prefer to avoid.

The point is, more and more travelers have become leery of leaving their one or two weeks a year to chance, the chance being that everything they clicked on a website was a good choice and went through correctly. It is, in short, a roll of the dice.

Here are a few other comparisons:

- *Time*. It takes time to browse, do research, and figure out an itinerary online. Some experienced travelers have become good at putting the pieces together, but many have not. Many travelers become frustrated bouncing from one site to another and filling in all the necessary fields, hoping they haven't screwed up somewhere in the process. As a travel agent, you can take over and save the traveler the time and aggravation of putting a trip together—that's your job.

- *Options*. Not only do you have access to all the options that are available to the client on the web, but you have more. A perfect example comes from American Airlines, which, as of early 2011, stopped putting its flights and vacation packages on a number of major travel booking sites.

Emergency Service

"Once I had a client get stranded on their way to Costa Rica," says Toni Lanotte-Day of Toni Tours Inc. in Levittown, New York. "Something happened with the flight and they were stuck so they called me. I called another carrier and got them re-booked and all they missed was maybe half a day. They could have been stuck for many hours or even overnight, but I got them on their way in a few hours. You need to provide service, and that's what differentiates us from them (the discount travel sites)."

- *Emergencies and advocacy.* What happens if a natural disaster leaves a tour group stranded in a foreign country? "A travel agent often is their best advocate," notes the Frommer's travel guide company, adding that the agent can make the various calls and do the research that can help get the group on its way quickly. This is also true of personal emergencies that may arise in which a traveler needs to make a change in plans quickly.

- *Expertise.* There are so many variables when it comes to travel that having the expertise of a professional is invaluable. Travel agents have experience getting people to where they want to go and adding the personal touches that make a vacation unique and memorable. Let's face it, someone in the business of travel has the expertise and knows more of the minor, yet important, details than the average traveler sitting at a computer picking and choosing components based primarily on prices.

Other advantages of a travel agent include:

- *Knowing local laws, traditions, and customs.* Knowing which locations and accommodations are best for families, seniors, and disabled travelers. Knowing exchange rates, tipping customs, and hidden costs. Knowing the lay of the land, and how to get around. In the end, travel agents sell more than 50 percent of all airline tickets and book 87 percent of all cruises.

- *Difficulty with online sites.* Many vacationers cite difficult navigation on websites and difficulty putting a package together as reasons why they become frustrated and have defected from the discount websites and returned to travel agents. People are willing to pay a little more to get the job done right.

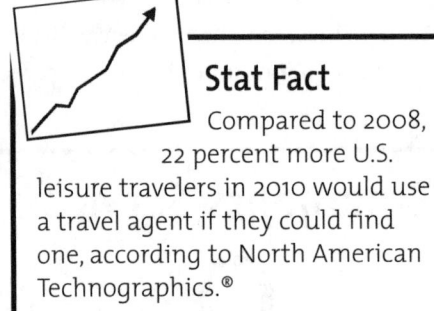

Stat Fact
Compared to 2008, 22 percent more U.S. leisure travelers in 2010 would use a travel agent if they could find one, according to North American Technographics.®

Thus, there is something to this travel agent thing. Of course, you need to be good at what you do, provide expert service, and, as mentioned earlier, stay one step ahead of your clients.

On the Job

Now that we've discussed the industry, and relieved some of your concern over those pesky discount internet websites, the questions arise: What exactly does a travel agent do? What does a tour operator do? Good questions! As a travel or tour professional, you can operate in one of two modes:

1. As a travel agent, you'll book clients on various tours at fabulous locations worldwide.
2. As a specialty tour operator, you will design and implement the tours your travel agent colleagues will sell.

We're going to cover both of these modes in this book, with a little more emphasis on the travel agent, since it is often somewhat easier to pursue and there are so many possibilities that await. However, since they're basically two sides of the same ticket, requiring much of the same knowledge and skills, we recommend that you read through everything to get the lay of the land.

The Travel Agent's World

The first thing to keep in mind is that the actual environment of the travel agent has changed radically in the past several years. You may recall seeing travel agencies as storefronts with various retail cubicles, decorated with shelves of Hawaiian cruise brochures and European vacation slicks, and tucked into downtown storefronts or out-of-the-way spaces at the local mall. As mentioned earlier, most of these are gone.

The new trend is toward the homebased, independent travel agent with no walk-in traffic and no airline tickets to write out. Homebased or independent travel agencies tend to focus on niche markets.

But we're getting ahead of ourselves. To explain the phenomenon of homebased travel agencies, let's step back in time, to the days before computers ran the world.

Dark-Age Ticketing

In ancient times (pre-1970s) when people wrote things out by hand, if you wanted to purchase an airline ticket, you had to trot on over to your local Pan Am or other air carrier's ticket counter—assuming there was a local counter or office—and stand in line until it was your turn. Then you had to wait while the ticket agent looked up flights in a book and wrote out your ticket in longhand.

Or—and this was a big time and effort saver—you could call your travel agent. He or she would then look up all the information in guides packed with eye-crossing small print, call the airline's agency desk, reserve your flight, and write the ticket by hand from a supply in his desk drawer. The agent didn't mind doing this because he or she got tidy commissions on all the fares.

As the World Turns

Then, in about 1975, the airline-ticketing world took a breathtaking turn with the introduction of the Computerized Reservation System or CRS. There are several CRS systems, each owned by a different airline or group of airlines; they all work in basically the same manner. Today, just about anybody with a home computer and internet access can reserve their own airline tickets; but back in the Brady Bunch era, computerized reservations were a major innovation.

With this online system, travel agencies could bypass the agency desk, make the reservations themselves and then print out not only your ticket but even a boarding pass and itinerary. At first, this benefited everyone. The airlines were delighted because they no longer had to pay a union employee to work the agency desk, and the travel agents were thrilled because they could offer lightning-fast automated service to their customers.

Travel agencies trumpeted the fact that they could give customers airline prices with no additional fees and with instant ticketing. And since even calling the airlines cost money, because they didn't have toll-free numbers, customers rushed to take advantage of travel agency ticketing. It was so easy; everybody won.

Of course, it wasn't all quite that simple. At first, travel agencies had to qualify to get a CRS. If they didn't show enough revenue to warrant a system, no amount of begging and pleading would get them one. By the time the '80s rolled around, more than 16,000 travel agencies boasted CRS systems.

Another Development

Eventually, however, the bloom fell off the rose. The airlines decided they could spring for toll-free numbers to regain customers lost to travel agencies and put a halt to at least some of those agency commissions they were paying out. By the mid-1990s, customers had discovered that they could reserve their own tickets right from home with their personal computers, which took another notch out of travel agencies' commissionable sales.

Then, in 1995, the domestic airlines pulled the rug out from under the agencies by placing a cap on the standard 10 percent commission. This meant that instead of earning as much as $200 or more for each business or first-class flyer, agents now were restricted to $25 for one-way tickets and $50 for round-trip tickets. Adding insult to injury, the airlines then began cutting the standard 10 percent commission down to

8 percent in 1997. That, however, wasn't the end. In October 1999, a number of air carriers dropped their commission rates to a dismal 5 percent, and in time eliminated commissions completely.

Put in its simplest form, this means that it now costs a travel agent money to write that airline ticket. Travel agencies spent almost two decades persuading consumers to come to them for their ticketing needs; now they can't afford to perform the service, and as noted earlier, this caused some travel agents to shut their doors and go into another business.

Your Host

Obviously, there is more to being a travel agent than writing airline tickets or booking hotel rooms. As we explained at the top of this section, homebased agents could not write airline tickets even if they wanted to. To do so, you have to have an

The E-Ticket

Back in the days when the Mousketeers still ruled Disneyland, an e-ticket was the one that got you on the fanciest and scariest rides, like the Matterhorn. Today, an e-ticket is the one that gets you into your airline seat without a boarding pass, at least without a traditional paper one. The e-ticket (aka "electronic" ticket) is paperless, which is great for those concerned about the environment and a time saver for passengers.

In 1996, all four major CRS programs made adjustments to allow for ticketless travel, and the major airlines began developing programs to implement it. There are currently several variations on the theme, but the basic idea is the same. When you make a reservation, you get a confirmation number instead of a paper ticket and boarding pass. You take this confirmation number and your photo ID (driver's license, for example) to the airport, and you're in. Having two IDs with you has become a good idea in an age of tighter security.

The beauty of this system is that passengers do not have to wait to receive tickets or worry about losing or forgetting them. The beauty for the air carrier is that it saves money, reportedly up to $2 per ticket, which amounts to several million dollars each year.

appointment (which is sort of like a license) from the Airlines Reporting Corporation, also known as the ARC. And the ARC doesn't hand out appointments to an agency unless it's housed in a commercial office space.

So why not just rent that commercial space and be done with it? Well, there's the overhead, for one thing. It's far less expensive to run your office from a room in your home, which costs you nothing in rent or additional utilities, than to go the commercial route and have to worry about monthly leasing fees and office utilities. Then there's the fact that, aside from the whims of the ARC, you really don't need a commercial office space. Today's independent travel agents conduct most of their business by phone, email, and even texts. They don't rely on random customers who may or may not wander in, lured by that poster in the window, so a formal retail office is an anachronism.

But how do you sell airline tickets if you can't get an ARC appointment? Most homebased travel agents affiliate themselves with a host agency, which is a commercially based outfit with an ARC appointment. The homebased agent is an independent contractor—sort of a freelance salesperson—finding and maintaining his or her own clients, selling travel products to them, and then splitting commissions with the host agency.

The real reason the new travel agent needs a host agency is that the host has established connections with numerous suppliers that would take an agent a long time and a lot of work to establish. In addition, the host agency can get far better discounts by booking in mass quantities. Then there is the training that is offered by host agencies.

So what is the split between host agency and homebased agent? Good question. It depends on the experience of the agent and how the contract is negotiated. Often a new agent will start with a lower commission and move up as they sell more packages.

Calculating

If, through a preferred supplier, a wholesaler, or a consortium (discussed later), the host agency has a package tour that sells for $3,000 per person and it receives a 15 percent commission, or $450, the agent getting a 70 percent commission would receive $315.

It's also faster and easier to collect money through a host agency than it is for a new agent to collect on his or her own.

Many commissions are 70/30 or 80/20 splits (with some as high as 90/10 or even 100 percent) with the host agency taking the lesser percentage. Since the host agency may be working with as many as 500 to 2,000-plus independent travel professionals such as yourself, the agency makes money off of the volume sold. In addition, independent agents typically pay an annual fee to affiliate with the host agency. This too is usually minimal but adds up for the host agency since it has so many agents working with one host. We will explore the relationship between host agencies and independent travel agents further throughout the book.

Most travel agents start with host agencies—some stay affiliated for many

Bright Idea
Do your homework! It's worth the investment in your business to visit your location(s) and learn the lay of the land inside out. For example, if you want to sell the Bahamas, visit the resorts, dine at the restaurants, talk to the locals, visit the shops, and go to the seminars (or take the webinars) offered by the tourist bureau or the local suppliers. This can help you gain the expertise you need to stay one step ahead of the clients who are surfing online at home to learn about the destination.

years, while others begin to make their own deals with suppliers after a few years in the business. Then, in time, they move away from their host agency. Some do a little of both. It's all up to you and how well you network, build up your knowledge of the industry, and enhance your skills. You also need the drive and desire to branch out on your own—some agents are perfectly happy working with a host agency and do very well, while others make a splash on their own.

You Can Also (Eventually) Do It Yourself

If you find the right niche market, you may want to offer tours specifically for that market, or you might opt for tours of a specific genre. Tour operators turn to travel agents to sell their products. They also sell their tours directly to consumers through magazines, direct mail, and by contacting associations and organizations that will be interested in their products. For instance, a tour operator would approach garden clubs to find consumers interested in tours of botanical gardens, or genealogy groups to find individuals interested in going on heritage tours. The reality is that today, you can make your own connections with all sorts of businesses that would love to have your travelers spend money in their establishments. This has become easier in recent years with the internet and the ability to reach out to groups and associations through the social media. You can also serve as a tour operator if you are very well versed in a location and the various offerings the location provides.

▲

Like travel agents, tour operators are carving out business from formerly unexplored territories, both in terms of geography and market niche. While the traditional tour once packaged tourists of all ages, interests, and inclinations onto a bus and gave them the expedited experience of seeing Europe, smart travel marketers today are narrowing their sights and increasing their revenues. Some specialty travel firms focus on a specific interest or hobbies such as bicycling, bird watching, art history, archaeology, or murder mysteries, and they organize tours designed specifically around them. Others hone in on a particular region, like the Scottish Highlands or the Greek Islands, and give their clients the full flavor of the area in ways they could never experience on the old If It's Tuesday tour.

Stat Fact
According to the United States Tour Operators Association, a 14-day, escorted first-class tour to China would have cost $1,782 in 1980—which in today's money would be $3,524. A similar tour now would cost less than $2,000.

Specialty tours can range from the rugged to the relaxed. Everything from a strenuous mountain trek, with all the thrills of altitude sickness and incipient frostbite, to a luxurious stay at a secluded European villa can be offered.

Adventure travel is a popular ticket, and includes trips focusing on a variety of pursuits, from hiking to rafting to trekking to learning about the culture and wildlife of a particular country. Sometimes these tours are the Rough Guide version, where you sleep in tents and eat around campfires. Sometimes they offer the best of both adventure and elegance, as on safaris where guests traverse the bush during the day, spotting lions and rhinos, but spend their nights in first-class hotels.

The ecotour is another hot ticket, featuring trips to ecologically sensitive areas like the Amazon or the Antarctic, to study the flora and fauna and interact with native people—just like on *The Discovery Channel*.

Read All About It!

The written word is a powerful learning tool. One of your first steps in your new venture should be reading everything you can. Blitz the bookstores, scour the websites, and read what the travel bloggers have to offer.

Some of the top travel blogs you may want to visit are included in Chapter 13.

We'll talk more about Tours and Adventure travel later on in the book. For now, you can just use these ideas as a springboard.

Of course, there's more to the business than the excitement of planning trips and tours. You also need to consider the weighty issues that come with starting up any business, including what to expect in the way of startup expenses, how much you can expect to earn, and whether you've got what it takes. So buckle up for the next exciting chapter—let's go!

2

Do You Have the Right Stuff?

As we discussed in our wind-up of Chapter 1, there's a lot more to being a travel specialist than just a love of travel or a desire to hop into a potentially lucrative industry. In this chapter, we'll explore the up-close and personal issues involved in starting a travel business, including the skills you'll need, as well as the startup expenses and potential profits before launching into any type of travel business.

Counting Your Coconuts

While there are a lot of questions to answer and factors to consider, we will answer the question of potential income early on, since you are curious. However, the answer covers a broad range and depends largely on how much time, effort, ingenuity, and due diligence you put into running your travel business. That being said, according to the Bureau of Labor Statistics, the median income for travel agents is roughly $31,000 per year. This includes part-timers and those who are in the business to earn extra income. There are those at the top of the field who are earning more than triple this amount.

The suggested ways of earning more money include building your own special niche market using all the tools possible to market your products and services, such as:

- Using preferred suppliers.
- Creating your own tours.

Jezper/www.shutterstock.com

- Selling high ticket, high commission items.
- Taking courses and getting certifications.
- Finding or creating products with high markups.
- Finding clients who have spending money.
- Providing exceptional customer service.
- Making sure you are collecting all commissions and payments due to you.
- Upselling additional products and services.
- Gaining a competitive edge over your competitors.

Most of these areas will be discussed throughout the book.

According to Tom Ogg, founder of CruiseReviews.com and TravelHomebased travelagent.com, income potential is largely a result of how much time and effort you put into your business and even more significantly, how much passion and knowledge you have for your product(s). "This is not a job where you just sit at a desk and sell trips all over the world to people. It's a job for many retired individuals and people in a second career who have a passion for something such as river cruises or scuba diving and they turn that passion into a lucrative business with a well thought out business plan and a marketing plan," says Ogg, who has now been in the travel industry for 42 years.

According to Ogg, the income potential is based on the efforts of serious and professional agents, not dabblers.

"I know outside agents who make $6,000 a year and some who make $70,000 a year," says Connie G., a travel agent with 25 years of experience in the industry. "It depends on how hard and how smart they want to work."

Not unlike any new business, starting a travel business of any type is slow going in the early stages. For that reason, many newcomers start handling travel as a part-time business while maintaining another job (with flexibility) to keep the money coming in.

Meanwhile, if a full-time travel business is your goal, you will likely want to build relationships with several suppliers and tour operators while evaluating which host agency with which to affiliate. Revenue figures can soar or plummet depending on many variables. A one-person operation that does half-day city walking tours will

Stat Fact

According to the United States Travel Association, the automobile was the primary means of transportation used by leisure visitors (76 percent) between August 2008 and July 2009. The percentage of leisure visitors traveling by auto varies by income, generation, and other demographic characteristics.

have a far different bottom line than a multi-employee company that runs 14-day European adventures.

As a startup, you shouldn't expect to earn big bucks immediately. "It's high risk, low return," says Jerry Mallett of the Adventure Travel Society, a nonprofit association for adventure travel professionals. But it's also a lot of fun, according to Mallett, who says, "It's a lifestyle situation."

"It looks easy, like you can just put an ad in a magazine and develop the idea," says Barry S., a specialist in car race tours who has been in the business for more than 20 years, and whose company boasts revenue in the millions. "But it isn't easy. It's a matter of really sticking at it. After about seven years, I was at a point where I was doing $1.2 million and not making any real profits and wondering why I was doing it. But I loved it and continued, and then it started growing from there."

This is not to say that as a tour operator, or booking agent, you won't earn a living for seven years, but you should be prepared to grow your company by degrees rather than expect an overnight success. To make the most of your new company—be it an independent travel agent or an adventure or specialty tour operator—find out as much as you can from the start. This book is a good beginning. Its pages will guide you through the many stages of starting a travel-oriented company. However, researching the specific type of business you want to run and the niche in which you want to specialize will be up to you.

Crank-Up Costs

One of the catch-22s of being in business for yourself, any business, is that you need money to make money. In other words, you need startup funds or seed money. For the travel and tour business, these costs typically range from $5,000 to $40,000. Starting out from your home means you won't have the high overhead from leasing an office space. Depending on how you choose to run your company, you probably won't need employees either, certainly not at the beginning. Your major outlays will be for your computers, software, printer, smartphone or BlackBerry, web design, and internet access. You'll also need to set aside money for advertising and marketing, which can be your most significant expense.

Are You the Travel Professional Type?

OK, you have decided that running a travel business is potentially profitable. You are willing to invest not only the money but also the time it will take to learn the ropes and become an established professional. What else should you consider? Personality and temperament. Not everybody is cut out to be in the travel business. This is not a career for the creatively challenged. It is not a career for someone who does not like to interact with other people. It is not a career for the chronically disorganized. It is not a career for someone who only wants to work from 9 to 5.

It takes a lot of foresight to figure out how to create a winning program, to design and construct it so that it turns a profit, and to promote it effectively. As a travel agent, you don't have to design tours, but you'll need the people skills to match clients with tours and make the sale. If you're one of those folks who'd rather undergo a root canal than have to come up with a peppy marketing plan, then you don't want to be in the tour business. If you are a sales-challenged type who cringes at the thought of persuading people to buy a product, you also might be happier doing something else.

Travel agents are largely marketers who want to sell the vacation experience they stand behind. You can create your own products, but you do not have to. You do need to sell products and give attention to detail to make sure everything falls into place and goes as planned.

Tours must be organized months in advance, with everything from the tour guide to the motor coach to the dining reservations nailed down early on. As a travel agent, you must be aware of deadlines for ticket, tour, and hotel reservations and must be able to pull all the varied segments of a client's trip into a cohesive whole. If you're a star procrastinator who can't seem to get started on anything until the 11th hour, then you should definitely look elsewhere for entrepreneurial satisfaction. But if you delight in dreaming up sparkling programs and star-spangled advertising and marketing ideas, if you're an efficient time manager and organizer, and if you love providing a dream vacation for your clients, then you'll love being a travel agent. And by the way, you need to be good with technology—not with knowing how it works or fixing it, but with using it to your benefit, whether it's laptops and iPhone apps or working the social media.

The Emergence of a Travel Agent

Travel professionals come from all walks of life. The travel agents we interviewed for this book came from a variety of alternate careers, from police captain to full-time mom. The tip here is that these entrepreneurs figured out how to make their backgrounds and interests work for them in their new careers in the travel business.

Cruising for Fun

"Our love of cruising is how this whole thing got started," says Jim T., who, along with his wife, Nancy, runs a cruise-oriented travel agency in Dunkirk, Maryland. "We

Traits of the Trade

Take this fun quiz and find out if you have what it takes to become a travel and tour specialist.

1. My idea of a fun evening is:
   a) watching five straight hours of the Travel Channel.
   b) snuggling up with a hot toddy and a rough draft of my advertising copy.
   c) cruising around town singing "Travelin' Man."

2. Here's how I usually send Christmas gifts to relatives living out of state:
   a) I wait until December 24th, stuff the gifts into bags with the addresses scribbled in crayon, then rush down to the post office and stand in a huge, snaky line with all the other procrastinators, hoping my gifts arrive in time and intact.
   b) I wrap my gifts carefully in specially selected packaging no later than December 10th, call my pre-designated FedEx or UPS courier (already checked to see which is cheaper and faster), and then follow up to make sure the gifts have arrived on time and intact.
   c) I hope no one notices I forgot to send gifts.

3. When it comes to social media, I:
   a) Let my 15-year-old handle all my texts and my Facebook page.
   b) Have my own Facebook page, belong to LinkedIn, and stay on top of all the latest mobile technology so I can text and tweet at a moment's notice.
   c) Remain anti-social (media).

4. When out-of-town guests arrive at my home for a week:
   a) I quarantine myself in the bedroom.
   b) I take them to several exciting local restaurants and drive them around town, showing them the sights, giving anecdotes about local features, and introducing them to interesting people.
   c) I leave a city map and some bus fare on the guest room nightstand.

5. I would best describe my self-motivational abilities as follows:
   a) I'll get to it eventually.
   b) I love setting and meeting goals and accomplishing tasks.
   c) My self-starter frequently gets stuck.

Answers: If you chose (b) for each answer, then you passed with flying colors! You've got what it takes to become a specialty travel and tour pro. You're organized, an efficient time manager, and self-motivated.

took our first Caribbean vacation to St. Thomas in 1989 and just absolutely fell in love with the area. We went back in 1990 on a cruise; and like the commercial about potato chips, we had one, and we were hooked."

What You Need to Know

"What you need to be successful in this business today is to understand business, understand and look for a niche market, know sales, and provide top quality customer service," says Geoff Millar with Ultimate All-Inclusive Vacations in Arizona.

As Millar points out, it is a business, and that means you need to treat it like a business and not a hobby. With that in mind, you need to be cognizant of state rules, regulations and licenses, business practices and policies, and understand your market and its needs.

If you don't like selling, this is probably not the business for you, and if you don't have good people skills, you'll have to bone up on putting your best foot forward—given the customers, suppliers, host agencies, and other important people involved in the travel business, you will be dealing with others on a steady basis.

You also need to understand the costs of doing business and how to determine if a vacation package will be profitable or put you in the red before you start offering it. Having a good sense of numbers and some knowledge of economics is a big plus—otherwise team with someone who does have these skills.

Many homebased travel agencies are husband and wife businesses, in part because it gets lonely working by yourself, in part because there is so much to do (if you really want to succeed), and in part because couples often complement one another when it comes to their skills. This doesn't mean saying "great job" or "I love how you punch numbers," but it does mean complementing one another by using your separate skills to run a business. In reality, few if any businesses are ever the work of one person alone. With that in mind, tap into the knowledge of your spouse or partner or bring in someone to work with you in areas in which you are not as proficient. "My wife had over 20 years in the travel business. I had the computer and technical know-how," says Millar. They teamed up in 2003, and today are booking more than $3 million in business. That's teamwork!

Fun Fact

The colossal Royal Caribbean cruise ships and the Allure of the Seas, are the largest cruise ships to date, both checking in at over 225,000 gross tons and able to accommodate more than 6,000 passengers each. The Allure features 3D theaters, a classic, full-sized carousel, an adults-only solarium, and a zipline across the boat, while the Oasis ship includes a full ice rink complete with spectacular ice shows.

▲

Making People Smile

Jim and Nancy both had high-stress careers; he was a police captain in greater metropolitan Washington, DC, and she was in a county finance department. "Cruising was the perfect answer," Jim explains, "getting away and letting somebody take care of us for a week. We started doing a cruise a year as a vacation and escape form, and it got to the point where several of our friends were coming to us for advice about cruise lines and destinations. After our reviews, a couple of them said jokingly that maybe we should do this for a living."

Jim was nearing retirement from the police department, and the idea of dealing with cruise ships instead of criminals began to sound pretty good. After researching the industry, Jim enrolled at a local travel school, took a 15-week course in the evenings and on weekends, and obtained his travel agent certification.

"We decided that, rather than go to work for somebody else as we'd been doing all our careers, we'd be our own entity—no franchises, no working for anybody, just doing it on our own," Jim says. "And, in February 1996, we started the company." Jim and Nancy hit their five-year goal of $500,000 in annual gross sales and, a decade later, are still going strong.

"After almost 25 years in law enforcement," Jim explains, "I wanted to get into something where people were coming to you with a smile on their faces and were hopefully leaving the same way. The travel business has lived up to that reputation."

From Navy Ships to Cruise Ships

Jesse M. MacKay spent more than 20 years in the U.S. Navy and lived in a wide range of places, from Japan to Hawaii to Newport, Rhode Island, to San Diego, California. After living in so many places, and with a passion for travel, MacKay used his GI Bill to attend the Carlson Travel Academy at night and on weekends in 1994/95 in San Diego. "My wife and I both liked to travel, so while I was working on a Navy contract I thought I'd learn about the travel business," says MacKay.

"Two Navy friends, against my recommendations, bought a travel agency and I went to work for them as an outside agency and director of marketing. Then around 2000 I was able to get the technology at home through Cox cable and got phone lines and high-speed internet," says MacKay, who was inspired to branch out on his own.

Fun Fact

Celebrity Cruises is known in the industry for its posh suite-type staterooms, which include such highfalutin extras as 24-hour butler service, personalized stationery, and private portrait sittings.

Today, MacKay and his wife run J&L Travel from Homosassa, Florida, which they launched in 2004. "We do mostly cruises and tours and put things together with package tours or build a tour through different suppliers. Some tours are escorted, others independent; it's all about what people want to do," says MacKay, who notes that most of his clients are seniors and many enjoy the riverboat cruise experiences. "We still do the trips for a local church group for 40 people to go to Ireland," adds MacKay, who is enjoying his post Navy life and second career.

Hooked On Travel

"I guess you could say as a kid I grew up hooked on travel," says Toni Lanotte-Day, travel consultant, Master Cruise Counselor (MCC) at Toni Tours Inc. in Levittown, New York. "My uncle was a foreign diplomat with lots of great travel stories and so I wanted to travel," says Lanotte-Day, who talked to the people in local travel agencies in the neighborhood and learned about the business. "I became a paramedic, but also went to Pan American travel school across from Madison Square Garden in Manhattan. I did double shifts with the fire department so I could make time for my classes," explains Lanotte-Day, who learned the tools of the trade well before the advent of modern technology. "I learned how to build relationships with suppliers and the airlines at the time in which they were huge for us. I learned the old TWA version of Sabre and got hired by a small agency. They set me up in a little back room office and told me to start calling family and friends. I did, but I also thought about what I would like to do on a trip. As an avid skier, I thought of seeing if I could get a group to go skiing in Italy. It was my first trip, and every year I took a group ranging from 10 to 40 people to Italy for skiing, working with Central Holidays as a supplier," says Lanotte-Day. She then continued working with various agencies until shortly after September 11, 2001, when the world changed and the travel industry was hit hard.

Lanotte-Day found another agency, but it too went out of business shortly thereafter, and she lost out on $5,000 she was owed in commissions. So she went out on her own.

She had learned the business well and pretty soon began putting together soft adventure trips that included hiking, whitewater rafting, and other fun activities. "Last year I had them all on the sidecars of motorcycles going through the Rockies," says Lanotte-Day. Meanwhile, she is always looking for the next unique adventure idea.

Today, Lanotte-Day clearly recognizes the significance of the 80-20 principle of business. The principle asserts that 80 percent of your business will come from the same clients, while 20 percent will come from new clients, in this case, mostly referrals. She knows the value of maintaining ongoing relationships and getting business from regular clientele and their families for years to come.

The Other Side of the Coin

On the other side of the travel coin are the tour operators. Like the travel agents we interviewed, the tour operators we spoke to have also come from varied backgrounds, and only one had any experience in tourism when starting out.

A Dream Come True

"I don't think I've done a tour or event where someone didn't ask 'How did you ever get started doing this?'" says Terry S., who runs city-walking tours and events in Seattle, Washington. "Most are just curious, but occasionally someone would like to do the same thing themselves. I encourage them but try to explain that there is much more to it than just walking around. My sound bite answer is something like 'I lost my computer industry job and decided to try something different.' But there's more to it than that."

The "more to it" is that Terry had a very successful career in computer programming and product management until 1989, when his employer decided to drop out of the computer business. The company handed out pink slips to all 7,000 of the information systems employees on a single red-letter (or pink-letter) day. They also asked Terry to stay on and "wind down" operations, which he did.

Terry explains, "During the wind-down, I pursued computer industry jobs but found that 1) the best opportunities—and I had some great offers—required I move from Seattle, which was a no-no for me; and 2) locally they wanted me to start at the bottom from whence I came. This circumstance caused me to think about what else I would like to do that I felt I could do well.

"I adopted the philosophy that there's more to life than computers and that I didn't need to make as much money as I had in the past. With this mindset, I reflected on the traveling I had done in the United States and around the world, both for business and on my own. When I got to a city, I would try to see as much as possible, often on a guided tour. And I would say to myself, 'What a great job these tour guides have. I'd like to do that.' But then, like waking from a pleasant dream, I'd be back at my computer job. Now I had a real chance to act on my dream—the real inspiration for me behind my company."

In 1993, Terry started by putting brochures in hotels, getting listed in the AAA (Automobile Association of America) Tour Book, and joining the Seattle-King County Convention and Visitors Bureau. "I made almost no money the first two years with just my walking tour. Then I created my Mystery & Scavenger Hunt and my website. Business picked up dramatically and continues so today," explains Terry.

Concorde Dreams

Farther down the West Coast, in Southern California, Barry S. also started off on a wing and prayer. Barry decided to get into the travel business nearly 25 years ago. "I worked for the Orange County Transit District," recalls the tour operator from Newport Beach. "We had a demand-responsive bus system with 70 to 80 buses out on the streets, running around like taxis, and a computer that crashed three times a day. At one stage I had 50 percent of my staff out on stress-related leave, and I thought 'This is crazy, living a life like this.'"

"I decided I had to do something for the rest of my life that I enjoyed doing," Barry explains. "It was really a matter of finding what I loved, which was car racing. So I went with the idea of doing car racing tours."

But it wasn't quite that simple. "There were other companies in other countries that were doing the same thing," Barry says. "I thought I'd copy what they were doing, but I had no experience in the travel industry. I spent a year and took in total

Fun Fact

The first Paris to New York nonstop flight was made in early September 1930, when Dieudonné Coste and Maurice Bellonte set the record with a 37-hour stint in a Breguet biplane.

Happy Days

When you plan your tours, consider the amount of vacation time your clients are likely to have—unless you're targeting retirees, and then there are no such worries. Tours that coincide with holidays are always popular because they can result in a few bonus vacation days. For instance, if July 4th falls on a Friday or Monday, your clients can tack that day onto the weekend for extra "free" time.

Most employers offer the same holiday calendar: New Year's, Memorial Day, Independence Day, Labor Day, Thanksgiving, and Christmas. Other popular days sometimes offered as holidays include Martin Luther King Jr. Day, Presidents Day, Good Friday, Columbus Day, and Veterans Day.

According to a survey by Hewitt Associates, a consulting firm in human resources management, only 1 percent of American businesses provide less than seven paid holidays in a year.

sales of $20,000. If you can imagine, it was pretty disastrous because my expenses were something like $40,000. I wasn't working at it full time; I carried on with my job and ran the company on the side. My brother came over from England. He worked, and I didn't pay him anything—it was a way of getting started.

"The second year we went out and found some more money and did $18,000 worth of business. I was working full time at it then, but it still didn't make any money, so I had to go out and get more funding. This went on for a few years. It was a struggle," explains Barry, adding that it took about ten years to turn the company into something he could really see a future in. "We developed a name, a logo, and we're known as the leading tour operator of our kind throughout the country. We grow 20 percent to 30 percent a year."

Today, Barry's company employs a staff of 12 and earns revenue of $5.8 million per year. He's chartered a cruise ship to stand off the coast of Monaco with a private maitre d' to greet his guests by name and pour wine while they watch the races on shore. He's had English lords invite his clients for tea and multimillionaires personally show them their private car museums.

Barry has worked hard to earn those champagne rewards. "When I started, I imagined within two years I'd be chartering the Concorde to go over to Europe for races," the car enthusiast says. "Those dreams did come true. We did charter the Concorde a couple of times. But we certainly didn't do it in two years. We didn't suddenly jump into millions—it took us a long, long time."

Future Forecast

It's easy to see that all the travel and tour specialists interviewed for this book have put their own passions together with creativity, and you can, and should, do the same. But in addition to personal background, creativity, startup costs, and annual revenue, there's one more thing to take into consideration: the industry prognosis. Will the specialty travel business be around for years to come?

Consumer travel expenditures are on the rise and will continue to rise for the foreseeable future, according to industry experts. If you can design unique adventure packages or cater to a specific market, such as cruise goers, or a more specific demographic group, such as seniors (all of which are discussed in the upcoming chapters), then you have a solid game plan for a successful business.

According to Tom Ogg, this is a great time for the travel business. While it is a people-centric business all about real people providing others with marvelous travel experiences, Ogg points out the latest in technology moving the business forward. "Technology lets people reach out and do things they could not have done in the past. The collector of ivory, for example, can probably find 2,000 other people who also collect ivory and can organize and package a trip for those people," explains Ogg. "Travel agents can now build packages themselves if they are resourceful," adds Ogg, noting that agents can bypass the middle people and have an internal yield of 30 to 40 percent. "It's a whole new world. So if you like something specific you can market it yourself. Of course, you've got to know more than the combined knowledge of the group you're booking. But you can call an inn located somewhere in France, get them on Skype, and make your plan with them. You couldn't do that even a few years ago," says Ogg, who also points out the improved settlement (payment) process.

Weather Wonders

Weather can play an important and sometimes unpredictable part in tour operations. "Public walking tours are very weather dependent," advises Dr. Phil S., an operator who offers tours of New York City. "If it's a very mild rain, people will show up. If it's moderate, people will show up. And if it's an unusual topic and the weather's bad, they'll still show up."

But there's no way to be certain—of the weather or your crowd capacity. The first year Phil did his Brooklyn Bridge tour, he had 17 reservations for the New Year's walk. Then the weather took a serious, unexpected plunge. "I couldn't blame people for not showing up, but nobody called to cancel," he recalls. "One person who didn't have a reservation showed up, and we looked at each other like we were crazy." A couple years later he had more than 150 people, on a clear and relatively mild night in New York, when the tour had been touted as one of the top 10 things to do for New Year's in New York.

▲

"PayPal, Checkout, and all the settlement processes out there make it easier to do business quickly. You can call someone in another part of the world, make a reservation, and settle it quickly using these processes," notes Ogg of how the latest in technology is benefiting the homebased travel agent more than ever before, and should continue to do so with forthcoming advances.

Risk Factors

The risk factor for independent travel agents is generally moderate—less risky than being a Hollywood stunt double but more risky than being a CPA. If you're willing to learn everything you can about your business and then strenuously promote it, you should do well. But it is important to know that just as in other professions, there are risks involved.

Financial Risk

Whether you have backers or investors, you will likely be putting some of your own money into your new travel business. This risk is lessened significantly if you are using funds that you have set aside for such a venture or you are borrowing money using collateral that does not include your home. Therefore, your financial investment into a new business venture (any business venture) should be money above and beyond that which you need to support yourself and your family. For some entrepreneurs it is the result of a few bonus checks at the corporate job they will soon be leaving, for some it comes from an inheritance, while for others, it simply means put aside money for such purposes. The bottom line is that you should neither be maxing out your credit cards nor banking your children's college funds to start a business.

Additionally, you can mitigate financial risks in the travel business by using a home office as your base, buying or using inexpensive furnishings or using those that you have, and being creative with marketing ideas that are cost effective. While every business has some financial risk, you can, and should, carefully map out your startup and ongoing expenses in advance so that you do not spend money unwisely.

Time Risk

Do you have the time to adequately start and grow a business? The time commitment for a new business is usually a significant one. The risk is

- whether you are "wasting" your time, and

- whether you can afford to put in the necessary hours.

If you cannot afford to take the time without bringing in a paycheck, you may not be ready to start a business. Likewise, if you have family and pressing obligations, then you may also be taking too big a personal risk to delve into a business endeavor. However, if you start by utilizing otherwise wasted time (in front of the TV set, or time spent on useless activities) and put that time to good use—in a part-time manner—you can mitigate the time risk factor by utilizing these hours to get started before quitting your full-time job. Determine how much time you can devote to a business venture, and if you cannot jump in full time, then start gradually.

Knowledge Risk

The only way to mitigate this risk is to do your homework. Someone who jumps into a business venture without having a thorough understanding of the industry is taking a very big (unnecessary) risk. Consider all the possible resource materials available on the internet, at seminars and webinars, at conferences, at newsstands and bookstores, and even at the library. In this industry, firsthand knowledge is also significant, so prepare to do some traveling to get the inside track on the excursions you plan to sell. Remember, your greatest strength is knowing more than your clients

At the Ready

Whether you decide to sell cruises, tours, or both, you should look into affiliation with the National Association of Career Travel Agents, familiarly known as NACTA. The association was developed in 1986 specifically for homebased, cruise-oriented, independent travel agents. NACTA stands at the ready with all sorts of helpful hints and assistance for the independent agent, including—when you join—a handbook packed with sample contracts and agreements and press releases. Membership also grants you discounts on legal counsel and a variety of industry publications and software, as well as lots of cruise- and land-based family trips.

The association also boasts 70+ host agency members and acts sort of as a Better Business Bureau of travel agencies. Host agencies must meet a set of criteria; one complaint and they're off NACTA's list—which makes life easier for you!

(who also have access to the internet) and being able to impart such knowledge whenever necessary.

Economic Risk

The economic climate is out of your hands. The best you can do is try to start a business at a time that is favorable for new businesses, particularly a business that falls into the "luxury" category. Mitigate economic risk by reading the latest economic news and having either enough variety, or a niche that draws enough customers even during a downturn in the economy. This may mean some low-cost, low-payoff tours that can still bring you a reasonable profit margin, while not being your more glamorous, high-priced offerings.

Natural Risks

For lack of a better term, these are risks that are out of your hands, such as natural disasters. Insurance will help mitigate such risks. You can also try to plan accordingly based on weather and other factors, but some risks will be out of your hands no matter what you do—this is inherent in every business. Prepare as best you can, and have offsite backups for all your important data files and account information. Should natural disasters impinge upon your tours, be prepared with plans to help your clients in any way possible.

Technology Risks

You need a wide array of technology at your fingertips to make it as a travel agent today. If you're not savvy in how to set up and use technology, talk to techies you know and/or take courses or online webinars.

Technology is marvelous when it works and a nightmare when it doesn't. Computers have their bad days, as do all modes of high-tech communication. You need to be prepared with an alternative plan for everything you do, since tech support is not as supportive as it once was and new technologies (being turned out at a rapid rate to keep tech companies in business) are not always better than the predecessors. In fact, it's advisable to consider the learning curve and possible glitches before buying each "new and improved" version of what you regularly use to your satisfaction. Keep in mind that newer and faster does not always interface well with older technology, making it slow and exasperating as you try for hours to get your new equipment to work.

The truth is, you need more than one of everything. If you have a desktop, get a laptop, and vice versa. Get an inexpensive backup printer. Have more than one cell phone and backup software. In other words, never be in a position where nonworking technology can shut you down. And do not network everything to each other—that's the kiss of death in business unless you need to work on a document with ten of your co-workers. But WAIT, you don't have co-workers! So don't network everything. That way if one high-tech marvel stops functioning, the rest of your business is fine.

You must always have the ways and means necessary to stay in constant contact with suppliers, clients, and anyone else with whom you need to be in contact.

Also have local repair services at the ready. And back up all your data offsite! "I'm sorry, I can't help you because the computer is down or my phone battery is dying," should never, ever come from your mouth.

3

Meet the Homebased Travel Agent

It's a new world, and thanks to technology, working from home is not only a plausible means of starting your newly founded travel business, but the most common course of action. In fact, Joanie Ogg, CTC (Certified Travel Counselor), MCC (Master Cruise Counselor), and president of the National Association of Career Travel Agents (NACTA), the travel industry's association for homebased and cruise travel agents, teamed with her husband, mentioned earlier, to write a book called *How to Start a Home Based Travel Agency* (Tom Ogg and Associates, 2001). While some of the information has changed over the past ten years, the Oggs' book is still a valuable read for would-be, and "soon-to-be" travel agents.

License or Not?

So how do you pass the tests and get the license to become a homebased travel agent? With the exception of a few states, there is no required "test" or license to be a travel agent. While this, however, answers the "travel agent" question, states and local municipalities have their own business licenses and some will have rules and licensing requirements to run a home business.

Often, other than having a business license, the biggest obstacles you may face are local zoning ordinances, whereby local government is trying to maintain separate commercial and residential neighborhoods. Typically, the concerns are related to signage, garbage removal, deliveries, and parking for customers. Since your business is 99 percent via internet and the telephone, none of these should apply to you. This does not mean we are telling you to break any laws; we're not. However, a homebased business can operate very smoothly without calling attention to itself. In other words, don't have tractor-trailer trucks delivering goods in your driveway and you may be just fine.

Find out from your city government whether any permits are necessary, and if they are, file them. If you need a zoning variance, apply for that too. And, while you're interfacing with your local authorities, be sure to ask about obtaining your business license. This generally consists of filling out a simple form and paying a nominal annual fee. Again, it's easier to get it upfront than to ignore it and have it nagging at the back of your brain. If you need advice, check with your attorney for all the general information you'll need about obtaining business licenses and permits. In many towns and cities, you can also get licensing information from the county clerk's office or from a local municipality website, which may be that belonging to city hall. Search under business licenses in your town or city.

Finally, unrelated to licensing, there are certifications in the travel industry that are available. Such certifications can be beneficial for dealing with host agencies that find a newcomer more of a risk than someone who has at least received some formal training. We'll talk more about host agencies later. There are also courses offered by some of the major cruise lines and by the AAA.

Home, But Not Alone

As more travel agents set up shop from home, a whole new world of interactions among travel agents has appeared. "Part of our focus is to educate members and to help them communicate with each other," says Joanie Ogg, adding that they offer chat groups for such communication among travel agents. Ogg, along with most people in the travel industry, emphasize the importance of building up a network to share ideas, information, and ask questions. Homebased travel agents are selling to so many different niche markets that most are not in direct competition with one another. There are, however, similarities in terms of their basic needs as travel industry professionals.

Tom Ogg's Travel Agent Community features 7,500 travel agents sharing with other travel agents at www.hbtacommunity.com.

Additionally, travel organizations, associations, and groups can be excellent sources for networking, along with the educational and social aspects that are vital to success for most entrepreneurs. "Finding a mentor in the industry can be a marvelous way of learning about the business," adds Ogg.

You can also contact SCORE (Service Corps of Retired Executives), where retired professionals work with newcomers free of charge, and it's very likely that you can find a retired travel agent among the many members of this national organization (www. score.org).

Taking on Ticketing

One of the first things to know is that there's more to the travel world than agents and customers. There are also suppliers.

They come in many forms: airlines, cruise lines, hotels, car rental agencies, and tour operators. Add to this mix a sprinkling of industry associations. One of these entities is the Airlines Reporting Corporation, commonly referred to as the ARC. The ARC is a closed corporation owned by a select group, all of whom are members of the Air Transport Association of America (aka the ATA), an industry group made up of the major domestic airlines.

Agents handling airline ticketing no longer need a host agency to get an ARC appointment. Not long ago, a commercial storefront and public access were requirements to get an ARC appointment.

Today, ARC has changed in order to embrace the homebased travel agent. However, since the airlines no longer pay commissions to travel agents, most agents are not in the business of selling airline tickets. In fact, if the customer wishes, many travel agents will simply book airline tickets using the customer's credit card.

"I'll tell people, here are the flights you'll want to book and this is how much you can spend, and you can save yourself the ticketing fee by doing it yourself," explains Toni Lanotte-Day of Toni Tours Inc. "But many of them still say 'No, no, you book it for me' because they just don't have the time."

Today, ARC is also the premier organization identifying nonairline-appointed travel agents. Individuals can also now obtain a Verified Travel Consultant (VTC) designation from ARC and be issued an ARC number. Since the VTC program was introduced in 2007, it has already grown in stature and Tom Ogg predicts that it will soon be the industry standard. Along with an ARC number, VTC members receive access to numerous products and services in what is called the VTC Tool Kit. This includes an ARC MarketPlace,® which provides access to more than 6,000 commissionable destination activities, products, and services and is available 24/7. The application process takes 30 to 60 days, which is because there is a background check to weed out fraudulent agents. Licenses and a tax identification number are also necessary. The biggest plus is that you are not working through ARC or VTC, but with your own travel agent, benefiting from their knowledge and background and most significantly, their contacts and even marketing.

What Is ARC All About?

The Airlines Reporting Corporation (ARC) began as part of the Air Transport Association (ATA) in 1964. Some 20 years later, thanks to the deregulation of the airline industry, they separated and incorporated as the Airlines Reporting Corporation. Today, ARC is an airline-owned company, based in Arlington, Virginia, that serves the travel industry with financial services, data products and services, ticket distribution, and settlement in the United States, Puerto Rico, and the U.S. Virgin Islands. It provides services for more than 20,000 ARC-accredited travel agency locations. Along with offering services to travel agencies, ARC offers a variety of services for carriers, corporate travel providers, and industry service providers.

While the actual joining of any other such groups and associations is a bit premature, this example provides an idea of how the industry is now becoming far more favorable to the homebased travel agent.

The Global Distribution System

A Global Distribution System (GDS), also known as an Automated Reservation System (ARS) or a Computerized Reservation System (CRS), is a worldwide computer reservation system using a single point of access for reserving airline seats, hotel rooms, car rentals, and other travel-related items. Such a system is used by travel agents, online reservation sites, and large corporations who handle their own in-house travel planning.

The best-known global distribution systems are Amadeus, Galileo, Sabre, and Worldspan. They are owned and operated as joint ventures by major airlines, car rental companies, and hotel groups.

Believe it or not, the GDS dates back to the 1950s when Trans-Canada Airlines, American Airlines, and other growing carriers started their efforts to formulate such a computer-based system. But it wasn't until the 1960s that such computer distribution systems came into being, and it was in the 1970s when United began offering its Apollo system to travel agents. Although they were not allowed to book tickets on United's competitors, the marketing value of the convenient terminal was remarkable. For a while, despite many battles within the industry regarding the control and use of the various systems, the GDS remained critical to the industry. The bottom line for travel agents was simple; they had computer access and their clients did not.

The GDS systems were formed by major airlines, including Delta, American, United, Air France, and many others, individually or by teaming up. Among the most prominent users in recent years have been the discount travel websites.

For several years the GDS systems were gaining in popularity among U.S. travel agents. Today, however, they remain more prominent for travel agents outside of the United States, where they are only used by roughly 35 percent of agents.

The biggest players in the GDS world are Amadeus, Sabre, and Travelport, which owns Galileo. Amadeus, which is used in more than 94,000 travel agency locations worldwide, by 86,000 hotels, and by 500 individual airlines and 24 rental car companies, is the fastest growing of the companies. Sabre, meanwhile, is used by more than 55,000 travel agencies around the world and features more than 400 airlines, 88,000 hotels, 24 car rental brands, and 13 cruise lines.

While the GDS systems play a huge role in the travel business, the rapid drop-off in their usage in the United States has been clear as U.S. travel agents have begun to

▲

corner niche markets, build their own contacts, and get much higher commissions with direct contact to preferred suppliers. Even through host agencies, the GDS has not been of major use for many homebased travel agents since they essentially stopped selling airline tickets.

It is anticipated that in the near future the GDS will be a thing of the past in the U.S. travel industry.

Host Agencies Revisited

As mentioned earlier, you may want to work with an accredited host agency to help provide your clients with many more possibilities. According to a study by ASTA (American Society of Travel Agents) and NACTA (National Association of Career Travel Agents), 91 percent of travel agents split commissions with a host agency. Most travel experts agree that it is a great way to start in the business, and many continue to successfully work with hosts for years to come.

Host agencies offer various important services, including overrides, control, and support. A good host agency can help you establish yourself more quickly at a much higher level and your clients will benefit from your new position in the industry. They typically have long established relationships in a very relationship-oriented industry. Host agencies can get preferred supplier commissions and special marketing incentives.

Peter Stilphen, CEO of Coral Sands Travel, one of the most successful host agencies, supports a large network of independent agents. "We feel so strongly about the importance of support that we have limited our growth to just 600 members. This will enable us to offer the highest tier commissions and still give our members full support," says Stilphen of the business that offers an agent-only website that provides agents with the tools to operate their businesses.

Stilphen, who came up through the hospitality industry, later owned a brick-and-mortar travel agency before the times changed. Today, Coral Sands does 60 percent cruise travel, according to Stilphen, and it charges agents annual rates on the lower end of the spectrum. It is also a host agency that takes on new agents. "Since we take on new agents, we have simple training programs to help them get started," says Stilphen, who is a big supporter of up and coming agents.

How to Choose a Host Agency

According to Stilphen, one of the best things you can do is to talk to other agents who work with a host agency and find out if they are paying their commissions on time and giving the support that a travel agent needs.

"You want to find out how long a host agency has been in business, if they are properly licensed, what kind of support and/or training they offer, what their commission breakdown is (and if there are any deductions), with what associations they are affiliated (ARC, CLIA, etc.), how many travel suppliers and preferred suppliers they work with, what fees they charge and how often they charge, and how they communicate with you. Also make sure they have emergency support and are up-to-date on the latest in technology. The Professional Association of Travel Hosts Inc. (PATH) also suggests that you check to see if they have $1,000,000 in E&O insurance," says Stilphen.

Tom Ogg recommends looking for the following traits in a host agency:

- It already works with successful independent agents.
- It does not have any unresolved formal complaints against the agency.
- It is committed to developing a professional independent agent network.

To Host or Not to Host

One of the potentially confusing aspects of starting off as a homebased travel agent is deciding whether you need a host agency. If you're considering a host merely as a source for airline tickets, think again. You don't have to have one to put your clients on a plane.

Connie G., who specializes in travel for the physically challenged and for Christians, doesn't use a host at all. "We specialize in cruises and tour packages," the Pennsylvania travel agent explains. "We don't do airline tickets just for people going to see their grandchildren or flying to a conference." When Connie needs to get her clients from Philadelphia to a tour starting point in Paris, she has the tour operator handle the airfares or she issues them through a consolidator.

This doesn't mean that you should dismiss a host agency without a second thought. Industry experts recommend that you go the host route—so that you've got somebody who knows the ropes to help with your learning curve. As you gain your sea (and land and air) legs, you can then strike out on your own, just like Connie G. did. "The first couple of years, I booked everything through another agency," she says. "About four years ago, I set up my own CLIA [Cruise Lines International Association] agency and started working directly with suppliers."

- It does not have a "travel agent recruiting" program.
- It does not tout "travel agent ID cards" to obtain travel discounts.
- It does offer meaningful commissions and overrides. You can understand what you are getting for your investment (if anything).
- It does offer ongoing support where it makes money if you do.

On www.homebasedtravelagent.com/hosts.htm, Ogg also offers his thoughts on finding a host travel agency and lists some of the industry leaders.

Agencies to Avoid

There are lots of folks out there who call themselves travel agents, even though their only clients are themselves and their Aunt Mildred or Uncle Fred. The reason? Fam trips (familiarization trips) and other perks like hotel rooms and attractions, which supposedly can be had at sizable discounts by anyone with a card that proclaims them a travel agent.

If you're not careful, you might end up getting your "official travel agent photo ID card" by signing on with a host agency that is—truth be known—more interested in selling memberships than in selling travel. They require you to pay a fee (usually something like $495) for a package that includes various training manuals or videos, and of course, the ID card. They offer little in the way of commission splits and sometimes pay no commissions at all for products like hotels and car rentals.

Peter Stilphen points out that you can usually spot the bad guys. "They often charge much more money, are not members of NACTA, and are essentially multi-level marketing companies," explains Stilphen. In addition, they don't have good reputations or are not known by other travel agents.

These unscrupulous companies are known in the industry as card mills because of the way they hold out ID cards like carrots to prospective buyers. They are not the kind of host agency you want! You will find them popping up on the internet and advertising in various magazines, and you can recognize them chiefly by the fact that they spend more space touting the delights of "official agent" freebies than discussing actual business opportunities. You can sometimes get discounts with a card from one of these mills, but suppliers are becoming increasingly more stringent, offering fams only to those they recognize as true travel professionals.

The way the card mills work is by offering business opportunities rather than focusing on travel opportunities. By signing up 500 agents at $495 and having them pay $30 per month, they are making money ($247,500 in this simple example) by

Detecting Card Mills

You can spot card mills if they are:

- ○ using excessive hype and soliciting

- ○ offering travel agent ID cards

- ○ making claims of "big money" or great wealth"—like the guys on the late night real estate commercials teaching you how to buy houses with no money down!!!!

- ○ more interested in getting you on board (offering a "career" opportunity) rather than providing you with concrete information about how they can help you sell travel.

Remember, card mills make money primarily by getting agents to join and pay monthly fees, not by actually selling very much travel.

"Some so-called host agencies, who are really marketing firms, usually send out misleading email broadcasts containing outrageous text to get your attention. They offer 'get the money' seminars that smell of the old 'get rich quick' schemes offered by such multilevel marketing companies. Beware of those marketing firms offering consumers discounted travel afforded the 'real' agents. An overabundance of testimonials is also a good tip-off of a marketing agency. Serious travel agents won't get fooled if they do their homework," adds Peter Stilphen of Coral Sands Travel.

accumulating a bevy of agents. While they may sell some travel as well, they don't need to do so for their revenue.

Card mills give everyone in the industry a bad name, and they're one of the reasons the IATAN (International Airlines Travel Agent Network) is so strict about who they appoint. They're striving to make sure that travel specialists—whether outside sales reps, traditional retail agencies, or tour operators who also sell airline tickets—are reliable, reputable, and earn the respect of the public.

Remember, most of the time if something sounds too good to be true, it typically is not worthwhile. Most industries have the card mill equivalent, such as the blue-sky schemers in the vending business. The best you can do is research a host agency before affiliating. Check with places like NACTA (www.nacta.com), *Travel Trade* magazine (www.traveltrade.com), and the Outside Sales Support Network (OSSN), a trade association established in 1990 to represent and support the Home Based Travel Agency, Independent Contractor Seller of Travel, and the Outside Sales Travel Agent.

Playing the Field

Keep in mind that you do not have to do all of your business with one host agency. While most agents do, you can also establish tours on your own or book with more than one host agency. In fact, because of tax purposes, host agencies will not give you an exclusive contract. The IRS has strict stipulations about who is considered an independent contractor and who is considered an employee. If, for example, you do all of your business through one host agency, the IRS could consider you an employee. However, other stipulations, such as not having office space at the host agency's establishment or hours set by the agency, can help show that you are indeed an independent agent—and host agencies prefer this so that they are not in a position of having to pay unemployment and payroll taxes on your behalf.

While you can benefit from host agencies, they can also benefit from you. Today, the host agency needs homebased travel agents to help market and build their business. The steadily rising overhead costs of running a host agency mean there is a need to bring in as much revenue as possible, and homebased travel agents can help generate sales. In some ways, this is not unlike a real estate agent helping to generate sales for a real estate broker while collecting commissions on his or her sales. The difference, however, is that as a travel agent, you remain independent, and not working for the host agency.

It is a trickle-down business in which there are numerous travel suppliers and wholesalers all over the map. Likewise, there are many independent travel agencies such as yours. The host agency is essentially the middleperson serving to make some sense of the two much larger ends of the business, much as a real estate agent brings the multitude of buyers and sellers together, or as a literary agent filters book proposals from numerous authors to numerous publishing houses by determining which manuscript should go to which house, and which ones should go no place at all.

However, there is nothing stopping you from establishing some direct relationships with travel suppliers. In fact, as you build your business, in an effort to establish your uniqueness in the industry, you may want to start building and fostering relationships with some unique niche travel suppliers.

While a lot of your work will be with a host agency, you can do some packages on your own. For example, you may establish a relationship with a new tour provider who will give you a higher commission. You will, therefore, need to determine the situations in which you can go your own way, while still maintaining your relationship with a host agency, ensuring access to their relationships with travel suppliers.

Your Home Base . . . Your Office

As a homebased agency, you can locate your office workspace anywhere in the house that's convenient; but ideally, you should have a dedicated office, a room that's reserved just for the business. You can locate this room in a den, a finished room over the garage, the garage itself, in a finished basement, or a spare bedroom. Keep in mind that whatever space you choose will be your workstation and command center. Use the Home Office Worksheet on page 46 to evaluate possible locations for your home office.

"We decided not to take on the overhead of a storefront," says Jim T., the Maryland-based cruise specialist. "It's worked to our advantage as well as our clients' because they're not paying our overhead." Jim, with his wife and partner, Nancy, started off utilizing one room of their suburban home as a dedicated office and later built on a special office space.

Jennifer Doncsecz, president of VIP Vacations Inc., which specializes in destination weddings, added onto her Hamburg, Pennsylvania, house to accommodate the rapidly growing business needs. "We look like a doctor's office," says Doncsecz of the added space that allowed for five employees at their own computers plus additional phone lines and BlackBerry access. "We got the proper permits from our township to build. We also got our company trademark in the state and became incorporated," adds Doncsecz, who pays workers' comp and unemployment insurance for her employees. In recognition of the community, VIP Vacations also partners with the chamber of commerce, donates to local charities, and has a sign up on one of the local highways noting that they help with cleanup programs. "It's important to give back to your community, especially if they are letting you grow your business," says Doncsecz.

If a dedicated office is not an option for you, you can also station yourself in a corner of the kitchen, at the dining room table, or in a part of the family room. If you have a boisterous family, however, a cubby hole in your bedroom is liable to be much more

> ### Bright Idea
> Some homes, especially older ones, have walk-in closets that are large enough to turn into a cozy little office—some even have windows. If you decide to turn your closet into an office, make sure it has adequate ventilation and light.

▲

The Home Office Worksheet

Start by listing three possible locations in your home for your office, which should include a work area for you and enough space for your desk, computer, and telephone.

1. _____

2. _____

3. _____

Make a physical survey of each location.

❑ Are phone and electrical outlets placed close enough to your equipment so they can be accessed if you need them? Or can you go 100 percent wireless?

❑ Measure your space. Will your current desk or table (or the one you have your eye on) fit?

❑ Do you have adequate lighting? Can you work natural sunlight into your plan?

❑ Is there proper ventilation?

❑ What is the noise factor?

❑ Is there room to spread out your work?

❑ Optional: How close is it to the coffee maker? Refrigerator? (This can be either a plus or minus, depending on your current waistline and jitter factor.)

If you'll have equipment like backpacks, food storage containers, or bikes, list three possible home locations for this stuff.

1. _____

2. _____

3. _____

Take a survey of each:

❑ Is there adequate lighting, ventilation, and space for you to easily access your stuff?

❑ Will you need to construct special shelving or add other storage space? If so, make notes here. _____

conducive to quiet, clear thinking than a nook in the family room with the TV blaring at all hours.

Organized and Efficient

When you're working at home, it's important to remember that you are a professional. Your work quarters, like yourself, should be organized and efficient. If at all possible, designate a separate room with four walls and a door. Aim for pleasant, quiet, well-lit surroundings. You're going to be spending a lot of time in this space, so you want it to be comfortable.

Make sure you have enough space to neatly file the papers you will need, including client data and brochures and other materials from suppliers. While most of your data will be stored electronically (and hopefully backed up), hard copies still exist and you'll need to hang on to them. The paperless office is not yet existent and probably won't be in the near future.

Defining Your Space

To facilitate any or all of these dreams, you will need to allocate the right space and arrange it properly. Before you start framing a few favorite photos to put on your desk or "work station," stop and consider why you are setting up your home office in the first place.

The idea is to save on overhead, enjoy a very easy commute, and be efficient at your new travel business. Therefore, you'll need to take some time to focus on establishing the following.

A Space that Facilitates Clear Thinking

Look for a spot in your home that is relatively distraction free and doesn't interfere with other activities taking place in the house—or where you can separate yourself from such activities. It's not fair to your family if they have to tiptoe around because you are on phone calls in the middle of the daily activity. It is also not conducive to having quiet, undisturbed phone conversations. This doesn't mean

Bright Idea
Good lighting is essential for productivity—and for your eyes. Don't depend strictly on overhead lighting for a lot of deskwork. Lamps can be of great benefit for your desk or workstation. Plus, you can move them around as necessary.

your surroundings need to replicate a library. Some people are very comfortable working with noises or distractions going on around them, while others are not. The ideal situation is an environment that suits your comfort level.

Communications and Connectivity

The travel industry was among the first to embrace the computer and use it as an integral part of their business. However, once the personal computer became a mainstay in the American home, and once the internet provided the same connectivity to the world at large, the storefront travel agent lost that "edge." No longer was he or she privy to a world of travel opportunities that the consumer was not. The homebased travel agent obviously must keep up to speed with the latest in connectivity and remain one step ahead of the customers by joining membership associations and utilizing the internet for research above and beyond what the home user will find on the discount travel sites.

The key to connectivity is your router, and today, since wireless is necessary for your laptop(s), you need a quality wifi router. The Wireless N routers, or 802.11n units, are considered particularly good because they have stronger antennas. You want to be able to pick up the signal at all times and have multiple computers going at once if your business grows substantially.

Jennifer Doncsecz, now has a staff of five full-timers and has six computers going at once in an extended office built onto her home. "We needed a rather substantial wifi system here," says Doncsecz. "When you have five or six computers a normal wifi system doesn't work. We also need to have steady BlackBerry access as well as a few phone lines. People want a price and don't care if it's Sunday night at 8:00, so you need to be ready at any time."

Wifi technology is enhanced by proximity to the equipment being used. The environment and type of materials in the building structure can also come into play, so make sure you don't have dead zones in your chosen work space. The standard antennas, which come with most wireless routers, are omnidirectional antennas that distribute their signal equally in all directions. These antennas provide more uniform coverage in a radius, but they also limit the signal's reach in any particular direction.

Along with cell phones, wireless routers, and laptops, the need for outlets and phone jacks still remains. You will need to plan out your electronic needs prior to selecting your home office environment.

A desktop, a laptop, a smartphone, and a backup cell phone, or second smartphone, plus a landline or two are your key communication devices. More on your tech needs will be discussed in Chapter 6.

Temperature

It's no fun working in the coldest, warmest, or driest part of the house. It's also not the best place for technical equipment. Determine where you'll physically be most comfortable, and whether you'll need to invest in additional air conditioning or supplementary heating units (aka electric space heater).

Office Furniture

Since you are not entertaining clients, you can utilize inexpensive furnishings or even use some of what is sitting in your basement, attic, or at local garage sales. Just make sure that you have something strong enough to hold your PC, printer, and any other peripherals you may have. Typically, you will need a computer table and a desk or extended work area to spread out your printed matter. Shelves and filing cabinets will usually round out the picture, plus, as mentioned earlier, good lighting. Measure your space and plan accordingly. If the space is tight, think vertically, with shelves above and filing cabinets that slide under the work area. Measure everything.

One area you should not ignore is your chair. Don't listen to the budget books that tell you to "just use a folding chair" or the one at the kitchen table. Hand, wrist, back, and even neck injuries are the results of sitting for hours in the wrong position at your computer keyboard. Many chiropractors and physical therapists are getting rich from such homebased workers. For less than $200 you can find a good office and/or computer chair, and it will be well worth it!

For desktop computer use, you want a comfortable, adjustable chair with a curvature that feels right for you. Armrests are a matter of choice. You should also be thinking ergonomics, meaning the chair is designed for your posture, with contoured lumbar back support. Most computer chairs have high backs and some come with headrest support. Top-of-the-line chairs include forward tilt adjustment position, which has the chair adjusting to your movements. Wheels are common, so that you have some mobility. Look for the features that make you feel most comfortable. Before you buy any chair, take it for a test drive by sitting in it and rolling around a little to see how smoothly the chair moves. Obviously, you want a chair that moves when you want it to and remains still while you work.

The Homebased Lifestyle

Working from home is a lifestyle all its own. As an entrepreneur, you need to remember that nobody is going to tell you what time to start your day or when to take lunch, or even whom you need to call. You need to be self-motivated and ready to jump-start your business. As a home baser, you need to be especially diligent about setting up a schedule and sticking to it.

Start off with a daily, or weekly, to-do list and stick closely to it. You need not spend an inordinate amount of time honing such a list—in fact, don't get into the trap of spending too much time planning out your day. Just do it and move on. Too many people spend half of their day working on their calendar and then wonder why they can't get everything done in a day.

Just make sure you have the general idea of what needs to get done, and then try to estimate how many hours for each task. No, you don't need to put in 50 hours a week to start a homebased business. There are no floors to be swept or inventory to put in the supply room every day before you lock up. You can do well with the more standardized 40-hour week if your 40 hours are productive. Most of the people who claim that they work 60-hour work weeks do not realize how many unnecessary meetings and short breaks, lunches, coffees, or personal phone calls fall into those "60" hours. Therefore, when you work at home, make your hours count. After all, the only one you have to be true to is yourself.

The hardest part of running a homebased business for many people is getting motivated every day. Therefore, set up a schedule and try to stick to it. Perhaps you start by returning calls and emails each morning and then begin work on your marketing efforts. Whatever your plan is, try to fall into good habits.

Also, make rules for yourself, such as NO TV before 6 o'clock unless it's to check on an impending snowstorm, hurricane, or similar type of emergency. Have rules for the family, such as no disturbances when you are working unless it is truly an emergency—and define what qualifies as an emergency to your kids. Of course you should also plan to take periodic breaks during the day. If your kids come home from school every day at 3 P.M., you might take 3 to 3:30 every day as a break time to check up on their day. Remember, you are not bound by a 9-to-5 schedule either. While most of your phone calls and many emails will take place during those hours, you may find yourself putting in an extra hour or so at any given time to answer a client's "urgent" question, such as whether they can find a Ben & Jerry's on Tahiti. Good travel agents today, thanks to BlackBerrys, Droids, iPhones, and other such smartphones, are never totally off duty. But you can try to integrate your business and personal life in such a way that you find important downtime as you go.

Also keep in mind that there will be many time zone differences to contend with, so be prepared to stretch out your days into evenings on occasion.

The key is to focus on getting into (and sticking with) a rhythm, one that gets your business off and rolling.

And finally, remember, even though you are homebased, you are running a legitimate business. Therefore, have a dedicated phone line, stationery, business cards, your own business computer or two, printer, and so forth.

In later chapters we'll talk more about some of the tools of the trade.

The Mobile Travel Agent

Most travel agents not only enjoy what they do, but they have a passion for travel. This means they want to visit the destinations they sell. Not only do they enjoy the trips, but more importantly, they learn the lay of the land, checking out all the possibilities for prospective clients and networking and meeting with the resort owners, tour operators, and others with whom they will be building packages on a regular basis.

Remember, you can't stop your business while you are away. Therefore, your BlackBerry, Droid, iPhone, or whatever smartphone you have is an essential component of your travel agent life along with your laptop. And don't forget the chargers to keep everything going. In fact, the longer the trip, the more important it is to have a backup phone at the ready.

Today, travel agents should be able to do business from any location worldwide. Use business centers of major hotels or find a comfy spot by the beach to curl up and use your BlackBerry to communicate with clients and suppliers.

You pay the price by needing 24/7 accessibility—but it's not so bad doing business from the beaches in the Caribbean or South of France.

4

Finding Your Travelers
Market Research

Every business needs consumers if its products or services are to "live long and prosper," as the Vulcans so eloquently put it in the original *Star Trek*. Your mission is to determine who your customers will be, or your target audience.

This is an all-important phase in building a travel business, or any successful business for that matter. The proper market research can help boost your business into a true profit center. The more research you do before you officially post your website, send out your first materials, or place that first ad, the less floundering you're likely to do. In this chapter, we'll hone in on market research tips and techniques for the budding travel entrepreneur.

Defining Your Market

To be successful in the travel business, you'll need to target your market carefully, deciding what sorts of products you'll specialize in and defining your customers. Travel agents often run into difficulties selling their services because they fail to take this crucial step into consideration. Despite the fact that travel is much more accessible to the average Joe or Jane than it once was, it is still a relatively expensive proposition and is still considered by many—including some travel agents—to be a luxury instead of a necessity. Hence the term "Luxury Travel." However, there are those among us for whom travel is not a "luxury" but a mental and physical health requirement. Few people can survive comfortably on the "all work and no play" plan.

Choosing Your Clients

Let's start by looking at the types of travelers you might target. Remember, we are living in a niche-oriented society, so the way to separate yourself from your competitors is to find a niche and become the best in that area. Gone are the days of generalist travel agents who could book a vacation in France for a young couple, a seniors cruise to Mexico, and a family trip to Disney World back-to-back and continue doing a little of everything. To find a niche, you need to select one, two, or perhaps three demographic groups from among this list of candidates:

- Business travelers
- Leisure travelers
- Adventure travelers
- Honeymooners
- High-income travelers
- Budget-conscious travelers
- Families
- Students
- Seniors

- Disabled travelers
- Travelers of a specific lifestyle (single, divorcees, gay/lesbian, etc.)

Remember, you don't have to target one of these groups to the exclusion of all others, but the more you specialize, the better your earnings are likely to be. Why? One reason is that you develop a reputation—and therefore a clientele—as an expert in that field. Another is that, as you gain expertise in your market, you learn where the best deals are so you can pass them along to your clients and meet their needs.

The Business Traveler

Business travelers can also mean big business for the travel agent, as well as for the tour operator. For the majority of businesspeople, travel means shuttling back and forth between airport, hotel, and meeting site, in an exhausting round of suitcase and briefcase toting. They need somebody to do the planning for them. As you know, you won't earn top dollar from the commissions, but rather from the convenience of your service and your specialization as an expert in your area. You'll also benefit from the contacts you make on your own.

In addition, commercial travelers may bring significant others along for the ride, and these folks need something to keep them occupied while hubby or wife is in a conference. A tour lasting an afternoon to a week can be just the ticket. Business travelers themselves often like to spend a morning or a day between appointments seeing the local sights. So business travel can be terrific for some travel specialists, although most focus on leisure travel.

Since major corporations usually have large corporate agencies making their bookings, your best bet, if you want to focus on the business crowd, is to concentrate on small to midsize companies. They don't need or want the vast computerized networks of mega-chain agencies, like American Express. What they do want is precisely what you can provide: the personal attention and counseling they can get only from a small agency. That's you!

Smart Tip

Don't assume business travelers—even frequent flyer types—know what they want. They don't. Beyond the basics of "Cleveland" or "Curacao," they usually have no idea of where to stay and what to see or even if there is anything to see. You can start with a host agency that is familiar with the needs and wants of business travelers or plan your own itineraries around a day of conferences and seminars. This might mean a hotel nearby the convention center, with a full business center for their work-related activities and perhaps shows, tours, or sporting events in the evening. Get to know the Convention & Visitors Travel Bureau in each of the major business travel markets and start making your own contacts as well.

The Leisure Traveler

Most experts agree that the future of the small travel agency or tour operator lies in serving the leisure traveler—not the guy in that retro '70s leisure suit, but the person traveling for fun rather than business. Leisure travelers range from those seeking sun and surf to those looking for adventurous activities. They want personalized attention and will benefit from your contacts.

Smart Tip

Tip...

Tourists interested in cultural and historic experiences tend to spend more, stay in hotels more often, visit more destinations, and be twice as likely to travel for entertainment purposes than other travelers, according to the Travel Industry Association of America.

There are many types of leisure travel, so your best bet is to zero in on what your demographic group wants to do. You might also choose an activity such as skiing and become the ultimate travel expert on ski trips in one place or in several locations.

Whether you are working with a host agency or have established relationships with suppliers on your own, or do both (which is not uncommon), the key is to listen closely to what your clients want and meet those details to the best of your ability. Show them that the cheapest way to plan a vacation is not always the best choice, since nobody wants to sacrifice the fun or enjoyment of a vacation to save a few bucks. The more trips you book, the more you will be able to anticipate your clients' needs and have offers ready for your niche market.

The Adventure Traveler

As you probably know, adventure and ecotourism are growing travel specialties, and we'll explore them in more detail in Chapters 8 and 11. For now, it is worth considering these as two very viable potential demographic groups. Keep in mind, however, that if you're not an expert in the field, you won't have much success. You can't very well take novices whitewater rafting if you don't know an oar from a paddle. Likewise, you can't lead a trek through the Alaskan bush if you yourself get lost going to the post office.

Many adventure and ecotour operators lead tours because of an overwhelming desire to share their experience and their love of the natural world with others. If this is you, then the adventure or ecotour route might just be the direction for you to take.

Again, don't try to bite off more than you can do. One travel agent focuses on skiing in the winter in Aspen and water skiing in the summer in Florida while another focuses on African Safaris. Of course, these travel experts also love what they do.

The Honeymooners

Newlyweds can be a big market for the travel agent, and today, because many of these couples are marrying a little later in life—having spent years as working singles—they have the funds to splurge on a splashy honeymoon package. Here, you can typically handle everything from soup to nuts. Since the couple is likely so immersed in wedding planning, they will typically be more than happy to have someone handle all of the honeymoon details, once they pick the place. You can make that easier by getting to know the suppliers in some of the most popular honeymoon destinations in the world. The more business you send them, the more favorable deals you will get. Many travel suppliers and hotels/resorts are very accommodating to newlyweds. If you want to have your clients tell all their soon-to-be-married friends about you, add some special romantic touches, such as champagne, fruit baskets, or some clever unique touch.

Fun Fact

The word "posh," according to some sources (and hotly contested by others) comes from the luxury liners of the 19th century. First-class passengers were assigned staterooms that were facing Port going Out and Starboard going Home, and thus on the sunny side during both legs of the voyage.

The High Roller

How about targeting your agency or tour package toward the upper-crust types? These are the folks who take the posh Orient Express instead of plebian British Rail, and opt for tea with Lady Whomever instead of cocoa from a thermos. High-income travelers represent the minority, but you can realize a high profit margin, both as an agent and/or as a tour operator, by catering to this market.

Like the adventure/ecotour specialist, you have to know your target audience and the specifics of the product you're selling. You also need to know where this target market enjoys vacationing and get to know those suppliers. However, since this group may already have established their own ties with resort owners and managers, you may benefit from looking for the next stunning location barely discovered by the high-end travelers. It's important to stay one step ahead whenever possible.

This is a specialty type of planning and you have no competition from the discount websites, since this crowd is willing to spend more to get more. Now it is up to you to learn where the wealthy crowd likes to gather and what they appreciate from a vacation. Your fee is for your expertise. Again, if you are working with a host agency, make sure they have strong relationships with suppliers that can cater to this market.

The Budget Traveler

Volumes have been written about traveling on a shoestring—everything from *Cost Conscious Cruiser: Champagne Cruising on a Beer Budget*, by Mary Lin Pardey and Larry Pardey, to the immensely popular and well-written *Let's Go* series, published by St. Martin's Press. These books never fall out of fashion, for a very good reason. There are always budget-conscious travelers, people who long to see the world but whose pocketbooks run more toward peanut butter and jelly than pheasant under glass.

Today, with the internet's bevy of discount travel websites, the only way to compete effectively in this market is to provide something different, based largely on your research of the market and your own creativity. For example, students frequently travel via the discount route. Therefore, you need to come up with the ultimate spring break package that is in line with the internet costs, but offers specific activities geared toward this crowd. Parties with fun finger foods, DJ's, contests, and other college favorites can put you on the map, provided you are conscious of keeping students out of trouble. Much of the success of catering to the budget travel crowd is in finding true off-the-beaten-path discounts at quality locations. Get to know the suppliers, many of whom will be happy to provide discounts if you can fill their rooms or pack their tours.

> **Bright Idea**
>
> You might also consider marketing to ethnic or religious groups. Connie G., the travel specialist in Pennsylvania, for instance, sells a lot of Christian pilgrimages and cruises. Other agents specialize in church or temple groups that have specific destinations they want to visit.

Family Ties

Family vacations usually focus on destinations with plenty of kid-friendly activities so parents can retain a semblance of sanity. You know the drill: Disneyland, Disney World, a Disney Cruise, and so on. But there's a whole other world of fun for both big and little kids. There's everything from dolphin spotting along the crystalline sands of Panama City Beach, Florida, to biking through the Czech Republic. If you're a kid at heart, you can target this growing market.

This is a very large market as family travel is growing as an important part of bonding and togetherness.

Keep in mind that there is tremendous competition for the families with little tykes. Therefore, you can find a very big target audience by also marketing trips for families with pre-teens and young teens, ages 10 to 14. And, if you can find great family trips where both teenagers and their parents want to go, you may hit the jackpot, since very often 15- to 17-year-olds don't really want to go along, but aren't ready to be left home alone. Cruises, family-friendly activities such as skiing, or trips to popular beach locations can be favorites with this market.

Targeting family reunions is another way to capture some of the family vacation market.

The Student Prince

Another (but vastly different) young niche market is student travel, which is sort of a sub-category of budget travel, with a twist. These are travel tours set up specifically for a group of students. Here you are marketing to high school and college kids. Actually, you are often marketing to their parents, who pay the way for graduation trips to Europe, surfing safaris to Costa Rica, and spring break madness.

There's yet another student market in the world of educational tours, the ones where a brave band of teachers and chaperones leads a group of kids on a tour of the "Wonders of Western Europe" or "Our Nation's Capital." These tours are aimed quite specifically at teachers, with the goal of having them sign up kids for the trips. Typically, the tour operator sends teachers a kit containing everything necessary to promote the package—invitational letters to parents, registration sheets, posters, videos, and even T-shirts. And some student-tour operators have special packages for home-schooled children so parents and kids can meet and learn with other home-scholars.

A Bit of Speculation

Terry S., the Seattle tour operator, says the best customers for his walking tours are seniors, along with the 40- and 50-something set, professionals, convention groups, and visitors to his fair city.

"I started my walking tours based on my observation that a) no one was doing such a tour in Seattle on a year-round basis (just van and bus tours), and b) my belief that there was a market for such a tour," says Terry. "A bit of speculation, but I was confident enough to give it a try. I did not conduct market research in the traditional sense. But I did informally ask a wide variety of individuals and organizations, 'If there were such a tour, would you or your group be interested?' Most all said yes."

The biggest incentive by far, however, is that the teacher or "tour leader" gets a free trip for signing on a certain number of kids and then also receives a cash bonus for any additional students she signs up. Who could refuse?

Golden Girls and Guys

Today's seniors are more active than ever before, and tours aimed for them encompass everything from snowmobiling in Alaska to attending traditional weddings in Indonesia. Post-retirement seniors are free of the constraints of jobs and school-age kids that fetter the rest of us, so they have plenty of time in which to travel and plenty of enthusiasm. Karen A., the tour operator in Savannah, Georgia, says her best customer group, besides Girl Scout troops and school groups, is the older set, prosperous people in their 50s and 60s with money and time to spare for specialty package tours. More on tours for this demographic group is coming up in Chapter 12.

The Physically Challenged Traveler

Not so long ago, people with physical disabilities had fewer travel options. Today, however, disabled wanderlusters can roam the world thanks to tour operators who arrange wheelchair-accessible transport and seek out accessible sights. Even adventure travel is a can-do, with everything from skiing to horseback riding to canoeing to hand cycling on the menu. If you're familiar with the demands and quirks of getting about in a wheelchair or walker, you might find this a rewarding target market.

"My agency specializes in disabled travel, specifically for blind and deaf travelers, wheelchair users, and slow walkers," says Connie G., the travel agent based in Pennsylvania, who's been interested in sign language since she was a child. "I took sign language classes, which automatically [led to] working with deaf clients. The more involved I got in the travel industry and with deaf clients, the more I had people coming to me with other disabilities saying, 'Why don't you handle us, too?' Most of it was friends saying 'If you can learn to work with a deaf client you can learn to work with a blind client or a wheelchair user.'"

Carving Your Own Niche

When Jennifer Doncsecz went into the travel business after finishing school, she knew she loved the business but didn't know which direction to take. In time, she decided to branch out on her own with a home office, and while searching for a niche, she discovered the growing popularity of destination weddings. A few years later, her company, VIP Vacations Inc., became the leading destination wedding travel agency in the nation, winning a number of awards along the way. To carve such a niche, Doncsecz researched and immersed herself in the wedding travel industry. Today, she has her own network of suppliers at the leading destination wedding locations worldwide. "We have our preferred resorts and most have a wedding liaison right there, since we're not Jennifer Lopez in *The Wedding Planner*, but still the travel agents," explains Doncsecz. "We're very close with Sandals Resorts. I make a phone call and have all the information at hand. They have a whole wedding team right in Miami. It's the same with some of the resorts in Mexico with wedding offices," adds Doncsecz, who also gets requests for some less popular destinations, where she has to find out the legalities associated with a wedding and the best accommodations for such a special occasion.

Finding a unique niche, such as destination weddings, and building a business around the niche doesn't happen by accident. It takes research, a lot of networking, and some visits to see exactly what is on hand at these destinations. It also helps to sell such marvelous destinations to friends of the bride and groom who may get married in a nondestination wedding and be looking for a great place to honeymoon. That's one of the ways in which Doncsecz expands her business. Remember, the travel industry is largely a word-of-mouth business.

Researching Your Market

There are two ways to go about doing research to zero in on your target market. You can either decide on the market based on your own passion and interests or explore where people are traveling and why and become an expert in that niche market. Explore the field and look for the market areas that are being underserved or find a group that you could appeal to from a sales and marketing perspective. Consider the resources and relationships you already have and those that you build during this discovery process, and that may help you hone in on the best market for you to pursue. For example, if you find a good host agency that has numerous cruise suppliers and you are personally familiar with cruises, then you might follow this path.

Once you have decided what sort of travel and tours you want to specialize in and who your participants will be, you might be tempted to stop there. But you are still not nearly finished with your market research! You will need to do specific research on this group to find out their income range, typical amount of vacation days, and what type of travel they are most likely to enjoy. You will combine both secondary resources, from books, the internet, and other published matter, with primary resources, which means going to the source and finding out what they like and why.

Find out how they feel about the products you plan to offer. Would they buy? How much would they spend? How frequently would they use your services?

One way to reach those potential customers is through online surveys. Some people are happy to fill out complete surveys, while others may only provide useless information. Therefore, you may need to find more inventive ways to go about your marketing, such as setting up (with permission) a booth in a mall and providing a giveaway or contest (for a small prize) that gives people incentive to answer a brief questionnaire. You might also make arrangements with a more established website that reaches the target market you are interested in and ask them to post a survey, again providing some sort of incentive. You might offer a special discount package or free ad on your site to the website owner who helps you with the survey.

What should you ask? Check out the sample "Focus Group Questionnaire" on page 64. Your queries will relate to your own target market and products, but you can use this as a starting point for what and how to ask. Remember, you should not ask for personal or identifying information, BUT, you can ask for their email address for sending future promotions. Keep your questions brief and to the point. People are not going to write essays!

You will most likely have better success today with emails than either snail mail or phone calls. One thing you can do is join organizations that allow you to contact the membership list (many will not give out the information for solicitations). Buying mailing lists may provide a lot of unwanted responses.

Often, the key is to just get out there and be in places where people in your demographic group will be found. Have a stack of questionnaires in hand, give an incentive (someone wins 30 percent off a vacation package), and talk to people—don't harass them. If you need permission to do this, at a fair or organized event, then get it. Barter your way in the door and do some market research.

Don't forget chat rooms and discussion boards on the web. Start threads in travel groups where you can discuss travel possibilities and see what people think.

Up Close and Personal

Another top technique for getting market research is to get up close and personal with a focus group. This is an informal gathering between you and a medley of potential travelers, usually 5 to 12 people. Try to hold several different focus groups. The more responses you have to work with, the better. Also, by holding several groups, you can change some of your questions based on what you've learned from the previous groups—this can help you generate more specific answers as you go. You can invite family (though they may be biased on your behalf), friends, friends of friends, co-workers, and colleagues in clubs or organizations you belong to. Keep in mind, however, that your focus groups should be composed of people who will have some connection with your proposed products. For instance, when researching family travel, you should invite people who travel with their families regularly— your co-workers or those of your spouse or sibling, or people from a local business

organization. Acquaintances whose only travel is taking the cross-town bus can be left out. Try to spread the word outside of your immediate circle and provide some food or some incentive for everyone who attends. Sandwiches and drinks for 12 people is a small investment in your marketing efforts, maybe $60.

Once you have your focus group assembled and you've distributed some sort of refreshment, you essentially have a captive audience to respond to your most pressing market concerns. Hand out questionnaires, have plenty of pens and pencils on tap, and encourage discussion.

Delve into the sample Focus Group Questionnaire for an idea of how to formulate your own question-and-answer sessions. Instead of family travel, you might be asking about New Age tours of Britain, honeymoon favorites, or business travel programs for small office/home office types. Ask as many questions as you feel your group can comfortably handle. Keep your questions focused on your objective: finding out what potential clients will want to see and do, what they will pay, and what travel products will draw them in. Let a discussion emerge and take notes. Then move on to the next question. Try not to direct answers to what you want to hear, but remain as objective as possible.

Just the Facts, Ma'am!

Besides going directly to your potential participants for market research, you'll also want to get some good statistical information—as Jack Webb on *Dragnet* would say, "Just the facts, ma'am." In other words, do you know how many families there are in the United States or how many there are in greater metropolitan Atlanta, for instance? How many retirees are there in the Midwest with sufficient income to travel? How many cooking enthusiasts are there in Anchorage, Alaska? The answers to questions like these will give you an idea of just how many potential participants there are for your products and if that number is large enough to be lucrative. Jennifer Doncsecz knew that the number of destination weddings had quadrupled in the years leading up to her decision to make that her niche. You need to know if your travel idea is potentially lucrative.

Focus Group Questionnaire for Family-Oriented Travel Agency

About Your Past Vacation Experiences

1. How many children are in your family?

   _____

2. What are their ages?

   _____

3. How many times a year do you travel with your kids?

   _____

4. Where do you usually vacation?

   _____

5. Where do you usually stay?

   _____

6. How long do your family vacations usually last?

   _____

7. What do you usually spend per family vacation?

   _____

About Future Vacations

1. Where would you like to vacation?

   _____

2. What types of activities does your family enjoy?

   _____

   _____

3. Are you interested in the history of the areas you visit?

   _____

4. Are you interested in the art or music of the areas you visit?

   _____

Focus Group Questionnaire for
Family-Oriented Travel Agency, continued

5. If you could extend a business trip to include vacation travel, would you be interested?

   _____

6. Would you be interested in a destination that allows adult-only time by providing daily child care?

   _____

7. How many hours of child care per day would you consider reasonable?

   _____

8. What is your family income?

   _____

   (Keep in mind that some of your group participants may not be willing to share income information with you.)

About Business Names

1. Please comment on the name Fun-For-All Family Travel (love, like, dislike, hate). (You could also use a 1–5 rating system from best to worst.)

   _____

2. Please comment on the name Intrepid Family Adventures (love, like, dislike, hate).

   _____

Please comment on the following tour packages:

(Here, you hand out three of your upcoming tour package ideas and find out whether the participants like any of them. You could ask for comments as to why they did or did not like the packages. If you are working with a host agency, list some of the packages offered by travel suppliers that you would like to promote.)

- *The internet.* A world library at your fingertips! For starters, check in with the U.S. Census Bureau at www.census.gov and the Department of Commerce at www.doc.gov (yes, they collect all that data for a reason—here's your chance to take advantage of it). Also go to travel bloggers, travel magazine websites, and those of the many travel associations (see the resources in the Appendix), or do a search for travel statistics and you'll find many places with numbers you can use. Hint: Check the dates and make sure they are fairly recent stats. Don't settle for numbers from 1996; look for something from 2010. The internet is also home to a world of interactive communications.

- *The social media.* Use Facebook, Twitter, LinkedIn, and other such tools of the social media to communicate with your target market about your area of interest. You need not say that you are a travel agent, but simply start a conversation about your topic. Get people talking, generate responses, and see what they think as you continue the conversation. The social media is interactive and that's your cue—keep the comments rolling in; you'll learn a lot.

- *Organizations and associations.* What better places to go for information on your specific market? If you're targeting senior citizens, for example, you could contact the American Association of Retired Persons for a count of its members.

Adding a Little Luxury

Carlson Wagonlit Travel boasts more than 3,000 locations in 150 countries or territories. The company began in 1872, when Belgian entrepreneur Georges Nagelmackers decided to give travelers a little luxury by adding sleeping compartments (wagons lits in French) to existing European railways. After creating his new firm, not coincidentally called Wagon-Lits, Nagelmackers went on to found the world-famous Orient Express.

Meanwhile, in 1888, Ward G. Foster opened his travel company, Ask Mr. Foster, in St. Augustine, Florida. By 1900, it was clear that lots of people were "asking Mr. Foster"—he had 160 offices in Europe and North Africa, from which he sold train tickets and hotel rooms. In 1972, Peter Ueberroth (you remember him, the baseball commissioner who later brought the Olympics to Los Angeles) bought Ask Mr. Foster for a mere $1 million. Then in 1979, Ueberroth sold the company to Carlson, which merged with Wagon Lit Travel in 1997 to form the international firm of Carlson Wagonlit. And it all started with sleeping compartments.

To find out the number of high school teachers, you'd talk to the folks at state and regional teachers' associations.

The Travel Agent's Competition

After you have decided on your target market, you'll need to find out what sort of competition you'll be up against. It's one thing to know that "Hey, there are 10 million potential clients out there." But it's another thing entirely to discover that there are thousands of other travel agents doing what you do. So you'll need to find out how many competitors you have in a particular niche market. There is room for several players within a given market, but you can't slice the pie too many ways and have anything left.

Your competitive edge will be in your network and the inroads you've made with suppliers. In the beginning, your inroads will be more in line with the suppliers your host offers. However, you will need to add your own expertise, personalized service, efficiency, and consistency to the mix. Then, as you begin to make your own contacts in the industry, you will start to set yourself apart from your competitors. The more specific your area of expertise, the smaller your competition will get. Of course, your market may get smaller as well. This means being aggressive. If, for example, you are offering family ski trip packages in Stowe, Vermont, then you need to be at every ski show in the Northeast and on every family vacation blog you can find. You need to have a creative package, priced accordingly, that includes everything the skiing family could want.

Research the family market, check out your competitor's offers and rates, and do what is done in every business—look for your competitive edge. What can you offer that your competitor doesn't?

As an agency with a niche market, you have another edge—the creative one. With no giant-corporation clients to appease and no impersonal rules to stick to, you can develop relationships with individual suppliers who will reward you with handsome commissions. There are an increasing number of carriers and suppliers who sell directly to the travel agents, and if they like working with you, it can allow you to build up your niche much more quickly.

The Tour Operator's Competition

As a tour operator, your competition will come primarily from existing firms that offer the types of specialty tours that you want to market. In a more general sense, however, you'll also face some competition from traditional tour packagers.

Preferred Suppliers

When you think about selling travel, either as an agent or as a tour operator, you need to think about preferred suppliers. As you know, suppliers are the companies that provide the travel products—cruise lines, tour packages, hotels, car rentals, and attractions. Preferred suppliers are those with whom you, or your host agency, build a special relationship: You send business their way and they reward you with higher commissions, which are often called overrides.

Here's basically how it works. Let's say you discover a wonderfully romantic getaway in Transylvania, an absolutely perfect destination for upscale singles. You develop a marketing program aimed at singles, and you start sending bevies of them to the resort. Because you're sending scads of business their way, the resort decides to give you higher than average commissions. It's now one of your preferred suppliers.

If Joe's Travel Agency down the street—which doesn't have a preferred supplier relationship—sells a Transylvanian package, Joe gets the regular 10 percent commission. You, however, as a preferred agent of the preferred supplier get a 5 percent override on top of the commission, which adds up to a heftier 15 percent in your pocket. Since host agencies, working with 300 or 400 independent travel agents, can send a supplier a tremendous amount of business, they typically have many preferred suppliers.

You, on the other hand, can create better deals with suppliers on your own—but it takes time and consistency in regard to making sure you fill their rooms.

A traditional tour company arranges transportation for its clients, shows off the sights of a given city, provides an evening's entertainment (i.e., Hawaiians performing traditional Hawaiian hula dances), and arranges lodging in a hotel or motel. These companies usually buy transportation and accommodations at group rates, which means they're often getting bargain-basement prices that they can pass along to their customers.

While smaller, niche tour operators technically have the ability to get the same deals, in actual operation it's difficult. Why? Because specialty tour packagers generally only purchase as much lodging and transportation as they need for the clients participating in a particular trip. Because the trip is more personalized, there are usually fewer travelers per journey. So specialty packagers don't buy in volume and don't get discounts to pass along to their clients. If, however, your clients are not looking at discount travel, but are willing to spend more to get more, then you are fine, and often in today's more selective environment, people are doing just that, paying for your expertise and for something that caters directly to their interests.

The Road Less Traveled

So, we've narrowed your primary competition down to existing specialty tour operators. Since there are roughly 8,000 adventure travel companies in the United States alone, that's more than a smidgen of rivalry. Not to worry, though! You can succeed, but you need to carefully target your market and develop your own niche.

In the specialty tour business, going off the beaten track or taking the road less traveled is a strong selling point, especially when it comes to adventure tours. As we've already explored, these tours typically take small but hardy groups to remote areas. The waters of the Amazon River, the steppes of the Russian Far East, and the slopes of the Himalayas are already on the books of a variety of tour operators. As expansive as these areas are, there may be a limit to the number of packagers that can run competing tours to them. You can't very well run an "exclusive" tour in a region overrun with a dozen other companies. And, as more visitors flood into remote locations, the less "unspoiled" they remain. So your challenge is to find unique and less crowded destinations.

Something Completely Different

If your goal is to succeed as a tour operator, one way to be competitive with existing operators is to offer something completely different. You could locate new or under-served destinations ("Midsummer Sahara Getaway!" or "Sing-Sing Like You've Never Seen It!"). Or you could offer a new twist on an already well-served destination, like "A Cook's Tour of Cook County," Illinois, featuring visits and lessons with famous Chicago-area chefs.

Offering a completely unique tour is probably the best way to compete with existing operators, but you can also vie for business by offering a tour fairly similar to those already on the market, if you can add

> **Fun Fact**
>
> There's more to see in North Dakota than you might imagine. This generally unsung area of the country boasts a bevy of oversized animals, scattered along the highways: a towering 40-foot sandhill crane; a massive Holstein cow, standing 38 feet tall; a buffalo weighing 60 tons; and a 36-foot-tall gorilla. Who says you can't sightsee in even the most featureless landscape?

something that distinguishes it from the others. Yours might differ through superior service; your personal knowledge of the terrain, people, culture, and history; or incomparable suppliers and outfitters.

Another approach is to cater to a different audience than the norm. While all around you operators are wooing young urban professionals or seniors, you might ply your tours among 30-something singles, empty nesters, or the many individuals looking to learn about a certain cultural heritage, such as Ireland for Irish Americans who have never been to the Emerald Isle. The key here is to look for a market otherwise not being reached by these types of travel offers.

Shopping the Competition

A little competition is healthy. If you do your homework properly, research your suppliers, and structure your company intelligently, you will shine despite—or because of—your rivals' lights.

The time to scrutinize your rivals is during your market research phase. What are they doing that's absolutely perfect? What can you successfully emulate? What are they doing that you can do better? What can you offer that will draw customers away from them and to you?

How can you answer all these questions? Start by performing these research tasks:

- Go ahead and shop, the competition, that is, find out what they are offering and what they charge. Take a tour if you can afford it. Then study them. What works? What doesn't? And why?
- Attend all the travel seminars and workshops you can. Ask questions. Don't be shy!
- Surf your competitors' websites. Send for brochures. Again, study what your rivals are doing. Explore what works and what doesn't work, and why.

Your Traveler's Trunk

Business Names, Structures, and More

OK, you've done your market research. You've decided on your target clients and your market niche. Terrific! Now, even though you may be living out of a suitcase for days at a time, you'll need to design a tight, sturdy "trunk" for your new company. You will need a structure that will keep it not only looking good, but solid enough to weather anything life might dish out. In this chapter, we'll guide you through that process, from choosing a company name to selecting a legal structure.

Name That Business

Every business has to have a name. You should devote as much thought to choosing an appellation for your company as you would for your kids. After all, you plan to have your business around for a long time. You want a name you can be proud of, one that identifies both the business and yourself. With a good name, you can identify who you are and what you are selling.

Many travel specialists incorporate the name of the products they sell into their business moniker—for example, Amazon Adventure Tours or Pack Up the Kids Travel Agency. This idea can be a blessing, or it can backfire. The blessing part is that it easily identifies your product; anybody can tell at a glance what your specialty is. But, if you call your company Alaska Outback Tours, for instance, and you later decide to branch out and offer Australian walkabouts, you're going to run into difficulties because your name won't have anything to do with your new product. This will make you harder to identify as a supplier of that Australian tour, and it will also cost you credibility.

This doesn't mean you shouldn't use your products in your business name; it just means you'll need to think about your long-range goals before you choose. This second option, Pack Up the Kids, still leaves a broad category of demographics, family vacations, while a specific name, such as Alaskan Tours, could possibly be too limiting, although the Alaskan tour market is booming. Only you can determine, in your research and planning, how much business you can get from a certain market. For example, some travel destinations, such as New York, Las Vegas, or Europe as a whole, are so rich with potential that you can build a business on them for years to come.

Some businesses simply offer a name that exudes confidence, such as A-1 Travel, Great Trips, or VIP Vacations. Others define themselves by their location, such as Boston Travel or San Francisco Travel. Let people know where you are or what you offer, or simply give them great expectations (Great Expectations Travel).

As a travel agent, you might consider naming your company for a large regional feature, like Sea Coast Travel if you are

> **Beware!**
> Your name not only has to look good; it has to sound good. Ellis Dee Tours for partners Ellis and Dee is fine on paper, but over the phone it will sound like LSD Tours, and while this may have been popular in 1967, it isn't the kind of trip you want to sell!

Business Name Brainstorming

List three ideas based on the travel products you plan to provide (i.e., honeymoon packages, cruises, eco-adventures).

1. _____

2. _____

3. _____

List three ideas combining a favorite theme with your planned products (i.e., cultural awareness, environmental awareness, kid-friendliness).

1. _____

2. _____

3. _____

After you've decided which name you like best, ask yourself, have you:

❑ Tried it aloud to make sure it's easily understood and pronounced? (Has it passed muster with your family? Have you had a friend call to see how it sounds over the phone?)

❑ Checked your local Yellow Pages to make sure the same or similar name is not already listed?

❑ Checked with your local business name authority to make sure it's available?

based by the sea or Bluegrass Travel if you're in Kentucky. As a tour operator, this doesn't always work, though. Sea Coast Tours is fine if you're leading groups along the nearby shore, but if your real mission is taking tourists to Outer Mongolia, then Sea Coast Tours is dead wrong.

For some top-notch ideas on choosing your own business name, take a look at the travel companies listed in the Appendix. You'll want to make yours as individual as you are, but these will get those creative gears turning. You can also look for travel agencies listed in your city (or any city) on Manta.com.

Eminent Domain

Another key factor in name selection is your website. You will need to register your domain name, that www.whatever.com address that people use to access your virtual office. There can be only one domain name per company, so you'll have to think up several versions of the name you want in case one's already been taken.

Here's what you do: Go to www.hostgator.com, www.networksolutions.com, or www.godaddy.com and check to see if your name choice is available. If it isn't, choose another. When you find a name that's available, register online and get your website. You can register for a domain name and actually get a site going with HostGator for $39 plus a monthly fee of around $6. There are various domain name registration sites, but typically, you won't pay more than $30 per year just for the domain name. You may also register some similar names if they are available, such as both the .com and .net suffixes of the name, or common misspelling. For example, if, while trying to go to Google.com, you type www.gogle.com, www.gooogle.com, or www.googel.com, you will still get www.google.com!

Keep in mind that when thinking of a name today, it not only has to look and sound right, but it needs to be easy to spell and to remember. And, for the sake of typing in a web address, don't make it too long. Nobody wants to type in the website address www.glenandmariesspectaculardominicanvacations.com.

Laying Your Foundation

There's more to laying the foundation of your business than choosing a name. You'll need to decide on a legal structure, check into zoning regulations and insurance coverage, and line up an attorney and an accountant—all the nitty-gritty stuff that will give your company a solid base on which to build.

There are a few business structures to consider, all of which need to be discussed with both your attorney and your accountant, as they can each contain legal and financial ramifications.

You can operate your business as a sole proprietorship, a partnership, or a corporation, with variations thereon. Many specialty travel startups go with the simplest version, the sole proprietorship. If you'll be starting out on your own, you may choose the same option. It's the least complicated and the least expensive. In fact, from a tax standpoint it is the easiest way to go, since your profits are recorded on your personal tax returns as income. Plus, you can take some deductions for business expenses. Of course, you may also likely need to pay self-employment taxes, so weigh the tax options with your accountant.

The biggest drawback of a sole proprietorship comes in the form of liability. If, on one of your tours, someone falls and decides to sue you, they could take a big handful of your personal savings. In fact, in this litigious society we find ourselves in today, you can get sued for much less than a real fall and injury.

One option is to incorporate. This, however, means a lot of paperwork and plenty of guidelines to follow. Each state has specific rules when it comes to incorporating, and you will definitely want a well-versed business attorney with whom to review this option. Again, your accountant will come into play, since incorporating can mean double taxation on income that shows up in the corporation and then later when you take it out for your own personal needs. The benefit of incorporating is that by setting up your business as a separate entity, it

> **Beware!**
> Some cities, such as New York, Niagara Falls, Washington, DC, and Montreal, require tour guides to be licensed. Contact the business license department in your city to find out if your guides need to be licensed.

At First Glance

Your customers' first contact with your company will probably be online. This means that your visual image is vitally important. Everything from the colors, graphics, and typefaces you choose for your website to the stationery and brochures you send out creates an impact. If your tours focus on kids, go all out for a logo that says children with bright primary colors and a bouncy, exuberant font style. If you're talking Europe, splash your materials with travel graphics—pictures of the Eiffel Tower or the Coliseum.

You can design just about anything with your trusty desktop-publishing program. But keep in mind that you're selling not only your special expertise, energy level, and ambience, but also an image of reliability. You want potential clients to know they're in good hands when they hire you.

Have friends or family look over your designs before you commit to a print run. Do they see typos? An amateurish look? Or do they see the sparkle of a travel professional?

Also, keep in mind that your website has to look good on the numerous mobile devices that your customers will use to find you—so check out the look of your website on your BlackBerry and have others look on their smartphones. We'll cover more on web design later.

is (typically) no longer your personal assets that are on the line if someone chooses to sue you. This serves as liability protection.

Naturally, there are hybrid solutions to almost everything these days. An LLC, or Limited Liability Corporation, is one such mixture, with less paperwork and restrictions than traditional incorporation, but also liability protection. Since the LLC is still fairly new, some states do not allow for such an option.

> **Tip...**
>
> **Smart Tip**
>
> If your first-choice domain name has been taken, get creative—but not so creative that your domain name has little or no relation to your company name. If your company is called Backwoods Tours, and there's already a www. backwoods.com, try something like www.goback-woods.com or www.bwoods.com.

For your purposes, you may be OK starting out as a sole proprietorship, but definitely review the options with your attorney and accountant.

As for partnerships, there are several possibilities, including full partnerships and variations thereof. One of the keys to a successful partnership falls in the area of personalities and temperament. Both parties need to determine the manner in which they will contribute to the business and who will be responsible for which tasks. In some cases, one partner is far more involved than the other, who serves primarily as a silent partner. In other partnerships, it is a 50–50 split, with each partner doing what he or she does best. The key is to establish the ground rules at the beginning to avoid later resentment and quarrels. Draw up partnership agreements, even with (or especially with) friends and family.

You can always switch to another format later on, if and when you take on partners and/or employees.

These laws, as they apply to independent agents working through a host agency, can be a tad murky. Some industry experts believe that if you're working through a host, you may be covered by its licensing; others do not. The bottom line is that it's up to you to check with your local governing body, your host agency, and your attorney—do your homework!

The main idea behind these Sellers of Travel Laws is to give consumers some sort of recourse if they bump up against an agent or tour operator who takes their money and runs.

Wilderness Pursuit Permits

If you're planning on operating as a tour packager, government licensing issues can get even more complicated. If you run an in-bound business, your state may require that you employ state-licensed (and bonded) guides. If you act as an outfitter, you will probably need a license. You will most likely need to get permits for activities like fishing or hunting, not only for your company, but also for the members of your group.

And that's not all. Some wilderness areas require that you obtain a permit before venturing inside. You may already know about passes to enter national parks, for example. But you should also be aware that if you run a river-rafting adventure, you might need a license to access a particular river. Keep in mind that some states limit the number of enthusiasts allowed on the water.

How do you determine if these rules apply to your operation? Ask. Always check with local and state authorities before proceeding. If you don't need special permits, you can rest easy. If you do, you'll know upfront, before you've spent valuable time, effort, and money developing a tour. Each tour activity and location needs to be checked out for permits and legal requirements in advance. Even as a travel agent, you may want to ask host agencies and/or travel suppliers if there is anything you need to know regarding licensing or other regulations on your end or if everything is taken care of. Most often, licenses will have been dealt with, but you will still need to know limits on how much you can sell. For example, a tour supplier will tell you that you can only fit 50 people on a given tour.

> **Tip...**
>
> **Smart Tip**
>
> Check with the National Association of Career Travel Agents or the American Society of Travel Agents, as well as your state attorney general, for the latest skinny on all things licensed.

Private Land

If you'll run tours on privately owned land, you will definitely need to get permission from the owner. If you're planning on including privately owned historic sites, like European castles, you'll need to contact the property owner and find out what his or her policies are regarding visitors. Ask these important questions:

- What are the property's hours of operation?
- How far in advance do you need to make reservations?
- How large a group can you bring?
- How long can you stay?
- Are there any restrictions on activities while on the property?
- Are they insured against liability or do you need to get a rider?

Attorneys and Plumbers

Attorneys are like plumbers—you don't want to think about them until you need one. But as a business owner, you should have a good attorney on call, one who knows small business. You'll want your attorney to check over any contracts you write with host agencies, suppliers, or outfitters and to advise you on the fine points of small business and tourism law. You won't need to call every week, or even every month. But there's no point in waiting until you've got a problem to establish a relationship. In the early stages, you will need to have several meetings with your attorney to review contracts, regulations, licenses, your business structure, and so on. Once you are off and running, you will have less frequent needs. Nonetheless, questions will arise. Don't hesitate to call.

> **Fun Fact**
>
> Don't be insulted if your English hotelier asks if you'd like to be knocked up in the morning. In Brit lingo, to "knock up" someone means to wake them up.

The money you spend on an attorney in the early stages can save you a lot of money later on in fines or lawsuits. If you're concerned about finding an attorney or the costs seem prohibitive, you might look for an attorney at www.nolo.com or consider LegalShield™ at www.LegalShield.com, which can be cost effective for routine ongoing legal services.

Along with that on-call attorney, you'll want to look into hiring an accountant to fill out those tax returns and advise you of any special ways you can save money with your business structure.

And don't forget your insurance agent! He or she can be an invaluable source of information and expertise. If you'll be homebased, you will need to find out if your homeowners' package covers your business assets, inventory, and equipment, or if you need additional coverage. If you'll be based outside the home, you will need coverage for these same items, as well as your physical location. If you plan to hire employees, you may need workers' compensation insurance, too.

Then, there's routine liability insurance. This covers you for things like a client slipping on a banana peel (or more likely, black ice), tripping over a tree root in your yard, walking into a wall, or in any other way damaging him or herself on your property and suing you for bodily injury. As a tour operator, you may also be required to carry a specified amount of liability insurance to qualify for some wilderness area permits (for rafting expeditions on various rivers, for example). Don't skimp on liability insurance if, for example, you are running adventure tours as a sole proprietor.

Bonding

Bonding was once a part of the travel business because agents were selling airline tickets. If you are affiliated with ARC, you typically do not need to be bonded. If you are on your own, few states still require that you be bonded—check with your state. Florida is one state that still requires bonding for travel agents.

Oops Insurance

Because people in today's society can be alarmingly lawsuit-happy, you should also consider errors and omissions insurance. This is a bit like malpractice insurance in that it covers you for mistakes that you might make or that a hyperactive client might think you made. For example, if you send a client abroad and she is injured by a bomb while there, she could conceivably sue you for putting her in harm's way. If, for example, despite your best efforts, a client gets bumped off a flight or misses his connection for a hot business meeting, he may sue you because he lost a $50 million account. Yes, it's ridiculous, but these things happen.

You may be able to tap into your host agency's errors and omissions policy; you simply pay the additional charge for being tacked onto the existing coverage. Alternatively, you can shop around for your own coverage or purchase coverage from an industry association like NACTA and get a tidy discount.

Business Interruption Insurance is another, less well-known, option. This means that if a power outage, snowstorm, or hurricane shuts down your homebased business for a week or a month or two, you will be insured for the time in which you could not operate your business.

For your clients, one of the newer types of insurance you can offer is cancel for any reason insurance. Geoff Millar, who, along with his wife, owns Ultimate All-Inclusive Vacations, which sells all-inclusive resort vacations in Mexico and the Caribbean, notes the significance of this insurance. "It's becoming more and more important, largely as a result of the recession," he says. "Before, there was insurance to cover you if you got sick and had to cancel a trip. Now you have people losing jobs or not being able to get out of a job commitment and can't change their schedule. This covers all sorts of reasons. I joke and say if you or your spouse wake up and have a bad hair day you can cancel your trip." The reality, however, is that there is a growing list of things that can go wrong that may interfere with a vacation. It used to be that money would be refunded except for the penalties, but now the penalties are covered. In addition, instead of having the airline give you a voucher for another flight, you can actually get a refund. "I offer it as something people can buy, rather than adding it in," says Millar, who offers the new insurance at $120 per person.

Staying Healthy

If you will be doing specialty tours, you have yet another insurance concern to consider: your clients' health. Specialty tour companies usually have had their tour members sign liability waivers, which state that the clients accept responsibility for their own health and physical conditions. You'll

> ### Smart Tip
>
> If you face a possible legal challenge or lawsuit, don't rush into battle. Statistics show that 90 percent of lawsuits are resolved through mediation or negotiations. Therefore, you want to do your best to avoid costly litigation. You also do not want to make settlements until you have all the facts, and you should settle only when you are at fault or your reputation is on the line. In those instances when someone is trying to take advantage of a situation, your attorneys can draft the necessary (strongly worded) letters to avoid legal action when you are not at fault. Lawsuit abuse runs rampant; don't become a victim based on a fraudulent claim.

want to do the same; have each client fill out a form describing his or her physical condition. This is very important in any type of trip, and is especially important for one that's physically demanding. Your clients should also provide statements signed by their doctors, asserting that the doctor knows and approves of the client's intended travel plans. And as a final safeguard, you should have all clients sign a form releasing you from any liability incurred due to their own ill health.

Some outbound operators ask to be named as co-insured parties on riders to outfitters' insurance policies, if the operator charters transportation and support personnel from the outfitter. Then, if catastrophe strikes a client while on a chartered vehicle, the tour operator is protected under the outfitters' insurance. This doesn't mean you should ignore insurance of your own—once again, check with your insurance agent for the best coverage for your particular operation.

Contract Smarts

While we're working away at the worry bone, what about that contract with your host agency? You do need one, and it should spell out everything including commission splits, when they're paid, and how overrides and bonuses are handled and split. Your host agency may have a standard contract on hand. You can obtain sample contracts

Know Before You Go

Don't forget that most foreign countries require both you and your tour members to have the appropriate visas before you can enter. Foreign locales may also require their own licenses and permits for fishing, hunting, or other activities. Also, in some countries, foreigners—that's you and your group—are limited in the amount of local currency they can carry into, or out of, the region.

Various regions of the world have their own customs, too, which are tantamount to laws. For instance, women are prohibited from entering some Middle Eastern religious sites. To know before your clients go, contact the American-based consulate of the country you plan to visit.

from professional associations like NACTA. Your friendly attorney can also put one together for you on her own or using one of these samples as a starting point.

If you decide to go with somebody else's "standard," make sure your attorney looks it over before you sign it, since there really is no such thing as a "one size fits all" standard contract. In many cases, you will be satisfied with the way the contract looks, but there may be a few fine points your attorney wants you to discuss with the host agency.

In the case of contracts, a cup of foresight is worth an ocean of afterthought.

Feeling Secure

In addition, stay on top of the latest in security measures, not only at American airports, but at airports in other countries. Since September 11th, 2001, most of the world is understandably much more security conscious. It is up to you to go to the travel trade magazines, websites, and any other sources of information (such as travel associations) and find out if any new security measures have been enacted. One of the big advantages a traveler has when working with you as a travel agent, or tour operator, over a discount travel website, is that you can provide the latest in "what to do" and "what not to do" when packing and boarding an aircraft. "Travel agents have to know what travelers should expect. They also need to teach clients the best use of caution," says Joanie Ogg, president of NACTA & TravelSellers.

The bottom line is that you want clients to be informed so that they can have as smooth and worry-free air travel as possible.

▲

Choosing a Location

As we've explained, one of the perks of running a travel business is that it lends itself ideally to the homebased entrepreneur. Travel agencies no longer require a high-traffic or high-visibility location, so you don't need to set up shop in a trendy part of town. Because your business operates largely in the virtual world, you won't need a mahogany-paneled office with a lobby and conference room in order to impress or entertain clients. The only space requirement is an area large enough for your desk, your chair, your filing cabinets, and perhaps a bookshelf. Here are a couple of points about home offices to consider:

1. *The home office is convenient.* You couldn't get any closer to your work unless you slept with your computer and your telephone, and many travel agents today do keep their BlackBerrys on their nightstand.

2. *It's economical.* You don't need to spend money on leased space, extra utilities, transportation costs, or lunches down at the corner grill. Working at home is not, however, mandatory. You may want to leave your laundry, your dog, and your loving-but-noisy family at home while you go off to an office space that's quiet, clean, and yours alone. Of course, since you can conduct business from almost anywhere, you can get into the habit of setting up shop in Starbucks and other local spots.

The Commercial Office

Although the trend is definitely toward homebased travel businesses, it's not necessarily the only way to go. In some instances, you can be successful with a commercial site, and for some tour operations, a "storefront" can be an even better alternative. Whether homebased or commercially based, it seems that most new travel entrepreneurs are not buying existing businesses, but rather starting their own from scratch. In fact, some of those agents who have worked in commercial travel agencies are making the shift to their own travel businesses, almost exclusively homebased.

If, however, you choose to open a commercial office, it must be well-situated to meet your needs. This doesn't necessarily mean that you are anticipating walk-in traffic. It means that you do not want to spend numerous hours commuting to and from the office or have a location that makes it difficult to attract employees should you expand. List your commercial requirements and seek out a place within your estimated price range that can accommodate those needs. Many commercial businesses are teaming up and sharing space. You should consider this as an option.

Tour Operator's Base

If you're looking at the homebased vs. commercial site question from the tour operator's point of view, things are a bit different. You may want to go the homebased route if you're doing tours that don't require much in the way of equipment or personnel—at least for starters—because it's by far the least expensive alternative. On the other hand, if you decide to run an operation such as whitewater rafting expeditions—where you'll have rafts, oars, life jackets, ice chests, tents, and sleeping bags to contend with—you might do far better with a commercial space where you can stash all your equipment. You can use this same space for meeting, greeting, and checking in your clients. A commercial space is also better for displaying and selling peripheral goodies like T-shirts, sweatshirts, coffee mugs, and caps emblazoned with your company name.

Equipment storage doesn't have to be your only reason for taking on a commercial space. As your company grows, you will also need room for employees. Barry S., the car race tour operator, houses his 12-employee company in 1,500 square feet of office space. Barry contracts the space within the offices of another tour operation that owns 20 percent of his company. He says, "Cost is below general market prices, and it is located in Newport Beach, California—a great address."

In Savannah, Georgia, Karen A. chose an office for her five-person tour company on the basis of price and location as well. "We have a gorgeous office," Karen says, "an 800-square-foot, two-room space in an 1824 stucco building. As additional space,

> **Beware!**
> Keeping everything on your computer's hard drive may seem like a wonderful paper-saving idea. However, if your computer crashes, you'll lose everything, including, temporarily, your mind. The same goes for computerized databases of clients, suppliers, and the like. Be sure to back up everything onto an external hard drive and/or flash drives that you keep in a secure, off-site location. We'll remind you of the importance of backing up your data yet again!

we get a private corridor, a walk-in closet, and a large private, rooftop patio. The main office has 14-foot ceilings, fireplaces, and huge windows. We chose it purely on price and location: $500 a month, right in the middle of the historic district. It fits our needs beautifully in that the location is perfect, the price is right, we have congenial neighbors, and lots of space to divide it into a dozen or so cubicles when we need more privacy for more office employees."

In many cases, it is your locale that brings in business for a tour operator. For example, if you are operating walking tours of Chinatown, what better place to be situated than smack in the middle of Chinatown. The same holds true for a historic part of town, or in any well-traveled, tourist-laden area.

Outfitting Commercial Space

Your office may be situated in a historic building, an upscale shopping plaza, a downtown office, or a barn by the river; nevertheless, you'll need the same basic setup as in a home office. Have a look at the worksheet provided on the next page for planning your commercial office.

You'll need plenty of room for all those files, plus your desk, chair, a few pieces of visitors' furniture, as well as desks and chairs for any employees you may hire. Whether in a home or commercial office, your computer should occupy a place of honor, away from dirt, drafts, and blinding sunlight. The same goes for your printer and fax machine.

In a commercial tour operation office, you may want a display area or counter for any retail products like T-shirts or tote bags, as well as a cash box or electronic credit card terminal for taking payments. You should also consider that altarpiece of American offices, the coffee maker. And of course, if you've got gear to stash—whether it is bungee cords, bicycles, or boat oars—you'll need sufficient storage space.

The Commercial Office Worksheet

Use this worksheet to help you plan your commercial office.

Start by listing three possible locations for your office based on your niche market. For an adventure travel agency, you could locate your office in a trendy shopping area next to a bookstore with a large travel section. For walking tours, you could have an office in a historical district. For rafting expeditions, you might want to locate yourself near the headwaters of a river. If part of your appeal is based on impulse buys, meaning tourists seeing your offer and saying "Hey, why not take a tour," then location , location, location is tantamount to your impending success. Therefore, you should first list the primary areas in which you would like to find a location.

1. _____

2. _____

3. _____

Make a physical survey of each location's exterior and access.

❑ Can clients find the location easily?

❑ Can clients easily access the location? Will they have to cross several lanes of heavy traffic or make unsafe or illegal U-turns?

❑ Is there adequate parking?

❑ Do local businesspeople, shoppers, and passersby conform to your niche market?

❑ Is signage a problem? Check with landlords and local zoning authorities to make sure the sign you have in mind will be accepted.

Make a physical survey of each location's interior office space. Make sure there is adequate room for work areas for you and your employees.

❑ Is there enough room for desks, computers, and telephones for you and for employees who may need their own units?

❑ Are phone and electrical outlets easily accessible at potential workstations? What is the cable access situation for your internet needs?

The Commercial Office Worksheet, continued

❑ Is there adequate lighting and proper ventilation?

❑ Is there adequate storage space for equipment?

If you'll conduct some sort of retail sales, like T-shirts and ball caps, list three possible spots to display and sell these items. You may want to consider a cash register, cash box, or electronic credit card machine as well.

1. _____

2. _____

3. _____

Figuring Your Finances and Your Equipment Needs

T hat old refrain, "The best things in life are free," does not quite apply when you are starting a new business. This chapter dips into the murky waters of budgeting, financing, and operating costs, and (hopefully) clears them up.

Startup Costs

One of the best things about the travel business is that the startup costs can be comparatively low. You have the advantage of being homebased, which cuts office lease expenses down to nothing. Except for any merchandise you might choose to develop (like T-shirts or tote bags emblazoned with your company name), you have no tangible inventory, and if you do have inventory, you won't need fancy display cabinets or trendy décor. Your major financial outlay will go toward office equipment, marketing, and promotion. In most scenarios you probably already have the most significant piece of office equipment—a computer.

But let's take it from the top. The following is a breakdown of everything that you'll need to get up and running, from heavy investment pieces to flyweight items:

- Education and certification (While certification and licenses aren't required in many states, they certainly help you stand out from the crowd.)
- Host agency (very important for starting out)
- Professional association fees
- Computers (laptop(s) and/or tablets and/or a desktop) and at least one printer
- Phones: at least one smartphone such as a BlackBerry, Android, or iPhone as well as a landline or two
- Fax machine (or a fax software program)
- Wifi internet access
- Website design and maintenance
- Marketing materials
- Software, including a CRM database
- Reference materials
- Business cards and office supplies
- Postage
- Add rent and utilities if you go the commercial office route

You can add all kinds of goodies with varying degrees of necessity to this list. As computers and electronic communication add more functionality, and hard copies become less significant, you may need less office equipment. For example, a copier was once a must, but now it's a maybe, depending on your needs. Many people today use Kinkos or another place to make multiple copies of a document since hard copies are not necessary in many transactions. It is, however, nice to have bona fide office furniture: a swiveling, rolling, leather-upholstered chair with lumbar support and so on.

But let's consider that you're starting from absolute scratch. You can always set up your computer on your kitchen table or on a card table in a corner of the bedroom. You can stash files in cardboard boxes. It's not glamorous, but it'll suffice until you get your business steaming ahead. The wisest way to go is to be thrifty, buying what is necessary while also bartering and bargaining to get what you need. Keep in mind that, as discussed earlier, a good chair is important for your back, shoulders, and arms.

Education

Since the travel business essentially does not require having a specific certificate or license, the amount of education you seek out is up to you. Once upon a time, travel agents started out working in established travel agencies, learning the ropes until they became proficient in their skills.

"When we started our business, my wife had 20 years of experience in a travel agency," says Geoff Millar of Ultimate All-Inclusive Vacations. "To get a job, you had to have some kind of training, so you would start in the business at an agency where you would do filing and answer the phones while learning the business. That kind of training doesn't exist anymore, so people need to take seminars, classes, and courses to know all about this business."

Some of the leading associations, such as the American Society of Travel Agents, offer courses, as do the cruise lines and CLIA. There are also many online training courses offered. The key is to find legitimate learning opportunities. With that in mind, look for reviews of travel schools and courses, ask other travel agents, and do your homework before going to school. Courses affiliated with the leading travel associations are typically among the most reputable. "I completed a program through the Travel Institute," says Margie Jordan of JETS & ASAP Travel. "I find that they have the most comprehensive programs besides the ones the cruise industry is doing." Jordan also notes that a lot of programs offered today lack the details. "They provide three quick programs and call you specialist," says Jordan, unimpressed with such travel schools.

The bottom line is that you need education and training to get ahead in this industry; you also need to look carefully for the best places from which to get it.

Get Certifiable

To sell cruises, you want to be certified by the Cruise Lines International Association (CLIA). While obtaining your CLIA certification definitely counts as fun, it doesn't come cheap. You've got to spring for cruises as well as travel to attend seminars and visit home ports on ship inspections. If you plan to add more credentials from CLIA or elsewhere, understand that there will be an expense, but the right certifications will pay for themselves over time.

Another option is to take the courses offered directly by the cruise lines. "There are a lot of educational opportunities," says Tom Ogg, adding that suppliers are interested in highly productive agents selling their product. "Every cruise line has their own university, and if you go through the training you may be able to build a direct link to the cruise line as a supplier."

Host Agency or Consortium Fees?

A travel consortium is a combination of agencies that pool together to get better rates from suppliers. Larger agencies and host agencies usually join a consortium, since there are typically necessary qualifications that need to be met. As for host agencies, discussed in a previous chapter, you are likely to start out with one and in time, if you are fortunate to build your own contacts within your chosen niche market, outgrow the host agency.

Most host agencies have annual fees, although some may have monthly fees. You will want to choose one based on what they can do for you, fees notwithstanding. Use some of the criteria discussed previously to decide among the various host agencies. To learn more about what makes a consortium useful, check out Vacation.com, Signature Travel Network, or The NEST. You may then see if your host agency of choice is part of a consortium.

Get Professional

Professional associations like the American Society of Travel Agents (ASTA) are important for both new and established agents. ASTA is an excellent place to see how the travel world interacts with Washington. The organization is a leader when it comes to lobbying for travel reform and laws to help the industry. ASTA is the world's largest association of travel professionals and also provides trade shows and plenty of important resources.

The National Association of Career Travel Agents (NACTA), the National Association of Cruise-Oriented Agents (NACOA), and the Adventure Travel Society (ATS) are among the other valuable resources for the travel specialist. (See the Appendix for a listing of professional associations for the travel business.)

The NEST

The NEST, based in Long Island, New York, is a leading travel-marketing consortium focused on you, the homebased travel agent. The goal is to bring homebased travel agents and travel suppliers together.

To join, you need to not only be homebased and independently owned, but also registered to book directly with suppliers. You also must be what The NEST refers to as a "strong producer," meaning you have already generated significant dollars through preferred suppliers.

The NEST is not for the brand-new agent, but is certainly a place to explore once you have launched your business and are already branching out on your own, beyond a host agency.

There are a number of features for members, such as turnkey sales promotions as part of an aggressive marketing calendar and use of Cruiseexpress, a direct-connect/real-time cruise booking engine. Beyond the $149 application fee, there is a $225 annual fee, which, as of August 2010, was being waived for the first two years for new members. So while you will not be ready to join The NEST when you start out, it is a popular and beneficial consortium to keep in mind for down the road.

There are typically membership fees for such organizations, but if you use what these associations have to offer, including seminars, webinars, trade shows, and a wealth of contacts and information, they can be extremely worthwhile.

Research and Reference Materials

Because the travel world changes so fast, you will need to surf, search, and visit familiar sites on the web constantly to stay on top of the latest news and innovations in technology. You may also want to stock up on books and reference materials that provide greater insight into your primary destinations.

Computer Needs

If you don't already have one, or if your current one has morphed into a dinosaur, buying a computer system will head the list of startup expenses. For a good quality system—hard drive, monitor, mouse, modem, and printer—you should allocate at

Dmitriy Shironosor/www.shutterstock.com

least $2,000. While laptops and tablets prevail these days, desktops still have their supporters, and in this business, you are probably best served by having at least one mobile computer plus a desktop at home to meet all your needs. Some requirements, however, apply to both.

Performance is important because you don't want to waste valuable time waiting for equipment to respond. Look for an Intel I3 or I5 processor with speed of 2.3 GHz or more. Equivalent CPUs from AMD (a leading maker of CPUs and computer parts) are also acceptable and are cost effective. RAM memory of 3 to 4 GB is sufficient for most applications. The Linux operating system, as an alternative to Windows, or in addition to Windows, is fine (Ubuntu with Open Office is free). Linux has far fewer viruses if you are searching the web often, which for travel agents is the case. However, it does not interface well with other users who typically have Windows.

Therefore, since you may be using software programs that only run on MS Windows, you will have to invest in Microsoft. The 32-bit versions of Windows are usually more compatible with older programs than the slightly faster 64-bit versions. If you must update huge Adobe graphical files, only then consider 64 bits. The "Professional" version of Windows 7 adds the ability to run older programs in "XP" mode if you have essential legacy programs; otherwise the "Home" version is typically OK for home business needs. The "standard" graphics chips built into

High Tech Integration Is Important

Margie Jordan, travel consultant and CEO of JETS & ASAP Travel, stresses the importance of having technologies that can integrate with one another. "The biggest thing is finding a way to manage your technology," she says. A lot of software and tools in the industry (and in general) don't talk to each other. Make sure that whatever systems you are using can allow you to move data from one place to another or you will spend a lot of time re-entering such data from one source to another." Jordan uses ClientBase to connect to suppliers' websites and to move information from a cruise line's database right into her own ClientBase. She points out, however, that many systems have not yet integrated social media into their formats. As social media becomes more significant, you'll want to look for technology that lets you pull necessary data from web-based social media sites into your data files.

systems today are adequate for most home businesses. However, if heavy graphical work is anticipated, look for the more advanced ATI or Nvidia graphics chips with dedicated graphics memory.

If you are growing and need to network with staff or suppliers' computers, you may be in better shape with the business version of Windows 7 Office 2010, which will give you more networking and integration options.

Your Desktop

Without worrying about battery life, you can have a desktop with a fast full-voltage processor. Likewise, if an advanced graphics card is required, there are many choices available that contain large amounts of dedicated graphics memory plus a big fan to keep the system cool. They can also be easily upgraded as graphics technology improves every couple of years. Laptops offer a smaller selection of advanced, but less powerful, graphics chips that cannot be changed. Desktops can also connect to the network by either Ethernet cable (faster) or your wireless connection.

One of the biggest advantages of a desktop is that the screen, mouse, and keyboard can be customized to each user's needs. A large luxurious screen can be used, which would be too expensive and heavy for a laptop. User comfort and ergonomics are important issues, especially considering that you will be spending lots of time in your homebased office.

Additionally, the components of a desktop are mostly modular, generic, and easy to replace. Therefore, the useful life of a desktop is much longer than that of a laptop. All the components are available on a desktop at a considerably lower price than they would be on an equivalently powered laptop.

Your Laptop

Some inexpensive laptops, "netbooks," and "ultra portables" are being offered with slow, low-voltage processors for longer battery life. Since you should have your necessary data and communications capabilities with you while traveling, or so that you can be mobile around your home office and in the community, you'll also want to have a laptop. With that in mind, look for one with a fast processor and a minimum 14-inch screen. Some other options on a laptop include wireless access to all standards: 802.11 a/b/g/n, which are all commonly used wifi technologies. Besides having backward compatibility at places such as airports, the "N" standard is several times faster and reaches farther distances than the other types. Get the biggest battery (usually 9 cell) the manufacturer offers to avoid panic on long flights. Don't worry about weight. Consider carrying an extra battery. If the data on the laptop is confidential, look into software that will encrypt the entire hard drive. Having just a logon password is not sufficient. Low-jack type software is also available. Keep in mind that some travel agents will not trust data, such as clients' Social Security numbers, to their laptops at all.

Take Good Care of Your Laptop

It should be understood with a laptop that a computer hard disk is constantly spinning a disk with a read/write head floating a hundredth of an inch over it on a cushion of air. Lifting a laptop just 2 inches above a desk and dropping it while Windows is running can permanently damage the disk and cause data to be lost. This kind of damage creeps up slowly until data loss is finally noticed. It is recommended that the laptop be set up to "sleep" when the cover is closed. A laptop should be in "sleep" or "hibernation" mode before moving it even a few feet. A recent development is the Solid State Drive (SSD). This drive replaces the traditional hard drives with an all-electronic device with no moving parts. An SSD is not only faster, but also more resistant to rough handling. However, it has a shorter life span and is more expensive.

Your laptop requirements depend on how it will be used and how much traveling you plan to do. Since laptop hard disks are obviously more fragile and more difficult to service, an extended warranty is highly recommended.

If you are only buying one computer—a laptop or desktop—you can try a hybrid solution. This involves using a laptop when you will be mobile and having a docking station at your office. A more comfortable mouse and keyboard can be plugged into the laptop. A larger monitor can also be plugged in. The downside is that you will make all the compromises necessary for a portable at extra cost and then pay double for the extra peripherals.

Other Options

Tablets, netbooks, and smartphones all have their markets. If the device has the appropriate jacks for docking, it can also serve as a hybrid solution. Be aware, however, that batteries need to be charged, so have a charger with you while traveling.

The iPad, and the multitude of various Android Tablets, can provide the connectivity for a quick internet hookup plus email. These devices use the SSD memory mentioned in the sidebar on page 94. Even with a conventional keyboard plugged in, these devices have little to offer that a laptop would not do better. The entry level cost is about $500 for a small amount of memory and wifi. The cost is high for larger amounts of SSD memory, you'll have the extra expense of slow 3G cell-phone style communication, and a screen of 7 or 10 inches does not compare favorably with a laptop. These devices do, however, meet your needs when you are out and about and a laptop is not practical.

Smart Tip *Tip...*

Recommended workstation requirements: Windows XP (Home or Professional) or Windows Vista, IE 6.0 or higher, Java 2 Platform Standard Edition 1.4.2_06 or higher, and Active X controls must be allowed.

Pocket Assistant

Don't discount the iPad. Especially for folks at upper levels, it's a status symbol not to be ignored. It's helpful for those who just need to do email and read news, and it can be a fantastic presentation tool for marketing meetings because all your "brochures" can now be at your fingertips instead of crumpled up in a briefcase.

With your trusty computers you can:

- Stay in constant contact with your clients through email and the social media such as Facebook and Twitter
- Stay in touch with suppliers and vendors
- Do your ongoing research
- Update your website regularly and visit those of your host agency, suppliers, and tour operators.
- Use your software programs to maintain a database and to perform accounting functions and generate financial reports.
- Maintain your customer database.
- Join discussions and forums, read blogs, and take webinars to learn more about the ever-changing travel industry.
- Link with others in the travel industry who can help you market your services.
- Create and distribute your online newsletter.
- Create your own stationery, brochures, Google ads, and so on.

Computer Peripherals

One "extra" you are going to need is a printer. Here, too, it's possible to go hog wild on the latest model. In all seriousness, think about what you're going to be using your printer for—printing fliers, signs, brochures, etc. The reason you want to think about it is because you have a couple of options. You will need a color printer. The choices, however, are inkjet versus laser. In short, inkjets are slower, but can produce sharper colors and are typically better for graphics—of course the cost of ink can be

---

Brochure—Lite

DVDs are in vogue these days as a vivid and enticing means of marketing travel destinations. All the major cruise lines now provide them and they are cost effective to mail. You can find premade DVDs offered by most preferred travel suppliers, replacing the brochures of old with a more exciting way of seeing the destinations of choice. Ask suppliers about what they have available. You can also check in at places such as the TravelVideoStore.com to build your own destination DVD library.

---

high. Lasers are fast and very reliable, but the quality of color materials is not as sharp. However, for running off 200 copies of a simple flier, a laser printer is more efficient. Many people in business today have one of each, which can be accomplished for $800 to $1,000, assuming you have neither one at present. You may find that your need for print is dwindling as customers look at your website, DVDs, and CDs rather than hard copies. Plus, you can send clients what they need electronically. Your printing needs will determine the level of printer you need.

The Software Skinny

A computer is only as good as the software inside. You will need Customer Relationship Management (CRM) software that allows you to maintain a database of clients and suppliers, while handling reservations and trip management. The two most popular software programs for travel agents are ClientBase® and ClientEase. ClientBase can be in the form of software or via the internet. It will allow you to manage trip details including reservations, itinerary printing, and inventory management as well as create detailed client and vendor profiles. The system also helps you maintain and track your marketing efforts. It will send electronic surveys, greeting cards, and reminders to regular customers.

An internet system, ClientEase lets you organize and operate your homebased agency entirely on the internet and is accessible from any internet connection. This allows you to get to your database from wherever you are. You can also create and manage itineraries, maintain databases, invoice clients, and create and maintain your marketing plans and strategies.

These are just two of the growing number of CRM programs available for homebased travel agents. Also available are Salesboom and Open Travel CRMs.

General Software

New computers typically come pre-loaded with all the software you'll need for basic office functions. If yours doesn't,

> **Smart Tip**
>
> Keep in mind that you do not need the latest and greatest computer. You can usually buy last year's hottest model for less money since dealers want to move them out to put the new ones on display. A good desktop with a monitor and keyboard can be had for under $2,000—so shop around. The year-to-year differences are not usually significant. It is a good idea, however, to buy a computer from a known entity (such as Best Buy, PC Richard, Comp USA, or directly from a manufacturer such as HP or Apple) because you want the warranty and the technical support for those instances when things do not work as they are supposed to.

you may want to look into the following programs. You'll need a word processing program, with which you can write correspondence, contracts, sales reports, and whatever else strikes your fancy. For a similar price, you may want to consider a spreadsheet program such as Microsoft Excel or a database program such as Microsoft Access to keep track of your clients and contacts. You might also opt for an office suite program. An accounting program such as Intuit QuickBooks or Microsoft Money can track your business finances. These make record keeping a breeze.

The last "must have" on the general software list is your anti-virus program. Often, you can have one loaded into your computer when you buy it, as part of the package. Norton Antivirus, Bit Defender, PC-cillin, McAfee Virus Scan Plus or Antivirus and Sophos Anti-Virus for Mac are among many possibilities. The point is, you MUST have one in your computer before you even think of hooking up with the internet. Viruses are rampant in cyberspace and you are jeopardizing your entire business without protecting it, just as you lock your doors and close your windows when you leave your home. Also, remember to update the anti-virus software frequently because new threats are constantly circulating as hackers continue to play the role of the villain in cyberspace. And don't think that Macs are immune to viruses—not anymore. As they become more popular, they also become targets of those who, for some odd reason, infect the business world with computer viruses. Your business is based on your computer(s), so, yes, protect them.

Smart Tip

Buy a surge protector. This is a device that protects you against a power outage that could wipe out the files you are working on. You can also opt for a UPS (uninterruptible power supply), which is even better than a surge protector because it serves as a short-term backup generator for the computer, letting you continue to work for a short time, saving, closing, and/or backing up the files you are working on.

Travel-Specific Software

As mentioned earlier, CRM software geared for the travel industry is becoming the hot item in the homebased travel agent's arsenal, whether it is actual software loaded onto your computers or web-based versions, whereby everything is safely stored in cyberspace.

While industry-specific software is not essential, it can help you simplify the process of planning itineraries, marketing your trips, and maintaining your database. Review various products and determine which ones meet your needs and are most user-friendly.

ISPs

A good internet service provider is a must for anyone in business today. Most internet service providers, or ISPs, charge about $10 to $20 per month and provide unlimited web and email access.

If you're going the tour operator route, you may not need specific software initially, but there are software suites that can make life easier, such as Tourplan, Peak15 Travel Booster, and Tour Tools. Again, it's a matter of looking at the features and determining what you need. Some programs help you make phone or online reservations and manage the tour planning process while also including surveys for customers and helping with everything from scheduling to invoicing to accounting.

The Internet

It's almost impossible to run a successful business today without some web presence. All the travel professionals we talked with for this book either had their own website or were in the process of getting one. The cost of putting up and maintaining a company site can vary considerably.

There are plenty of places on the internet that will help you set up an inexpensive website. Wordpress, for example, allows you to create a site and/or a blog. Many such websites let you create a good-looking site that can meet your online needs. However, in a competitive market, you may prefer something built with a little more pizzazz. To get a more professional looking site up and running, you can expect to spend at least $2,500 and possibly a few thousand more.

Don't feel bad if you start off with something inexpensive—as long as it looks decent and showcases your travel offers, it will work. You can always grow to the more elaborate site in time.

You may be lucky enough to know someone who can design a site. However, make sure that you're not dealing with someone whose biggest claim to web design fame is

> **Tip...**
>
> **Smart Tip**
> No matter how user-friendly technology is, there will still be times when you'll need hand-holding. So when you shop, be sure to ask what sort of technical support comes with anything you buy, from hardware (computers) to software.

their Facebook page. It is essential that your site looks professional and loads quickly. There are too many competing sites out there, so if you do not put forth a quality website, people will simply move on to another. More on designing a website, and what should and should not be included, are found in Chapter 13.

Electronic Money

According to www.charge.com, by accepting credit cards online you can increase your sales by an astounding 50 to 400 percent. These days, you simply can't compete if you don't accept credit cards. Charge.com is one of a number of companies that can help you add a credit card platform to your website.

You can also process credit card transactions through your host agency's merchant account. With ClientBase and ClientEase, you can directly connect to a supplier's website and use a client's credit card as payment on the supplier's website. Or you can simply visit the supplier's website outside of ClientBase or ClientEase and make a credit card transaction.

If you opt to have your own merchant account, there may be a monthly fee and then a per-transaction fee of roughly 2.25 percent or more. It depends on what you are able to negotiate.

Margie Jordan of JETS & ASAP Travel, based in Florida, notes that agents should keep in mind the Seller of Travel Laws when deciding how to handle client payments. For instance, in the state of Florida, independent contractors are prohibited from accepting any client payments or checks written to or processed by the independent contractor unless the independent contractor is the registered seller of travel. "In most instances, Florida homebased agents simply register in Florida under the host agency's name," says Jordan. "In this instance, we would not be allowed to accept payments or process credit cards as ASAP Travel, for instance. Payments and credit cards would need to be processed in the name of the host agency, which is the registered seller of travel in Florida." It's important to know your state laws.

Phone Fun

We'll assume that you already have a landline, in which case you already know all about phone bills. You should install a separate dedicated line, or two, for your business. You'll want one landline for handling phone calls, and if you have a stand-alone fax machine, you'll probably need a separate line for that as well. Faxes are becoming obsolete, however, so you might manage if your landline is tied up on occasion with a rare fax.

Keep in mind that costs vary with the number of features you add to your telephone service, and which local and long distance carriers you go with; but for the purposes of startup budgeting, let's say you should allocate about $150 for a good phone, including installation.

It's also important that you have voice mail set up and are able to forward your calls to your mobile phone so you are reachable at all times.

Cell Phones and Smartphones

Who doesn't have a cell phone today? Cell phones are a part of life and smartphones are a key component of the travel agent's arsenal. Most likely, you'll want to have a phone that can operate as your office while you are in transit. And BlackBerries, Androids, and iPhones can do just that.

For less than $300 you can have the world at your fingertips with the latest in smartphones.

Of course, there are some must-haves that you should be on the lookout for. These include:

- A 3G or 4G phone for memory and internet capacity
- Integration capabilities with your PCs or Macs
- An MP3 player
- A high-resolution display screen
- A camera. Many smartphones offer zooms and video features
- An easy-to-use keyboard: You can decide whether or not you prefer a touch-screen keyboard or a button-press slide-out
- Wifi and Mobile Broadband access
- An earpiece to use for talking while driving

Smart Shopping for Smartphones

When searching for a cellular plan, look at the various offers, ask friends and family, and scout around a little before buying. Many companies, including AT&T, Verizon, Sprint, and T-Mobile, are quite competitive, so as you search, you will usually find a good deal with the best coverage in the main area in which you will be using the phone.

The basic costs of cell phones and smartphones are in the minute plans. Most offer unlimited nights and weekends, which is great for you since many clients call during nontraditional business hours and you may need to talk with people in different time zones at all hours of the day or night.

▲

Costs can range from $30 per month for 200 anytime minutes to $80 for $1,500 anytime minutes, so you will need to determine how much you plan to use your smartphone or cell phone. Some plans let you roll unused minutes over; others do not. Since rates become roughly $.45 per minute once you are over your plan limit, you'll need to make a good estimate as to what you will need—you can always change the

Applications

Apps, as they are called, are inexpensive, and sometimes free. They are the special "programs" of sorts that provide you with a wealth of information at your fingertips on your smartphone. Verizon's VZ Navigator, for example, is an app that provides accurate and clear turn-by-turn directions, points of interest, and traffic updates. You can even search for fuel by price and peruse movie times and local event listings. Some of the numerous apps available (with new ones coming out every day) include:

- *FlightView*, which lets you track upcoming and en-route planes.

- *Evernote*, which shoots a camera phone photo of a handwritten note, records audio clips, or types in text. Evernote stores all your snippets online for quick search and anytime retrieval.

- *HNHSoft 2Go Talking Phrase Books*, which let you read or listen to phrase translations from English to many foreign languages.

- *AccuWeather*, which gives iPhone customers both local forecasts and those of various travel destinations.

- *GateGuru*, which provides information on where to go and what to eat while waiting at airports or on layovers.

Remember, different apps will work on different phones, but there are similar versions of popular ones, such as those for maps, weather, and local restaurants. Seek and you shall find!

Of course, apps are generally available to your clients as well. But it's advantageous for you to have the latest information handy for those who do not have the apps or even a smartphone. The senior crowd can typically benefit from your app-based "wisdom."

plan. Also, if you have co-workers and are paying for several lines, you will need to pay extra per phone, usually about $10 extra per line per month. You can also save money on multiyear plans.

Consider your needs, which may include texting. If you plan to do a lot of texting, you can get an unlimited plan that will cost roughly $20 to $30 per month.

Most plans will also include voice mail, call forwarding, and caller ID.

Remember to shop around, as there are many carriers and plans. Incentives are frequently offered to lure you in. Visit the websites of some of the leading carriers and check out PC World for phone comparisons (as well as computer comparisons). Mobiledia also has comparisons of the latest in cell phones, and Consumer Reports is a good place to browse as well.

Your Calling Card

Your business card is as important to your travel image as a well-answered phone. You will need business cards that promote your business and image, and plenty of them so you can hand them out at conferences, conventions, seminars and to clients and anyone else who may be potentially interested in your business.

You want to build a business image with everything you send out, from checks to thank-you notes. Make sure you get a design that you like, one that shows what your business is about. Be careful not to "over" design, or your look can become tacky and your message can be lost in the design—this goes for all your branding, from your website to your brochures or DVDs.

You can purchase blank stationery, including business cards, and print everything yourself using a desktop publishing program. Or you can have a set of stationery and business cards printed for you at a copy center like Kinko's or Office Depot. Either way, you should allocate about $300. If you know a professional printer, strike up a barter deal and give them a good price on a much-needed vacation in exchange for some printing—it works in your favor, because they can tell their friends about you if they love their vacation, and you need to make sure that they do.

All That Jazz

Other expenses you'll need to plug into your startup expense chart include business licenses, business insurance, legal advice, and all that jazz—the costs intrinsic to any company's beginning. If you plan to go with a commercial location, you'll also need to consider rent, utilities, and signage; and if you'll hire employees, you'll have to add in payroll and workers' compensation fees. To give you an idea of what to budget for, we have provided a sample page of startup costs on page 105 and a worksheet for projected monthly income and expenses on page 109. Look over the sample page and then use the blank worksheet to fill in some of your own numbers. Work in pencil so you can erase and make changes as you go.

Expenses begin to increase once you take on employees. Besides salaries, you will need additional office equipment and perhaps a network setup for your computers so that you can all work on the same client material. In addition, you will have to pay your payroll taxes, unemployment taxes, and workers' compensation insurance. To attract good people to work for your business, you may also need to pay for a medical plan and/or other benefits.

Some startup costs are one time only, while others morph into monthly expenses. While you can get yourself started, in good shape, for anywhere from $5,000 to $15,000, including some marketing, insurance, and all of your licensing, there will also be ongoing monthly expenses that you will need to factor against your projected income. That will be your bottom line and from where you will need to grow your business.

Operating Expenses

These are the various and sundry costs that make up the backbone of every travel professional's operation. Subtracted from your projected gross profits, these operating expenses will tell the true tale of how much profit you will be making. Since tour operators expense out each tour to determine costs and net profits per program, operating expenses for tour operators and travel agents are about the same.

So here we go. We're going to assume once again that you'll be homebased and won't have to worry about expenses for office rent or utilities. We do, however, need to consider the following ongoing expenses:

If you already have a computer and internet connection you might be able to design your own website. You can minimize marketing expenses by honing your expertise in the social media. You can save money on your office setup with inexpensive furnishings.

When listing your monthly expenses, you will find that you have both fixed and variable expenses. For example, your cellular plan will have a fixed monthly rate, unless you go over your allotted minutes, in which case you will have some additional, variable expenses. Likewise, subscriptions will have fixed monthly rates.

Your variables will include advertising and marketing expenses, which will likely change as you pursue different routes for spreading the word about your products and services. For the variable entries, which will also include travel for your business, you may

Startup Costs: Independent Travel Agents

Items	Homebased Travel Agent Costs
Education/certification	$2,000 (including webinars/ seminars, courses, etc.)
Professional associations	$700
Office setup, including a new computer	$3,000
Licenses	$150
Phones (including installation of a dedicated landline plus a smartphone and service plan)	$450
Legal services	$500
Advertising and marketing (roughly 15 percent of your budget should go to marketing)	$1,750
Insurance	$1,000
Software (including ClientBase, ClientEase, or a similar data system)	$300
Miscellaneous expenses	$800
Digital camera	$800
Total startup costs	**$11,450**

find that one month the total may be $5,000, while the next month, nothing. For these expenses, you will want to make a good estimate of your annual total and divide by 12 for your monthly expense listings. Therefore, if you run ads and do marketing campaigns four times a year for about $3,000 each time, then your total would be $12,000, or $1,000 per month on your expense sheet. This is important, because many businesses have seasonal highs and lows with both income and variable expenses. You need to account for such variance, especially if your niche is winter wonderland destinations.

Independent Travel Agent Startup Costs Worksheet

Fill in your own numbers below

Items	Costs
Education/certification	$
Professional associations	$
Office setup (including computer)	$
Licenses	$
Phones (including cell phones)	$
Legal services	$
Advertising and marketing	$
Insurance	$
Software	$
Miscellaneous expenses	$
Digital camera	$
Total startup costs	$

Fixed expenses will still show up both during the good months and the off months, and you can't tell the phone company, "Wait until next month when ski season begins, that's when we do much more business." Therefore, you need to look at your income in a similar fashion so that you spread it out over the 12 months. If you bring in $48,000, but almost all of it comes during busier months, you will need to stretch it out over the calendar year at $4,000 per month so you know what you need to cover yourself during the off-season months. While you may be running a business that does well all year round, most businesses have seasonal ups and downs, and travel is no exception. With the possible exception of the senior crowd, it's harder to book vacations during certain months, such as January through March. School and work schedules will factor into your income, so be prepared to let the good months, like June, July, August, and December, cover the slower ones. Create a budget and work within the confines of that framework. In time, you will learn to adjust more easily for busier and slower cycles.

Paying the Piper

We've set aside a fixed expense called loan repayment. If you don't borrow money to start your business, you won't need to bother with this one. If, however, you finance your startup costs through loans, you'll need to repay the piper. Here's where you pencil in whatever your monthly fee will be for paying back the loan. For a homebased business, the startup costs are relatively low, so your loan may likely be fairly minimal. Nonetheless, if you get a loan through a commercial lender, you will need to start repaying—with interest, on a regular basis. More about loans will come up later when we discuss getting your financing together.

Putting It Together

Use the "Projected Income/Operating Expenses" worksheet to pencil in your own income and expense figures and determine your new company's projected monthly bottom line. If some of these items won't apply to you—like rent if you'll be homebased or employees and workers' compensation, then pass them by.

A few interesting things to note. First, we did not include taxes, such as self-employment taxes (some of which can be claimed as a deduction on your tax return) and quarterly estimates. So before jumping up and down about a tidy profit every month, set aside roughly 30 percent of your income for personal tax purposes (or corporate taxes if you have incorporated)—which you will review with your accountant. On $4,000 income, as a sole proprietor, you could be paying close to $1,200 in taxes, although probably not, once you factor in business deductions, so save all business receipts.

> ### Dollar Stretcher
>
> Be environmentally and economically smart.
> Reuse that printer paper. Instead of practicing hoop shots into the trash with all those versions of letters, evaluation sheets, and other printed materials that you decided you didn't like, set the pages aside. When you've compiled a tidy stack, load them back into your printer and print on the blank side. Save your "good" paper for the final draft that goes out in the mail. Or send as much as you can via email and avoid paper completely!

During your first year, all the equipment you purchase that is used solely for business purposes can be claimed as a business deduction. As you buy new equipment over the years, that will also be deductible as long as it is solely for business use.

You will notice that utilities are included in this list of expenses. This is the increase in your home utility costs because of your office. More heat, more lighting, more electricity. The percentage of utilities used strictly for your business can also be considered a business tax deduction. Therefore, if one-tenth of your 1,500-square-foot home (or 150 square feet/a 10-by-15 foot room) is your office, then 10 percent of your utility bills would be factored in as a business expense.

As you start listing some of your own anticipated monthly income and expenses, include all sources of income besides booking the trips and receiving commissions. If, for example, you're a tour operator selling T-shirts and travel mementos, you need to include this income as well. In this case, use the line "for-sale products" since you will need to pay for the materials that you are selling. In this case, you will also have to pay sales tax and file a sales tax return. In most other cases, the sales tax is added on by the travel supplier, such as the cruise line, so you do not have to figure out sales taxes.

Your Digital Camera

For your website, or for your advertising materials, or both, you will definitely want a digital camera. This will allow you to snap those breathtaking photos of majestic scenery or those of your tour participants having a ball, and then load them onto your computer where you can edit them.

A good single lens reflex (SLR) digital camera from Canon or Nikon can cost you upwards of $700, but can be worthwhile for your business. While travel suppliers often offer photographs, DVDs, and brochures, you'll want to have your own materials as well with your design and your business name on them.

Adobe's Photoshop, which costs roughly $150 to $200, depending on the version, lets you do all sorts of editing and manipulating to get the most out of your photos before you post them on your website or in your marketing materials. Yes, you may want to incorporate some professional photos onto your site, but they may be costly unless you work out a deal with a photographer you know. In the meantime, you can shoot some of your own photos.

Projected Income/Operating Expenses

Projected Monthly Income		$
Monthly income from tours	$	
Monthly income from product sales		
Total Projected Monthly Income		
Projected Monthly Operating Expenses		
Rent		
Utilities		
Phone		
License renewals		
Electronic terminal		
Employee payroll*		
Workers' compensation insurance*		
Legal services		
Accounting services		
Reference materials/subscription renewals		
Bonding—annual renewal		
Postage		
Web hosting		
Internet service provider		
Advertising/promotions		
Travel		
Loan repayment		
Stationery/office supplies		
Insurance		
For-sale products		
Miscellaneous		
Total Projected Monthly Expenses	$	
Projected Net Monthly Income		$

Only applicable if you have hired employees

▲

Let's Go Shopping

Sure, the expense categories include office equipment, but you will at some point actually have to go out and purchase that equipment. So, here's a lowdown on buying some of the remaining essentials that have not already been mentioned.

We've provided a handy checklist on page 112, which will help you determine what you will need and what you already have on hand. Die-hard shoppers may want to rush out and buy every item brand-new; but don't be too quick with the old credit card. You can use a lot of what you have on hand or find inexpensive alternatives for some of your office needs. Checklist in hand, let's take a whirlwind virtual shopping spree.

Office Equipment

Keep in mind that there's always the buy of a lifetime, and there's always the ultimate top-of-the-line model. What you're looking for are the low- and middle-of-the-road models. You can trade up to the Rolls Royce of computers and other equipment after your business is up and running, and once you're able to pay for upgrades. Just make sure your computers are fast, accommodate your software, and meet your needs. Many new business owners use their current computer and buy a new one as well. The best scenario is to have one desktop and one laptop (or notebook) as mentioned earlier. Buy the one you don't already have and make sure the two machines are easily compatible.

When shopping for equipment or furniture, it's advantageous to go to the larger, more recognizable stores for three reasons. First, they are more likely to have a larger selection. Secondly, they are more likely to stay in business. Third, they are more likely to have a customer service department that is well-versed in dealing with problems that may arise. This is not to say a local mom-and-pop store cannot be a great place to shop, complete with handholding. However, if mom and pop decide to retire and move to Florida or take one of your very long

> **Beware!**
> Voice mail has replaced answering machines for most businesses, but no matter which you use, make sure your message sounds professional. Give your business name—spoken clearly and carefully—and ask callers to leave a short message and a phone number. Thank them for calling and assure them that someone from your office will return their call as soon as possible. Then return all messages within 24 hours, especially since you should be able to get your messages from anyplace in the world.

⚠ Beware!

Remember that you can't scan (or use) anything for which somebody else holds a copyright. This includes graphics, artwork, and text. Make sure the content you use in your marketing materials is public domain or you have permission to use it—this includes photos and other materials you find on the web. Many people believe that if it's on the internet it's fair game. That is not true. You have to have permission to use the material before you import it and post it on your own site, on a DVD, or in your brochures.

vacation packages, who will be there for you when your computer doesn't work or your swivel chair no longer swivels?

Also, get warranties on larger items, save all paperwork, and make sure to have phone numbers for tech support on any item you buy that falls into the "tech" category. Many people shop around and buy online. Again, look for the familiar name stores or websites, such as Compusa.com or Bestbuy.com. You can also go directly to the source, such as Dell.com or Apple.com. Use the Office Equipment Checklist on pages 112 to 113 to price out supplies.

You can also do a great deal of research on the internet for any product—so shop around, compare prices, and ask friends and family (particularly those people who are in business) what has worked for them.

While you're shopping for resources, you might want to take a look at Weissman Travel Reports (www.weissmann.com). This is not a reservation and booking system but instead spins out all sorts of relevant travel information on 10,000 different cities around the world. With this great product—which you update online monthly—you can generate brochures and reports tailored to specific clients and their particular travel destinations, or to your particular tours.

"It's very, very in-depth, like an almanac on computer," says Jim T. in Maryland, who recently added Weissman Travel Reports to his software library. "It gives you vast areas of information on each destination: background, crime, tourist locations, places to go, economics. You can get in there and commingle information, put together itineraries, and print them out for your client. It's a really nice document. Our clients have been ecstatic about it because it gives them so much background on where they're going."

Smart Tip 💡 *Tip...*

You should never send a piece of paper out of your office unless you have kept a copy. You can always print two copies of every document you generate on your computer, keeping one as a file copy. The same goes for emails. Take time to move all important emails into separate folders so you can verify what you sent to a client or travel supplier whenever necessary.

Your Office Equipment Checklist

Use this handy list as a shopping guide for equipping your office. It's been designed with the one-person home office in mind. If you have partners, employees, or you just inherited a million dollars from a mysterious foundation with the stipulation that you spend at least half on office equipment, you may want to make modifications.

After you've done your shopping, fill in the purchase price next to each item and add up the total to give you an idea of what your office expenses will be.

Items

- ❑ Computer $_____
- ❑ Software programs
   - Client relationship management   _____
   - Desktop publishing   _____
   - Accounting   _____
   - Antivirus   _____
   - Other   _____
- ❑ Laser or inkjet printer or both   _____
- ❑ Phones (two lines + cell/smartphone)   _____
- ❑ Scanner   _____
- ❑ Voice mail or answering machine   _____
- ❑ Uninterruptible power supply   _____
- ❑ Surge protector   _____
- ❑ Digital camera   _____
- ❑ Reference materials   _____
- ❑ Office supplies   _____
- ❑ Business cards   _____
- ❑ Blank letterhead stationery   _____
- ❑ Matching envelopes   _____

Your Office Equipment Checklist, continued

Items

- ❑ Cabinets and/or or storage _____
- ❑ Office furniture including
  workstation and chair _____
- ❑ Extra printer cartridge _____
- ❑ Miscellaneous office supplies
  (pens, mousepads, flash drives, etc.) _____

Not on the critical list and probably unnecessary

- ❑ Fax machine _____
- ❑ Copier _____
- ❑ Bookcase _____

**Total Office Equipment and
Furniture Expenditures** $_____

Choose from four types of profiles, or reports:

1. *International profiles.* These are reports on every country in the world. They include elements like "What to Do There," "Transportation," "Accommodations and Health Advisories," and also "What to Buy," "What to Eat" (which can be extremely entertaining), "Dos and Don'ts," and "Potpourri" (of fascinating tidbits about local customs).

2. *United States and Canadian Provinces.* These reports are similar in style and tone to the international profiles.

3. *City profiles.* These profiles include information for the city of your choice, including features such as Bird's-Eye View, Must See or Do, Especially for Kids, and Day Trips. You will also find CityScan, FAQs from average temperatures and rainfall to proper business attire, areas in which to be on crime-guard, and city holidays.

4. *Ports of call.* This includes destination information geared for the cruise passenger voyaging the Americas and the Caribbean, with Fun Facts, Insider Tips (covering everything from whether the water is safe to drink to native slang), and a calendar of events.

You have lots of options with this information, and you can combine several profiles into a single report. Add your clients' itinerary or your own text into the report and even print the reports with your company name, contact information, logo, and your clients' names on the cover page. This has a terrific, personalized impact and makes you look pretty darn slick!

How much should you expect to pay for all this? The basic package runs in the neighborhood of $100 per month. You may be able to wrangle a discount if you belong to NACTA or other groups, including some consortiums—be sure to ask when you call for a subscription.

Funding Your Business

The startup costs of a homebased travel business are not extraordinary. For this reason, you may be able to set aside enough money (perhaps $5,000 to $15,000) to get off the ground comfortably without having to borrow very much money. If you foresee yourself looking for outside funding, start by estimating how much you think you will need. If you list your startup expenses and your total necessary to get off the ground, with some marketing and promotion, as $11,000, perhaps you will then need to borrow half, or $5,500. You may look for some personal loans from family or friends, or you may approach the bank. Either way, you should have a capsule version of a business plan mapped out, including:

- A short executive summary of the overall business
- A summary of the travel industry
- A review of your needs (what you will be spending the money on)
- How your business will operate (booking through a host agency, running your own tours, etc.)
- How you will make money (pricing, any other inventory)
- Competition—Review some of the businesses out there doing what you do and explain what you can do better. Explain how you differ from the budget discount sites in general.
- Bio—Briefly explain your background as it pertains to your new business. This is important for a bank or other commercial lender.

- Financials—Show profit and loss projections for the coming years—be conservative.

A short business plan can help you see all of the aspects of the business and serve as a personal guide. It can show investors that you literally mean business and can provide a snapshot of what it is your business will do—and how you will make money.

If you seek outside funding from a lending institution, you should make sure your credit rating is good. Make sure to check with the three major credit bureaus:

1. *Equifax*: 1-800-685-1111 (general) or 1-800-525-6285 (fraud); PO Box 740241, Atlanta, GA 30374, www.equifax.com

2. *Experian*: 1-888-397-3742 (general and fraud); PO Box 2002, Allen, TX 75013, www.experian.com

3. *TransUnion*: 1-800-888-4213 (general) or 1-800-680-7289 (fraud); PO Box 2000, Chester, PA 19022, www.transunion.com

If you are behind in payments or in debt, get yourself aboveboard prior to seeking out a loan. Even if you don't think you need to borrow, sometimes a small business loan can be beneficial if you pay it back promptly—this shows the bank you are a good credit risk, which can be a benefit in a year or two when you want to borrow money for a major promotional campaign or to expand from a home base into an office location.

Also, check out the SBA at www.sba.gov for information on loans.

Note: If you borrow from family and friends, work out a contract of sorts and discuss the plan from an emotional and relationship standpoint in advance. Borrowing money from family and friends can be very tricky—evaluate the relationship first.

Daily Operations

By this time, you're probably wondering, what exactly does an independent travel agent do all day? Well, in this chapter we answer that question, and take a look at what tour operators do as well.

The Travel Agent: A Day in the Life

As an independent travel agent, in the early stages, your day will generally consist of research, educating yourself, networking, marketing, and (you hope) finding and interacting with suppliers and potential clients. Being fairly well organized helps, so you can move from one task to the next smoothly and not keep clients on hold.

Your first order of business should be responding to phone calls, emails, and texts, since communications and maintaining relationships is the cornerstone of your business. Such phone and email messages may come from potential clients or from your host agency, or travel suppliers. All of these are important relationships and ones that you want to maintain by responding in a timely manner. However, before you reply, you need to prepare yourself with answers. For example, if the client's text says something like "Looking at your great family tours of the Grand Canyon. What are your offerings for June?" you can first check your schedule, or that of your host agency, to see what you have during June and if you have availability before responding. The point is that you will want to be prepared.

Once you are in contact with the customer, or should your phone ring with a caller who has heard about you from a mutual friend, you immediately want to get an idea of what it is they are seeking.

Ultimately, your goal is to send your clients on a marvelous vacation. To do this you will want to:

- Get to know a little about the clients, without giving them the third degree.
- Find out how much your clients are willing to spend.
- Book them.
- Close the deal.
- Settle the transaction.
- Make sure any and all necessary travel data and documents get to your client.
- Collect your commission!

Of course that is a very simplistic version of how the scenario plays out, and this won't happen on one phone call.

First, you will want to meet with, talk with, or exchange emails or texts with a new client. One of the benefits of having a homebased business today is that you can handle all of your business needs through email, text, and telephone communications. If your client is more comfortable meeting with you in person, you can certainly offer a house call, whereby you meet at his or her office, or at a restaurant or coffee emporium, such as a Starbucks, where you can hang out and talk for a little while. Typically, someone who wants to meet in person is more serious about making major travel plans, so you need to be on your most cordial and professional behavior. You will only meet a small percentage of your clients face to face.

Once upon a time, the first contact, or meeting, with your new client was the time to find out all the nitty-gritty you could about his or her travel habits and preferences, as well as personal information. This may seem a bit like the old name, rank, and serial number routine, but it provided valuable insight into your client's travel wants and needs.

Today, the business has changed from the generalist travel agents to your niche markets. Sure, you will have to narrow down the particulars, especially since a niche can cover a wide variety of choices.

A travel agent offering romantic cruises, for example, will still need to find out the basics of when, where, and for how long the loving couple wishes to travel. The difference is, for the most part, fewer travel agents are dealing with a world of possibilities than in the past. Of course, even with a niche, you still want to be able to help anyone seeking your services. While Jennifer Doncsecz, president of VIP Vacations Inc., is mostly booking destination weddings and honeymoons, should one

Use the Phone!

In an age of smartphones and cell-phone service that connects you instantly and clearly (in most cases) with almost anyone around the world, many people have shunned phone conversations—only using emails or texts. This can become cumbersome and slow moving for back-and-forth communication.

Emails are marvelous, but phone calls are still a great way to communicate effectively and quickly when there is a lot of back-and-forth interaction required. The new tendency to never pick up a phone or to not return phone calls often comes back to hurt businesses as their customer service and reputation suffer. A big business can get away with some "bad" or rude behavior because it will make up for it somewhere else (not that it is acceptable). However, a small business, especially one that relies heavily on word-of-mouth, needs to be as careful as possible not to alienate anyone.

Also, the manner in which something is communicated in an email can cause the meaning to be misinterpreted or lost entirely.

of the wedding guests call her and ask about taking their family to Disney World, she will be accommodating, rather than turn away their business. Therefore, no matter what your specialty, you should have a broad research database that you can tap into.

Getting personal information can also be a plus, as it lets you recommend possible vacation options. For example, anniversary dates give you the chance to suggest romantic destinations for a rekindled honeymoon. Finding out about club memberships and hobbies gives you the chance to suggest group travel or special tours. When a client contacts you, their profile will be at your fingertips to help you give them the kind of personalized service they want and a trip they will love.

You do need to play each and every situation by ear. If someone is pressed for time, you may need to stick to his or her immediate needs. Remember, gathering a ton of information on a client is completely useless if you do not satisfy his or her vacation needs. Generally speaking, you'll want to get some basic information on the first communication and then dazzle them with a marvelous trip. After that, they will be glad to provide you with plenty for their travel folder. Therefore, don't jump into a long-term relationship before you've had a wonderful first date.

The Wish List

The major key to success in this business is personalized service, and that means listening and listening closely. There's nothing worse than a travel agent who:

- Books what he or she thinks is the best package regardless of what the customer says.
- Books based on his or her own commissions (in the financial industry this is called churning and will destroy your reputation).
- Doesn't pay attention to the needs of the customer. Remember, if he or she is not happy, you not only lose the customer, but you also lose business from his or her friends, family, and neighbors as well.

Each time you book a tour, cruise, or any type of vacation, you are putting your reputation out there for everyone to see because people love to talk about their vacations—good ones and bad ones. Word of mouth can be a blessing or a nightmare.

The wish list should include the type of accommodations that they would like, the style of vacation they prefer (busy and active, tightly scheduled, free style, relaxing a lot around the pool or by the beach, etc.), the activities they are looking for, and the time frame that best suits them to travel (morning flights, late-night travel, etc.). Make sure you want to know when they plan to leave and return and what flexibility if any they have in those areas. Even within your vacation packages, there should always be some flexibility.

Go, Go, Gigi!

If you say "GG," it sounds like you're referring to the character Leslie Caron played in the old movie, GiGi, the sweet young French girl serenaded by Maurice Chevalier and Louis Jourdan. But in cruising parlance, GG rates mean guaranteed group rates. When a cruise line offers GG rates to a consortium or host travel agency, it has put another feather in its preferred supplier cap by giving that consortium or host agency the same bargain prices for Joe and Jane Doe as it gives to large groups.

As part of the larger group, being a host agency or a consortium, you can pass this along to your customers. If you don't know of such an offer, this is something you want to find out about—which is why, as mentioned earlier, you want to call clients back with well-researched answers.

Give the People What They Want

Now it's your turn to do what you do best: Play matchmaker, or specialist. You need to find the right package tour for your clients. Look at what they have requested in conjunction with what you offer and start putting the pieces together. If you're selling luxury resorts, there are different levels of luxury and different styles that appeal to discerning clients. Likewise, if you sell adventure, there are varying degrees of what your clients find adventurous.

It's important that you start to build a preferred client profile, which you can typically do in your travel software database (i.e., ClientBase or ClientEase).

You will want to have as much data available as possible so that once you have booked that first trip, you can maintain an ongoing relationship with your clients. The first trip is the toughest. This is when you need to prove your worth. Doing so means listening closely to your clients' wants and needs and making sure to cover that wish list as closely as possible. It also means having the confidence to believe in and sell your products. Remember, you are not the travel agent of old, primarily there to meet any travel needs a customer throws at you.

Today, you are a specialist, and a salesperson, with well-prepared and researched travel packages that you want to sell—packages you know all about and are confident can provide an excellent quality vacation (otherwise, you wouldn't be selling them). In

Preferred Client Profile

Remember, you need not fill this out in one sitting or when you first meet a client. Make a sale first—WOW them, and then they'll be a preferred client! The first part of this list is basic information you will need for all clients. Then it becomes "Preferred."

Personal Information

Name: _____

Home address: _____

Office address: _____

Home telephone: _____

Cell phone: _____

Email address: _____

Spouse or significant other: _____

And now it gets to the preferred part—some of which you may learn upfront, the rest you'll gather later on.

Birth dates: _____

Anniversary date: _____

Honeymoon haven: _____

Children's names: _____

Children's birth dates: _____

Household income: _____

Any special health or diet considerations? _____

For which family member(s)? _____

Preferred Client Profile, continued

Family interests: _____

Club and organization memberships: _____

Average number of trips per year: _____

Average length: _____

Favorite travel activities: _____

What times of year do they like to travel? _____

How many vacations do they take in a particular year? _____

Length of average trip: _____

Favorite destinations: _____

Dream destinations: _____

Car rental preferences: _____

Airline preferences: _____

Hotel and resort preferences: _____

Room preference: _____

Cruises

Preferred cruise lines: _____

Favorite ship style: _____

Cabin category preference: _____

Meal seating preference: _____

Additional comments: _____

_____

some cases, this may also mean you are not the travel agent for everyone who calls. With this in mind, you should get to know other agents catering to different niche markets and you should be able to point customers to them, and they to you.

Price Your Time and Package

Travel agents were once the ones with the computers and the travel contacts, booking trips for people with no resources available. Customers relied on the travel agent to find things they could not possibly find on their own. Now, your customers are finding all sorts of places to go and things to do—they are coming to you because you are the expert on Caribbean resorts, cruises to Alaska, kayaking adventures, skiing in the Swiss Alps, safaris in Africa, or whatever packages you offer. Therefore, your first weeks or months will be all about learning and knowing more about these destinations than your customers can find online. Like Margie Jordan of Jordan Executive Travel (JETS) and ASAP Travel, who visited and fell in love with Africa before booking African adventures, you need to visit and research your destinations of choice.

"My first trip to Africa was based on what I had learned from my training online. It was an 11-day trip I took with my boyfriend," says Jordan, who adds that it was an amazing experience. "When I got another opportunity to go, I went back to Africa with another travel agent and had the most amazing time. For me it was a love of the culture, the foods, the cuisine, the people, mixing with the locals, and getting to be in the middle of it. I got to experience what life was really all about for these people," explains Jordan, who immediately started booking trips to Africa.

She soon attained specialist designations for Africa, and is now booking Australia as well. In addition, Jordan holds the position of travel advisor for the Florida Black Chamber of Commerce, assisting travelers in discovering their African American heritage domestically and abroad.

Today, this is how travel agents spend their time, getting to know their destinations of choice through visits and plenty of research. Most of the time they love these destinations.

The next step is to prepare your packages and start looking at pricing. You need to carefully price your trips to meet consumer demands. Remember, when pricing, you need to stay competitive and know your clients' limits. Certainly, if they only want to spend $2,700 and you can come up with a fabulous trip for $3,000, you should pitch it to them . . . along with other alternatives.

Know All the Other Details

Besides providing information on hotels and resorts, tours, rental cars, and all sorts of activities, you also need to know the other details about the destinations you are selling trips to.

If you are sending travelers to other parts of the United States, you won't have to deal with passports (whew!). But you will need to know when hurricane season is, when to expect extreme cold, when the area is crowded or empty, and about local customs. There are plenty of differences between regions and even cities, such as Boston and New Orleans, ranging from the food to the slang. While the currency is the same coast to coast, the economy can also be better or worse in certain regions.

If you are booking international getaways, you will have to know that much more, including currency conversions plus laws and customs of the country and more specifically the regions in that country. The more off the beaten path you are sending people in a foreign land, the more you will need to supply local guides. While some travelers are happy to see the sites as designated on the most popular tours, others like to go far off course to the lesser-traveled regions of a country. Not unlike a parent letting their youngsters have more independence, you can send people into the obscure regions of a country (providing it's not dangerous or simply not permitted) while still making sure someone is keeping an eye on them.

Passport Readiness

Some countries, like Bali, will refuse entry to visitors whose passports are even six months from expiration. If your clients are heading out of the United States, make sure your clients' passports are travel-ready. Know the country's requirements, if any, before sending them on their way.

Even our neighbor to the north, Canada, has been more diligent in recent years about making sure people have proper passports and checking their arrest records and history of other bad behavior before they enter the country. Let your travelers know what the requirements are to cross any border.

Talk to Your Clients

Once you have everything in hand, give your clients the lowdown on what you can do for them. Be positive and enthusiastic, but like any good salesperson, listen. Your clients will have questions and you will either have answers at the ready or be able to ask your travel supplier or host agency for answers quickly. With email, texts, and of course phones, you should be able to respond to customers in a reasonable amount of time. It's best to have some options available to your clients unless they have dictated so specifically what they want that there are no alternatives.

The other crucial aspect of client communication is the post-trip conversation. How did the trip go? Take a deep breath before inquiring, since the negatives will certainly come up. The hope is that the positives of their journey will outweigh any minor glitches and you will hear their smiles over the phone or even see them via Skype.

If clients do point out some areas in which they were disappointed, be attentive and take notes. Minor inconveniences can usually be easily adjusted. In some cases, such as bad weather, you can only listen and commiserate, while trying to nudge people to talk about the positives. The more positives, the more chance you will work with this client again.

Always follow up within a few days of your clients' return. You may also elect to speak briefly with them and let them know you will send a quick follow-up survey. In such a survey, you'll want to ask how the clients would rate the accommodations, the check-in and check-out process, the quality of service, the cleanliness of the room, and the facility, and then ask about some of the activities. Take a mental walk through each major aspect of the vacation and ask general questions to get the the clients' rating or comment. Always ask for comments and/or suggestions. However, note whether or not the resort or cruise also has such a satisfaction survey—often they do, so you will not want to duplicate their efforts. Talk to your contacts about seeing the results and then tailor your survey to your services. And keep it short! You can email clients a survey, and to entice them to participate, you can offer an incentive, such as a discount on their next trip.

Fun Fact

FIT for travel! In travel lingo, a FIT is not something you throw if things don't go your way, but a foreign independent tour, or one in which the tourist explores on his own instead of with a group.

Book the Trip

Let's say your clients love your Grand Canyon vacation package, and you've done the proper amount of tweaking to make sure it suits their specific needs. Now what do you do? You book it! This means you contact your host agency or supplier(s) if you have established the relationship directly.

If you have established your own relationship with the packager you will likely get the best deal and best commission.

If there is a problem in getting exactly what the client wants, then you have two options: One is to book something similar and the other is to ask the packager to hold on or wait while you ask the client about this change. You do not want to do this often, so know ahead of time what tends to "sell out"

so you can let your clients know in advance that such and such may not be easy to get on short notice or at a certain time of year (again, know as much as possible about the area). This way, you can get alternative options from your client ahead of time.

Some clients will be more flexible than others, so you will have to go with their level of flexibility and try to work within those parameters. Some clients want what they want no matter how difficult it is to attain. However, if you can please the most discerning clients, they may be with you for years to come . . . and so may their friends and families.

Payment (or Settlement)

There are various ways to handle payment, or settlement as it is called in the trade. This will depend on your relationships with your host agency and/or the service providers involved. In some cases, the host agency will handle payment, sending it to the supplier and giving you a percentage. If you are working directly with a supplier, then you will send payment directly to them. By whatever means you are set up to make payments, make sure you handle them quickly and have a paper trail to verify that you sent the payments. Tom Ogg notes that thanks to technology and services such as PayPal and Checkout, it's easier than ever to complete travel transactions.

"You can call someone in another part of the world, make a reservation, and settle it using these processes within a matter of hours," says Ogg.

So, What Else Will You Be Doing During Your Day?

While the bulk of your day will hopefully be focused on helping travelers find the vacations that they are dreaming of, you will also be doing some in-house activities, so to speak (actually all of your business activities are in your house, but that's just a matter of semantics). This type of in-house activity means making sure that your entire database is up to date and that you have the latest news on all of your suppliers' offerings.

Travel agents agree that there is plenty to do when you are not communicating with clients or suppliers, and that ongoing education (taking webinars or seminars or simply reading web-based articles or even magazines) is important. Also, checking to see that data is where it belongs, and that your website is constantly current, are important aspects of your day-to-day activities. This means making sure your website is running smoothly and keeping it updated with new information—maybe not on a daily basis,

> **Beware!**
> Try to get a feel for how serious your prospect is before you commit too much counseling time. If the person is a vacation looky-loo (and you'll learn the signs as you grow), you can send him politely on his way with a few brochures. If he is serious later, he can call on you again. The more potential clients you speak to, the more quickly you will be able to discern those who simply want information and those who might actually be interested in using your services.

but certainly on a frequent basis so it doesn't look stale. You don't want to have mid-winter getaways still on your home page as you approach April.

Your day will often include working on and/or placing ads, sending marketing materials, and maintaining your presence in the social media on Facebook and Twitter. You may also be handling paperwork, which can include anything from paying monthly bills to ordering new supplies. You should designate some time every day for your in-house work, the kind that keeps your business running smoothly on a day-to-day basis.

The Tour Operator: A Day in the Life

We've peeked into the daily life of the independent travel agent. Now, what's your day going to be like as a tour operator? Do you put the phone on voice mail, lock up the office, and spend the day out on the river or exploring the city with your clients? Do you spend all day on the phone trying to line up a ground operator who will pick up your group at the airport at 3 A.M.? Or is your time taken up designing tours that will tempt people to sign on?

All of these scenarios are realistic, plus many more.

Designing Tours

A significant part of your early days as a tour operator will be spent designing your tours. One of the most important aspects of a winning tour—the one that garners rave reviews and keeps clients coming back for new offerings—is its design. You can take tourists to the Taj Mahal and bore them silly or to downtown Ozona, Texas, and get oohs of approval, depending on how you structure your program.

You want your tours to give your clients new and intriguing sights, sounds, and scents; but you also want to make sure they reflect the personalities and desires of your target market. A home-schooling group, made up of a dozen 10-year-olds and their parents, will want to whiz through the cathedral of Notre Dame in ten minutes; while a group of a dozen art historians may happily spend an entire day poring over ceilings and floors. Seniors tend to want more hand-holding on a tour than Gen Xers. More savvy tourists from sophisticated areas like New York City or San Francisco may need less coaching on travel etiquette than tourists who have not often ventured into big cities.

The Mystery Tour

Your tours can be as creative as you are. Don't be afraid to break the mold and try something different, as Terry S. did in Seattle. Terry started his business giving walking tours and later branched out to running four different themed tours. Each was a result of a request from one of the groups that took his original tour.

But about two years into running his business, the former computer programmer realized that walking tours were just not going to attract a certain demographic group—namely Gen Xers and local corporate groups. "So I created an alternative way to see the city," Terry explains, "a competitive event that I call Mystery & Scavenger Hunt."

"These sleuthing contests are great morale events, social mixers, team builders, and entertainment for large or small groups," says Terry. "They are conducted in Seattle with chauffeured limousines or on foot—the Inspector Clouseau types vs. the Dirty Harrys. This is the most successful part of my business. Corporate and other groups use it as a morale event, and my most frequent customer is Microsoft."

Practice, Practice

If you are leading the tours yourself, then your tours should also reflect your own personality. There's no need to hit people over the head with your comic timing or your encyclopedic knowledge of Roman history, but your interests and enthusiasm will contribute a great deal to your clients' sense of fulfillment and fun. This is not to say that leading a tour is a no-brainer, as long as you, or your tour guides, have charm.

As a tour operator, you need to do your homework, making sure you are well versed in each area of the tour you offer. You will then spend a lot of time refining each of your tours, whether it is a murder and mystery tour or a Chinatown at twilight tour.

Phil S., a tour operator in New York City, starts each of his tours based on information found in guidebooks and gradually develops a specific theme or approach. "From there you can find out what works and what doesn't," he says. That also includes pacing. The original version of Phil's East Village tour covered a three-mile area in two-and-a-half hours—a hike that the history professor soon whittled down to just one mile. "It's not a marathon anymore," he says with a smile.

Sell What You Know

Let's face it, there are hundreds, if not thousands, of tour companies, and to compete effectively in this crowded market means doing something special and presenting it with a personal touch.

Barry, the car race tour operator, uses his expertise in his chosen field to give his clients a unique experience. "We may have a driver spend some time with people," he says. "We may have a race commentator give them special information. We'll put on theme parties—we did one in Canada for a thousand people. We may have an auction of car parts in which the money goes to charity. We do many different things in these areas. If we're charging a premium, there has to be a reason for somebody to go on our tours."

Some of Barry's tours are hosted by celebrities, and sometimes the celebs put in a surprise appearance. "Things will happen that you don't envision," he explains. "You can't tell clients that this or that will happen. Somebody invites you where you never expected to go, as when an English lord invites a tour group for tea or the owner of a museum personally shows you his magnificent cars."

> **Tip...**
>
> ## Smart Tip
>
> "The whole goal in running a tour," says car race tour promoter Barry S., "is to give people something they can't do on their own. If you can do something that's impossible for people to achieve alone, then you have them as customers."

It sounds like serendipity, and it is. But these unexpected delights also happen because Barry has developed a friendship and rapport with the people involved—the windfalls of which he's able to pass along to his lucky clients.

Debrief and Distill

"Specialize," advises Karen A., the tour operator in Savannah, Georgia. "Whether your customers are Girl Scouts or music students, whether your tours are bird watching or gambling, you will never get really good at giving a tour unless you give the same kind of tour to the same kind of people over and over and iron out the kinks. If you get really good at it, people will spread the word; and you'll get much of your new business from return customers and by word-of-mouth.

"Hold debriefing meetings after every tour and distill what you have learned into policies that will make the next tour run more smoothly."

Primary Research

If you are a travel agent booking tours, you can more easily stay in the comfort of your homebased office and match the traveler to the best tour based on all that is offered by suppliers. If you are a tour operator, however, you are the supplier. Therefore, as you piece a tour together, you will need to walk or ride through the tour as you build it to make sure it is feasible. This means making all the stops and determining what can and cannot be worked into x number of minutes, hours, or days.

From Leading Tours to Entrepreneur

Many tour operators go from leading tours to running a company that handles numerous tours and serves as a supplier. This means putting together tours that meet the needs of visitors to your town, city, region, or country. The more tours you create and market successfully, the more business owners (from tour bus companies to hotels) will want to be included in your tours. In time, you can be selling full-scale tours, complete with accommodations, transportation, and dining, which travel agents will market to their clients. You can become a "middle person" of sorts, putting tours together and selling them.

Permissions

Along with designing the tour, which we will discuss in greater detail later on, you will need to spend some of your days making sure the tour works and is interesting. You will also need to make sure that you have received permissions for entry to buildings, parking for vehicles, photographing private property, and so on. You cannot leave one stone unturned when making sure that no part of the tour will have you or your clients breaking laws, ordinances, or causing a fire hazard. In addition, you will need to make sure that you follow the rules and requirements of any facility—no matter how big or small—that you are planning to enter. For example, if the 700-year-old church that boasts spectacular architecture informs you that no more than 40 people at a time can be inside the structure, then you are limited to 39 plus yourself. No eating or photography in specific locations means just that! You will spend a part of your day establishing very solid relationships with the people who own, run, and/or manage the sites and activities on your tour, making sure you know exactly what to expect when you arrive. There are way too many stories of tour operators not being able to gain access to a key site because nobody informed the guard at the front gate that a tour was coming. Therefore, double and triple check exactly how access will be determined.

Ready to Roll!

Once your tours are set up, you will spend a good portion of your days doing marketing and finding new and innovative ways of selling your product. This may mean contacting travel agents, since you are a supplier, or booking the tours yourself. Either way, you need to spend your time evaluating the best, most cost-efficient means of reaching your target market.

As your business grows you will more than likely hire others to conduct the actual tours while you run the business, which includes handling all the paperwork and doing everything from paying taxes and insurance premiums to making sure your website is up-to-date with your latest tour offerings. Your day will include making sure the travel agents and any online travel companies with whom you work are up-to-date on your latest tours. Also, it is even more important for you to have photographs of your tours, whether it means using your own digital camera or hiring a professional photographer to take photos for you. Remember, the tour business is sales oriented. You can have the most incredible tour offerings in the world, but if you don't focus a lot of your time and efforts on sales and marketing, you won't succeed.

When marketing, it will help if you write succinct, inviting copy for brochures and for your website to make the tour sound exciting, enchanting, educational, thought-provoking, or whatever it is you want your clients to get from the experience.

Bounce marketing ideas off of people around you and make sure you work and re-work your copy until it makes the tour jump off the page or screen. Don't forget the photos!

Go to trade shows, conferences, seminars, and any other places where you can let other travel professionals know that you have something that may interest their clients.

Then, much like the travel agent, make sure you answer all inquiries promptly and try to close as many deals for the tour as possible.

8

All About Tours

Tours are big business worldwide, and if you have locations that people want to visit, to learn about, or to explore, then your tours will be in demand. Today, for the most part, travel agents book tours, but do not run them—which is why we have been separately discussing your option of going into the travel business as a tour operator.

What You Need to Know

First, as a travel agent, you are looking at thousands of possible tours offered by travel suppliers. As mentioned throughout the book, you will need to either start getting to know travel suppliers—who may or may not have time to build relationships with independent travel agents—or hook up with a host agency which provides the type of tours that meet your needs and serve your target market. You can also work directly with tour operators who put tours together or with wholesalers who sell tour operators' products.

Evaluating tours is the key to providing what your audience wants. Remember, you are providing a service. From your perspective, you need to read the fine print, and ask questions wherever you are unsure. You want to know:

- When the tour is offered—year round? Certain months only?
- What is the tour itinerary and are there variations?
- How long does the tour last?
- What specifically is and (more importantly) is not part of the tour package? (i.e., Air? Meals? Ground transportation?)
- What is the price and what are the additional fees/costs, if any?
- What are the tour parameters? (No kids under 12? Nobody who is scared of alligators?) Whatever they are, you need to know them.
- What does the traveler need to bring, if anything, on such a tour?
- What is the cancellation policy? How much is charged if the tour is canceled?
- What happens if the tour operator has to cancel a tour due to circumstances out of their control (i.e., war or threat of war, riots, civil unrest, terrorist activity, natural disaster, fire, adverse weather conditions, etc.)?
- What are the tour payment or settlement policies?
- How many people can go on this tour?
- How often are these tours booked?
- What kind of marketing is the tour supplier and/or your host agency doing?
- What does the tour operator or supplier provide you in terms of marketing materials for the tour?
- How far in advance must you book and how quickly do these tours fill up?

These are the basics that you will need to know as a travel agent before you can book the tour. Your goal will be to find as many tours that fit your genre or niche as possible. You will then want to talk to other travel agents (which is one good reason for joining associations) about this tour supplier. What have they heard? A host agency that has been working with a tour operator or packager for 20 years is a good sign. It means that they have a trusting relationship.

You can also arrange your own tours by putting together the various components yourself. This gives you the freedom to pick and choose the various elements of the tours(s) you wish to offer and make them your own. However, it's hard to run a travel agency and handle the specific aspects of the tours yourself. Additionally, you will not get the discounts that a tour operator will get because he or she is buying in bulk to sell tours to many travel agents.

So let's learn a little more about tour operators, another avenue you might pursue, which will have you working with travel agents.

Tour Operators

The primary focus of a tour operator is to create, arrange, and market tour packages, which may or may not include all the key elements, transportation, accommodations, and tours/activities. Tour operators may also include dining and other special services in their packages. A good tour operator needs to be on top of each aspect of their product—the tour—at all times and know the business (and the destinations) inside out.

Jeff Adam, vice president of sales and marketing for AAT Kings North America, based in Anaheim, California, promotes fully guided coach tours and sightseeing day tours throughout his homeland of Australia and in New Zealand. "As a tour operator, one of the things I do is train travel agents on how to sell Australia," says Adam, who runs numerous webinars on the topic.

In the process of assembling a variety of tours, AAT Kings includes accommodations, guided sightseeing tours, transfers, and meals in a variety of locations and time frames. Like other tour operators, they put together itineraries through their knowledge and contacts in each of numerous locations, which in their case cover a wide range of possibilities in Australia and New Zealand. "We also offer Flexi itineraries," says Adam, explaining that these are AAT Kings short tours that bring the highlights of a specific region or city to life. "Designed as modules, these short tours can be attached so that different ten-day or two-week tours can be created," says Adam of the build-your-own tour aspect of the Flexi tours. "This way, you can grab a packaged three nights, four-day tour of Sydney and then add on a two-night, three-day tour of somewhere else, for example," explains Adam, adding that it would be much more difficult for a travel agent to build tours like this from scratch largely because as a tour operator a company like AAT Kings can get much better rates.

Tour Operator Skills

The most important skills for a tour operator include:

- Organizational skills
- General management skills
- Time management skills
- People skills
- Sales and marketing skills
- Customer service skills
- Financial management skills
- Communications skills

Along with all these skills, being savvy in social media and the latest in all forms of high-tech communications is also helpful. Not unlike a travel agent, a tour operator needs to take advantage of as many courses, seminars, webinars, and other educational opportunities as possible.

For example, along with giving webinars about touring Australia and New Zealand, Jeff Adam of AAT Kings recommends that those travel agents looking to sell tours in Australia become Aussie specialists and join the ASP Social Network, which provides a chance to interact with other travel agents and tour operators selling in Australia (http://aussiespecialist.ning.com).

Whether it's a skill or not, the ability to think fast and handle all situations is part of the job. It is also imperative to have an excellent knowledge of each aspect of your tour packages, including history, geography, and anything else travelers could possibly want to know about the destination. You will want to do your homework regarding the going rate for tours such as yours to remain competitive in the industry. It is advantageous if you can create tour packages that are cost effective for the travelers. The more packages you sell, the better discounts you can pass along. Volume purchasing often enables you to secure accommodations and travel arrangements that would be virtually impossible for travel agents to obtain on their own.

Lots of Options

While you are creating the best tour possibilities for your clients, make sure you consider the following:

- *Dinner or not?* Tour operators will often design their programs around a MAP, which is not a street or topographic map, but the Modified American Plan, or meal plan in which customers are fed two out of three meals a day (usually breakfast and dinner) as part of the tour price. Make sure clients are aware that lunch isn't included, so they are ready to spring for that midday meal if they so choose. Since dining out can be part of the lure of some areas, you need to determine whether it is advantageous to include meals in a tour package, or make it an option. If your mountain climbers are going to be tired at the

Smart Tip

Tip...

Some tour operators design their packages with two prices—air-inclusive and land-only. As you can surmise, the former includes airfare to the tour origination city, while the latter is for the tour only so clients can make their own arrival arrangements.

end of the day, having planned meals included at their luxury resort may be a smart idea. Likewise, should the choices for dining be limited in an out-of-the-way location, you may want to have dining already accounted for, so your clients are not left searching for local eateries, which may be overpriced and/or less than satisfying. If your tour is to New York City, or anyplace with an amazing array of five-star eateries, travelers won't want to be restricted in their dining choices. However, you can strike up deals with some restaurants for discounts; again, you have volume as your bargaining tool if you are selling a lot of tours.

- *Optional adventures*. Sometimes tour brochures can be a bit misleading. If that Transylvania package has a line like, "Day 3 includes a scenic mountain drive to the quaint village of Igor Abbey, location of the famous Vampire's Kiss Winery," it doesn't necessarily mean that a winery tour is included. Make sure your client understands exactly what is included. Then suggest the winery tour—it's added fun for them and can add more commission for you! People like to have activities and flexibility. With that in mind, take a page from the cruise liners that offer a host of daily excursions at every port (and make a fortune doing so) and include some choices.

- *Extra perks*. Tour operators often add extra perks to make the tour a special experience. If the package includes goodies like dinner with a celebrity ("Count Vlad at your table!"), be sure your client knows about this, too. Anticipation is part of the fun. Look for perks that are cost effective but fit nicely into your tour package motif. This is where you can add "creativity" to the list of tour operator skills.

Marketing Tours

The best way to sell tours to your niche market is to go back to your initial marketing study—the one that you did to determine your target audience and see what

United States Tour Operators Association

The United States Tour Operators Association (USTOA) is the professional association of the tour operator industry. Tour operators and suppliers may all join USTOA, although membership requirements are stringent, asking tour operators for 18 or more references from a variety of industry sources and financial institutions. Operators also must meet specific minimums in terms of tour passengers and/or dollar volume. The company must have been in business at least three years under the same management in the U.S. and must carry a minimum of $1,000,000 professional liability insurance.

Those who meet the criteria are considered among the top travel businesses in the U.S., and are responsible for a majority of tours and vacations sold by U.S. travel agents. According to the American Tourism Society, a recent survey showed that USTOA companies move more than 10 million passengers annually and account for an annual sales volume of more than $8 billion.

The USTOA is dedicated to providing the travel industry with education and to protecting customers from financial loss in the event of a member filing for bankruptcy.

Terry Dale, president of USTOA, notes that the 40-year-old association also focuses on advocacy. "One of our top priorities is advocacy. We want to be more effective in how we educate elected officials on what our segment of the travel industry is all about and our impact on the economy around the world," explains Dale, who worked with USTOA to engage a government affairs firm in Washington, DC, to help educate them on the tour industry and find ways to help federal agencies such as the Department of Labor and the Department of Transportation better understand the needs of tour operators so that they can operate profitably.

The other major priority of the USTOA today is dealing with issues regarding safety and security. "Not only is the economy a challenge, but if you think about our industry, every global issue touches and impacts how we operate," says Dale, referring to such issues and events as the civil unrest in Egypt, the tsunami and earthquake in Japan, the flooding in Australia, and earthquakes in New Zealand. "We have tours going on all over the world, so we need to be able to help tour operators anywhere when it comes to the safety and security of their clients," says Dale regarding the need to get customers out of a region and into a safe territory as quickly as possible.

USTOA, continued

The USTOA also holds an annual conference where suppliers and tour opera-tor members can meet face to face and gather information about one another in hopes of forming connections.

---

it is that would pique their interest. What is of greatest importance to your travelers? Accommodations? Low rates? Adventure? History? Scenic beauty? Breathtaking beaches? Give them—or the travel agents who sell to the customers—what they want in bold print and with the photos to match. Also, give yourself time to book in advance.

Travel agents want to have as much promotional material as possible from the tour suppliers and/or through their host agency. As you are putting the tours together, get promotional materials from the resort, the cruise lines, the folks who rent the kayaks, and anyone else involved in your tour. If you are putting much of it together yourself, hire a photographer and get whatever photos you believe will best sell your tours.

 **Beware!**
Some states have rules about who can sell insurance, including travel agents who offer it to their clients through an independent insurance agent. Be sure to check with your state's regulatory body before proceeding.

You may want to hire graphic designers, web designers, photographers, travel writers, copywriters, or whomever you feel can help you best sell your tours. Remember, as mentioned earlier, the best and most successful entrepreneurs (in all fields) know when to ask for help. So if you are not convinced that your marketing materials (including your website) are first rate, hire help.

Also, don't forget to market through the social media. Talk to travel agents, travelers, and anyone else who can become, or guide you to, a customer.

Ecotourism

According to the International Ecotourism Society (TIES), ecotourism is "responsible travel to natural areas that conserves the environment and improves the well-being of local people."

Short for ecological tourism, an ecotour usually includes background information, education, and even hands-on activities designed to illustrate the benefits of environmentally sound areas and cultures. Among the goals of ecotourism are building environmental and cultural awareness and providing positive experiences for the participants, as well as financial benefits for conservation and for the local people in the area.

Along with evaluating environmental and cultural factors, initiatives by hospitality providers to promote recycling, energy efficiency, water re-use, and the creation of economic opportunities for local communities are an integral part of ecotourism.

When looking for the best ecological tours, look for those that fit the above criteria and not ones that are simply taking travelers to a five-star luxury hotel plunked down in the middle of an otherwise lavish natural setting.

You can also find some "green hotels." Typically they:

- Reduce laundry water temperatures from 90° C to 60° C
- Install low-flow showerheads and low-flow toilets
- Install solar panels to heat water
- Implement hotel-wide recycling programs
- Replace individual soaps and lotions with wall dispensers

Adopting of green practices typically helps hotels realize considerable savings that can range from several thousand to hundreds of thousands of dollars per year.

Popular New Ecotourism Locations

Popular current locations for ecotourism include:

Ecotourism Facts and Figures

Ecotourism captures $77 billion of the global market, according to the Center for Responsible Travel.

According to *Travel Weekly*, sustainable tourism could grow to 25 percent of the world's travel market by 2012, taking the value of the sector to approximately $473 billion a year.

- *Borneo*, filled with dense jungles, cavernous caves, exotic wildlife, and thousands of species of Himalayan, Australasian, and Indomalayan plant life, plus eco-lodges that use rain water and solar power.
- *Belize*, home to rainforests and numerous species of wildlife. It is a magnificent place to scuba dive and get a glimpse of stingrays, sharks, dolphins, coral, and turtles in the waters below, while also enjoying the hospitality of eco-lodges.
- *Guyana*, home to the Karanambu Ranch where orphaned giant river otters are rehabilitated so they can be released back into the wild. Travelers can explore the magnificent mountain ranges or get a glimpse into the lives of exotic birds, red howler monkeys, and other wildlife that call the rainforests home.
- *Scandinavia*, including Sweden, Norway, and Denmark. This is also home to amazing natural wonders across a widespread region that awaits the ecotourism crowd.

Those who implement and participate in ecotourism activities should adhere to the following ecotourism principles:

- Minimize impact.
- Build environmental and cultural awareness and respect.
- Provide positive experiences for both visitors and hosts.
- Provide direct financial benefits for conservation.
- Provide financial benefits and empowerment for local people.
- Raise sensitivity to host countries' political, environmental, and social climate.

Group Tours

Travel agents can benefit from tours on which they book groups, such as lodge members, a large family for a reunion, or other such possibilities. Clearly, the advantages of booking a large group are a greater discount for them, yet more commissions for you. After all, even at a lower rate, booking 25 people at one time is terrific.

There are, however, some added concerns when booking groups. First, you will need to get a "joint wish list" for the entire crowd. This means that you will need to work with one representative on behalf of everyone involved, whether it's the school administrator or the patriarch or matriarch of the family. That person will need to be in charge of gathering the information—wants, likes, and dislikes from the group as a whole—and forwarding it to you. This person is your contact point and he or she should get the answers to the questions, such as the type of tour the group is looking for and favorite activities.

You will now be able to work with the group sales representative at the travel supplier or your host agent will provide you with such group sales information and possible tours that work well for the demographics and interests of the group.

If you are not buying a tour from an operator, but are actually building one yourself, group planning means spending a lot of time and effort on logistics, since travelers may need their own bus or van, depending on the size of the group and their tours of interest. If the tour is for a specific purpose, such as a family traveling to celebrate a special anniversary, you will then want to inquire about the guests of honor and try to find specialty items that may add that unique touch. This may mean doing some legwork above and beyond booking the tour package.

Knowing your group and knowing a lot about their interests and wishes can make booking group tours very worthwhile. Having tour operators at the ready with various packages can make your life a lot easier—however, if you can build a tour yourself, without too many headaches, it can be worthwhile.

Tour Possibilities

- *Bus tours* (or as travel specialists prefer to call it, motor coach). This takes us back to the old *If It's Tuesday, This Must Be Belgium* model, except that these days motor coach tours are more leisurely than frenzied. These tours can encompass anything from a two-week trip through France to a two-hour jaunt through Kenosha, Wisconsin. In an age where airline travel security slows down the flow of multicity touring, this can be a very welcome and relaxing way for travelers to see not only the major cities and key attractions, but some of the beautiful landscape in between. The drawback today of bus tours is the rising price of gas, but many operators still offer such tours.

- *Rail tours.* The romance of the rails, once nearly extinct, is back in a big way, outside of the United States. Travelers can choose super-luxury tours aboard the old Orient Express à la Agatha Christie (minus the murder), breathtaking journeys through Mexico's Copper Canyon, or traveling by train along coastal Nova Scotia, among a myriad of other offerings. The savings of traveling by train can allow you to creatively add some additional activities to their itinerary, and benefit from commissions or service fees.

- *Your own wheels.* People with a penchant for motor homes, motorcycles, or off-road vehicles can take part in tours, which might more aptly be called caravans, organized around their favorite sets of wheels. Tour operators lead groups of RVs through Mexico, for instance, stopping at sites along the way just as you'd do in a motor coach, except that you have your own vehicle.

- *Adventure tours.* Featured in more detail in Chapter 11, these are the tours that have travelers climbing Mt. Kilimanjaro, skiing an Alaskan glacier, or cave-diving in Kentucky. This type of tour is not for the faint of heart or flat of feet.

- *Extreme tours* (X-Tours). These tours are about adventure and excitement. They let people who spend much of their time behind desks get out and raise their heart rates. And today, as people's workloads increase, there is a greater desire than ever among travelers to strap on skis, surf the waves, climb aboard a camel, ride the rapids, or glide down a zip line. The concept is adventure, and by incorporating it within a trip to a spectacular destination, such as Morocco, Bali, Borneo, or Maui, your clients can indulge in their passion for excitement, while adding the perfect setting.

- *Wine tours.* You don't look at overseas itineraries to find wine tours; in fact, you can build some yourself. Just keep in mind that you will have a lot of competition. The Napa Valley in California, including Napa, Oakville, Rutherford, Yountville, St. Helena, and Calistoga, as well as Sonoma County, the California Central Coast, and the Sierra Foothills, offers great choices of wineries. You'll want to offer first-rate accommodations (perhaps in a quaint bed and breakfast) and sumptuous dining as well as sightseeing excursions and even something special such as hot air balloon rides. It's also imperative that you provide safe transportation from tasting to tasting.

- *Bike tours.* There are bikers and then there are bikers. The daily distance, topography, and overall scope of the trip will vary greatly depending on whether you are making plans for experienced riders or newbies. So before you book bike tours with operators or create your own, determine which market or markets you are going after. Bike tours can encompass great sightseeing and a wide range of accommodations, from camping to bed and breakfasts to five-star hotels.

- *Romantic tours.* Whether it's a dreamy island paradise or a secluded spot with all the amenities, romantic getaways are big business. The tours are the diversion, or the "date" part of the evening, perhaps in the jazz clubs of Bourbon Street or on a carriage ride through Central Park. Of course if your clients want to move beyond the romance, you can send them to Hedonism Resorts and the clothing optional tours, which are big business for companies such as AdultOnlyTours. com. Whatever you are planning, romance or otherwise, privacy and tranquility are two of the selling points. Think: opposite of a Disney trip.

- *Golf and sports tours.* Golf is in a class by itself. Spectacular and challenging courses can be found all over the United States, particularly in California, Arizona, Florida, and Myrtle Beach and even in the Northeast. You can also send your golf lovers to other parts of the globe. Golfers can be a fussy group,

▲

so make sure you know what they like to a tee (pun intended) and plan accordingly. Also consider the level of the golfers you are marketing to. You might try finding the best courses for the up and coming golfers or the casual players since there are countless packaged tours for serious golfers.

- *Sports fan tours.* Traveling the country to see sporting events such as NASCAR racing or golf tournaments can pique the interest of fans, as can stadium hopping, a favorite of baseball fans who want to see as many of the great ballparks as they can.

> **Smart Tip** *Tip...*
>
> An inbound tour operator brings tourists into her locality, while an outbound operator specializes in ferrying locals to someplace far away. If you're based in San Antonio, for instance, and you are shepherding groups from Paris to the Alamo, you're an inbound operator. If you're based in San Antonio and you take an American group to the Eiffel Tower, you're acting as an outbound operator.

Timing and scheduling are of prime importance when piecing together such a tour. Sports Travel and Tours, for example, offers spring training tours in Arizona and Florida. They also have a spring training cruise during which baseball lovers go to spring training games in Florida, take a seventh inning stretch for a week or so aboard a cruise ship that travels to Jamaica and Grand

The Do-It-Yourself Package for Travel Agents

An alternative to the pre-packaged tour is to design a custom tour for your clients.

It requires some legwork (or phone and email work) but can be a tremendous means of finding, creating, and selling to your own niche market. In addition, it is almost imperative that you first get to know the area intimately and establish contacts with local travel suppliers (which don't have to be quite as intimate).

The savvy travel agent can double as a tour operator by putting together each piece of the puzzle step by step if she is extremely detail oriented. You probably won't be able to do this when you are starting out, but many travel agents are reaping the major benefits of building their own tours once they become established and confident in both their planning skills and their ability to network with preferred suppliers.

Caymen in Mexico, and then return to Florida for more baseball. For some couples, this can be a great compromise vacation.

- *Island hopping.* Yes, many cruise ships stop at ports in the Caribbean, but the focus is primarily on the cruise and the ports are typically one-day stops. You could, however, package tours that take your clients to a few island resorts for several days at a time, letting them bask in the sun and play in the sand of not just one beautiful island, but several.

- *Theme tours.* These are the multitude of tours designed with a specific theme in mind, like "Beer Lover's Germany" or "Haunted Hollywood." Instead of just taking travelers to Germany or plain old Hollywood, each facet of the itinerary is planned around a theme. These are particularly great excursions for the right group and are offered by various tour operators.

- *City tours.* While most of the tours we've described last from several days to a couple of weeks, a city tour is usually a quickie that takes a few hours to one day. Although sometimes it can be a three-day package of day tours. "Haunted Hollywood" is a good example, as is "Sherlock Holmes' London" or "Discover Detroit." You get the idea—this is a motor coach or walking tour that gives visitors the flavor of a town and a peek into its particular sights and sounds.

> **Beware!**
> There are a million tour operators out there, and not all of them are in the best financial shape. As a travel agent, it's your responsibility to be as certain as possible that these businesses won't collapse, taking your clients' money and vacation plans along with them. As always, do your homework and keep abreast of industry news. You'll often read about those on shaky ground long before they hit the dirt. Also look for tour operators who are affiliated with the USTOA, where they will be insured against such disasters as bankruptcy.

Making Your Own Tours: Structural Elements

Whether you are a tour operator or a travel agent determined to create tours yourself, you need to first determine what the theme of your tour will be and how you will use your knowledge and expertise to make it special. Now how do you give it a structure? Take a look at the following elements, for starters.

- *Holiday rambling.* Decide what the best time of year is for your particular tour. As one fishing aficionado points out, some activities—like king salmon fishing in September—insist on their own time frames. Often, clients have time frames that are better or worse for them as well. Obviously, family vacation tours play better during school and work holiday periods, traditional summer vacations, weeklong breaks, such as Christmas break, and short-hop holidays, such as Memorial Day and Labor Day.

> **Bright Idea**
>
> If you'll target a particular professional organization, try scheduling a short tour right before or after your tourists' national convention. People who'll be in town to attend the big meeting can include your tour without adding in extra travel expenses or significantly more time away from work. It will also offer a nice change of pace from work-related activities.

- *Paint the town.* Unless a special event is the focus of your tour, make sure your program doesn't coincide with paint-the-town-red events. These would be events like the Olympics; Mardi Gras; Le Mans; the running of the bulls at Pamplona; or other annual feasts, festivals, and general mayhem that can tie up traffic and hotel rooms—and make the latter much less available and much more expensive.

- *Weather wrinkles.* Whether it's hurricane season in the Florida Keys, blizzard conditions in the Midwest or Northeast, or monsoon season in India, you need to be aware of seasonal weather patterns. You can't know precisely when some of these weather events will occur, but you can definitely take them into consideration when planning and marketing tours.

- *Time redux.* One more timing element to take into consideration is the length of your tour. A half-day tour of Apalachicola, Florida, is probably long enough to see all there is in this small fishing town, but you can easily schedule a full week in San Francisco or two weeks in China. Consider how much there is to see, how long they will stay interested, the costs per day, and the typical length of a tour vacation. Typically one week domestically for a major city or two weeks abroad are common, but there are no set rules.

High Concept

Give your tours a high-concept title. In Hollywood terms, this means a title that paints an immediate and intriguing picture. "Midnight, Moonlight, and Magnolias" sounds far more interesting than "The Charleston, Beaufort, and Savannah Tour." Think of your products in terms of how they'll sound in a brochure and the romance or excitement (or both) they'll conjure up in potential clients' minds. However, don't be so "cutesy" with your tour names that you baffle your target audience.

Keep these high-concept pointers in mind as you design your tours:

- *Stick with the program.* Don't wander away from that unique concept. If your theme is "Midnight, Moonlight, and Magnolias," and you're packaging seafront cities of the Old South, you can't suddenly throw in Chicago as well–even if your clients will be changing planes there en route to Charleston.

- *Act smart.* Planning a tour is like writing a three- or four-act play. You need to give it a kick-start, an exciting end, and not let it fall somewhere in the middle. Plan an itinerary that's full of surprises but that also has enough pleasant lulls to keep your clients from feeling overwhelmed. A two-week trip—as well as a two-hour walking tour—should be stimulating but also allow time for relaxation.

Supplier Smarts

"Hotels demand deposits for group reservations and payment in full before the group arrives," advises Karen A. in Savannah, Georgia. "Motor coach owners also require deposits. In theory, so do many other attractions. Everything, however, is negotiable, and your reputation as a tour operator or travel agent is all-important. (One Savannah tour operator has been banned from a Savannah museum for paying their bills too slowly and booking too many no-show groups.) In practice, we pay hotels in full a couple of weeks in advance. In our second year, we paid some of the more prosperous restaurants by invoice after the event and most other restaurants and attractions at the time of the tour. In our third year, with a reputation for paying our bills, we are being billed after the event by nearly all our vendors except hotels," explains Karen.

Today, with the ramped-up high-tech means of making fast payments, being sure suppliers are paid and happy should not be a problem.

> **Tip...**
>
> ## Smart Tip
> Be sure to explain facets of foreign cultures to your clients before they encounter certain situations—everything from the fact that you can't always get unsweetened iced tea in Southern restaurants to the fact that bowing in Japan is common courtesy. It makes for a more comfortable tour and also reduces the insecurity factor. Remember that as a tour operator or travel agent you can provide information on nuances that travelers don't often get from discount travel websites, and this is important to your business.

Lodging Logistics

Your choice of lodgings will play a large part in how your clients view your tour. Your choices can range from a quaint bed and breakfast in the country to a suite at the Ritz. Naturally, one is going to be pricier than the other, but your choices will also appeal to different clients. So how do you choose?

First, realize that your hotel price will be built into the price of your tour, as we explained previously.

Even though you build lodging into the cost of your tours, you still have a lot of decisions to make. Do you go with the hotel that's in the middle of the action or one that is off the beaten path? And if you choose the latter, how do your clients get around? Your accommodations need to fit the mode, purpose, and logistics of the tour. If sightseeing by foot is the activity of choice, then look for a lodging location within walking distance of the sites. If biking is the theme of the tour, then housing 60 people with their bicycles in the middle of downtown Chicago might not be feasible.

Take a look at these tips for making the right decision:

- *Compatibility*. Choose a hotel that's a good match with your clients and your subject matter. If you're doing a tour for business executives, you might choose an upscale, modern hotel near the airport or a fashionable, upscale semi-burb like Beverly Hills. These are the types of environments the suit crowd feels comfortable in and considers worth its time and money. On the other hand, if your market niche is the paranormal, you might seek out an old downtown hotel with an ambiance of emanations and possibly even a resident ghost or two.

- *Minimize packing and unpacking*. Most travelers are not enamored with the idea of packing and unpacking every night (which is one of the selling points of a cruise—that you don't have to). So if your tour will encompass several cities or regions, it's a good idea to check clients into a centrally located hotel and plan day trips for the surrounding areas. For example, you might choose a hotel in Dana Point, California, and take minivan excursions to Los Angeles, San Diego, and Ensenada, Mexico, instead of shuttling people to three different hotels.

The Lodging Wish List

Once you've chosen your ideal lodging, it's time to talk price with the sales manager. Hotels—especially larger properties that are used to dealing with seminars, conventions, weddings, and other groups—tend to operate something like car dealers, fully expecting that in any negotiations they'll come out ahead. Therefore, they may (and probably will) quote rates that are higher than they actually need to turn a profit, insist that they can't help with certain requests because it's not "hotel policy," and otherwise drag their feet.

Your part in dealing with hotels is to build relationships in advance—the more business you send their way, the more accommodating they should be (pun intended again). They get lots of rooms filled in one fell swoop, along with the stellar opportunity to have you bring groups back over and over again. So stick to your guns in the negotiating process. Don't be rude or aggressive; you're trying to win longtime contacts. But do be prepared to bargain. Of course, they may also want you to "put your money where your mouth is" so to speak. Which means, prove to them that you can bring them regular business—if you do build up a steady run of tours, they will be your best friends.

But, first, you need to know what you want. Take a look at this lodging wish list:

- *A room with a view.* Tell the sales manager how many rooms you will need and stress that they must be rooms with a view of the sea, the park, the city lights, or whatever defines the best views. Your clients will not be impressed by a view of the dumpsters or the brick wall next door and neither will you.

- *Dining delights.* Find out if the hotel will include breakfast as part of the room rate. Then make sure you're negotiating for either a continental breakfast, which is the European version with just coffee and rolls; a full dining room meal of bacon and eggs; or a special room for a buffet-type breakfast.

- *Dining delights part deux.* If the hotel won't go for complimentary breakfasts, make sure it does have a dining room or that there's a breakfast eatery somewhere nearby so that your clients can eat before departing for the day's activity. Ditto this for evening meals, unless you will arrange for them to eat out as part of the program or make it a meals-not-included package. As mentioned earlier, the more dining options there are in a particular place, such as Manhattan, the less you'll need to concern yourself with meals. In such cases, you may strike up some bargains with popular eateries and let the travelers decide for themselves where they want to dine.

- *Meeting room.* You may want a sizable room if your tour will include any sort of workshop or seminar. Discuss this with the hotel well in advance.

Dollar Stretcher

Don't forget that airlines, hotels, attractions, and many other suppliers offer senior discounts. If you'll have seniors on your tour, negotiate this into your costs.

- *Party.* If you will include a welcome reception or farewell bash, you will want the hotel to spring for eats and drinks (at a reasonable cost), as well as provide an appointed room in which to hold the affair.

- *Cool comps.* Ask for comps, which are complimentary, i.e., freebie rooms, for your coach driver and tour guide.

And in the End

Whether you are booking tours as a tour operator, or as a travel agent working through travel suppliers via your host agency or through your own connections, or you are planning and marketing your very own tours, it is essential that you get feedback from your travelers once they return. In fact, feedback is so valuable that you should consider offering an incentive, such as a 10 or 15 percent discount on their next trip. By learning what travelers did and did not like about the tour, you will know whether to use the same tour provider in the future or how to make appropriate changes, if this is your own itinerary.

Simple, short questionnaires can be mailed, emailed, or made available on your website. You can also opt for a quick phone survey if that suits your client. However you manage to do it, you need to get some data on how they felt about the accommodations, the transportation (airline, rail, bus, or boat), the meals, the entertainment, and the tour guide or guides.

Destination Driven

The travel industry today is largely destination driven. There are locations all over the globe that have been drawing tourists for centuries and others that are just emerging as travelers seek out unusual, off-the-beaten-path localities.

In this chapter we look in brief at just a few of the many possibilities, and offer some notes on what you may find and subsequently offer to customers traveling to these locations. Of course, this is a concise overview, meaning you will have to start digging deeper to pinpoint your selected vacation offerings.

Know Your Geography

The travel business provides a world of opportunity. To successfully carve out your own niche you will need to know the type of vacations you want to offer and where to find them. If you have traveled to certain parts of the world and truly enjoyed your visits, then you can consider what it would take to send other vacationers off to have a similarly wonderful experience. If you have great ideas for active vacationers, you will need to start matching up activities with destinations. To do so, you must determine where to find the information you are seeking. Do some research: Where are the rainforests? Which countries have the most challenging golf courses? Where are the most spectacular mountain ranges for climbing or skiing? Whatever you are looking for, it can be found, either here in the United States or in some corner of the world.

Most travel professionals would advise you to get a hands-on feel for wherever you plan to specialize, if at all possible. Remember, if you are booking a region—any region—you need to know more about it than your customers do. So no matter how you do it, get to know the lay of the land. You'll be embarrassed and lose customers if they know more than you do about the time zones, climate, topography, travel

Never Too Old to Learn

While you may have studied geography in school, a lot has changed over the years and there is much more detail you will need to know now. With that in mind, look for courses that include geography in their curriculum, such as IATA's "Foundation in Travel and Tourism" course, which helps you put together efficient customer itineraries using polished geography skills. *Selling Destinations*, a book updated in 2008, by Marc Mancini, can also help the travel agent find their way around the world for their clients. If it's apps you prefer, GeographyAllTheWay (for Android users) can keep you abreast of the latest geographical events.

distances, neighboring countries, historical sites, or best ways to navigate the terrain in a particular area.

All About Security

National and international security affects your clients whenever and wherever they travel, particularly if they are flying. While you may not be booking plane tickets, you do need to remind travelers what to expect when they get to the airport and when they land.

Security measures at airports have tightened in recent years to include pat-downs and full body scans. While such measures will vary from country to country, the goal is the same: to maintain safe travel for all passengers.

Airport Security

You should take some time to fill your travelers in on what to expect at airport security. Being prepared can help passengers move along more quickly. For international flights, and most domestic flights, remind passengers to get to the airport two hours in advance of departure time, especially on busy travel days. Travelers can also bring only one carry-on item onboard, and it must fit in its allotted space. This typically means it must be 45 linear inches in size, meaning that the total length of the bag's height, width, and depth must not exceed 45 inches. Nobody wants to wait while the plane is delayed because someone is trying to shove a baby grand piano into the overhead compartment. It's also important to remind travelers that they will pay more for heavier bags. Know the baggage weight limits. Travelers should have photo IDs (typically a driver's license and/or passport) easily accessible.

Also remind passengers to travel light and keep important items such as medicines and eyeglasses in their carry-on bags. And if the medicine is unusual or contains narcotics,

> ### Smart Tip
>
> **Tip...**
>
> The U.S. State Department has recommended the following tips for safe travel. Passengers should take copies of their passport identification page, airline tickets, driver's license, and credit cards in case they are robbed or lose any of these items. In addition they should have their name, address, and telephone number on the inside and outside of each piece of checked luggage and the luggage should be locked if possible. Travelers should also have their travel insurance documents, noting the travel assistance services number and policy number in case they need to call for help.

the passenger should get a letter from their doctor so that the medication will not be confiscated.

Note: Remind travelers what they can and cannot bring on an airplane.

Travel Abroad

It's advantageous to know any additional security concerns your travelers will likely face outside of the United States. Familiarize yourself with the procedures at airports in other countries. Also, familiarize yourself with local laws and customs in other countries and apprise travelers of those you feel are important for them to know. Even in the United States, there will be certain state laws that you may want to pass along to your clients.

You should have copies of your travelers' itineraries and pertinent contact information.

It never hurts to give the American embassy contact information to travelers going overseas. In a changing world, you also want to stay abreast of the political climate in any region where you may be sending travelers. Keep up with news reports and be ready to contact your travelers if something should arise, such as the uprising in Egypt in early 2011.

Security for Domestic Travel

Even for domestic travel, airport security is tight, and travelers need to give themselves ample time, be prepared to pass through security checkpoints, and have a sense of awareness about them at all times, which includes keeping an eye on their luggage and all personal belongings. Buses, railroads, and other means of travel have few security measures. You still need to be diligent about knowing what is going on in specific regions and cities in which you are planning trips. Whether it's learning about possible hurricanes, rallies and protests, or increases in local criminal activities, you should be one step ahead of your clients. Travelers have written about areas that were once quite safe but no longer provide the same secure ambience. Economic downturns can affect neighborhoods in which your vacation packages are booked. If an area becomes depressed, so might your vacationers if you send them there. Be aware.

Otherwise, most nonairline security measures fall under the common sense heading, such as not carrying expensive jewelry and leaving it lying around the hotel room.

Destinations

It's difficult—make that impossible—to sum up the world in a chapter. But it is worth a brief overview of a few of the popular destinations to spark some vacation package ideas as you consider your options, activities, and potential niche market(s). Consider how you can put your personal slant on some of these and other possibilities.

Australia

Six states, two territories, and two minor territories make up what we call "the land down under," complete with koala bears, kangaroos, and dingoes. Within this country, where people are primarily of British or Irish ethnicity, are a variety of amazing destinations characterized by old world charm, modern cities, and spectacular natural beauty.

Sydney Harbor, a natural harbor, is for kayaking under the Harbour Bridge, or taking a leisurely ferry ride across to Manly. The opera house, the markets, the restaurants, the cafes, the national parks, historic Fort Denison, numerous beaches, and local festivals are all what make this a marvelous destination city to which you will want to send your clientele.

The biodiversity of the Great Barrier Reef, off the Queensland coast, makes it a spectacular destination for those interested in ecotourism. The humpback dolphin, dwarf minke whale, flatback turtle, olive ridley turtle, and salt-water crocodile, plus many varieties of birds, are among the many species found here.

You may interest skiers or hikers in Mount Kosciuszko, the highest mountain in Australia, at 2,228 meters, or 7,310 feet. It is located in New South Wales.

Aussie travel specialist Kerrie Strumolo, who runs KS Travel in Wayne, New Jersey, loves talking about tours to her native homeland. "Silky Oaks is just beautiful," says Strumolo, referring to the Silky Oaks Lodge, a beautiful luxury treehouse-style boutique resort and spa in the Daintree Rainforest—the world's oldest rainforest. "Located on the Mossman River, this property is perfect for honeymooners and those seeking romance or even for a girls getaway. It's the 'wow factor' of any Australian itinerary," says Strumolo of this unique Australian experience.

For those with a sense of adventure and limited time, Strumolo recommends Discovery Air Tours, which offer travelers a perfect way to see Australia's highlights as the tours focus on seasonal attractions. "Various itineraries allow guests to travel in small groups in their own plane to places like the Outback, the Great Barrier Reef, the wilderness, and the southern wonders," says Strumolo of this aerial way to tour the countryside.

For a taste of Aboriginal culture, you may want to take a day tour from Darwin to the Tiwi Islands with AAT Kings. "Visiting with the Tiwi people and seeing their unique culture is a once-in-a-lifetime opportunity to experience a modern-day Aboriginal community, with an insight into the Tiwi people's rich culture and lifestyle," says Strumolo of this marvelous way to get up close and personal in Australia.

France and Italy

Some 477 million tourists visited Europe in 2010, with France leading all nations in the world with more than 76 million visitors. The cultural heritage, including the food, is rich and the art, fashion, and scenic beauty from Paris to the French Riviera are second to none.

While La Tour Eiffel can easily fit into any Paris itinerary, you can also send your travelers off to smile back at Leonardo da Vinci's Mona Lisa and check out more than 35,000 pieces of art at the Louvre as part of a tour of the museums of France.

A trip to the Palace of Versailles remains a marvelous way to spend a day seeing the Hall of Mirrors, lavish gardens, and fountains. Your guests will also find sumptuous dining in the region. If your clients prefer the visual medium of film, they might enjoy a trip to Cannes if you can work out a visit during the famed film festival. Among

A Trio of European Travel Favorites

Three other European countries are among the top travel destinations in the world, combining to host more than 100 million visitors annually. Spain, Great Britain, and Germany offer history, culture, nightlife, adventure, and much more for a wide range of travelers. You'll find plenty of options for vacation packages.

other themes that characterize excursions to France, you'll find visiting the wineries or taking bicycle tours high on the list. And if people want luxurious hotels, glamour, fine dining, and exotic beaches, the French Riviera will certainly impress and delight your clientele. For those who prefer an all-over tan, Cap d'Agde features a nudist beach plus a full resort, dubbed France's Naked City, complete with shopping. Imagine dining and even banking while in the buff along with as many as 40,000 visitors in the warmest weather.

From biking tours through Pisa to visit the Leaning Tower to walking tours through the ruins in Pompeii, Italy, has a wide variety of vacation possibilities. The rolling hills of Tuscany are the backdrop for fantastic wine-tasting tours, not to mention visits to numerous galleries. The water-bound country hosted nearly 45 million travelers in 2010, landing it among the top five tourist locations in the world.

More than 150 canals weave their way through the magnificent city of Venice, making it ideal for your more romantically inclined clientele. Florence, meanwhile, remains a popular destination, rich with culture, museums, cathedrals, and elegant buildings, which line the streets of this Renaissance city.

Then of course there is Rome, the capital city and home to the Vatican. Palatial old palaces, historic monuments, and medieval churches are among the rich cultural attractions by day, and authentic restaurants and eclectic clubs provide a different ambience to unwind at night.

From sightseeing in the major cities to biking the Tuscan countryside to frolicking at the beach along the spectacular Amalfi Coast, you have numerous choices if you plan to sell Italy vacation packages.

China

In 2010, China was the third most visited country, behind France and the United States, with more than 55 million tourists. The sheer size of China, home to nearly 20 percent of the world's population, makes it challenging when deciding how much your clients can take in on a single journey. This is typically a place to tour, explore, and see an amazing array of sites, from the Great Wall to the classic Yuyuan Garden of Shanghai. The language barrier and size of China can make it difficult to branch away from the more familiar tourist locations, but that's OK because there is so much to see.

Beijing, the capital of the People's Republic, has a long and illustrious history and has been home to nearly three dozen emperors. The Great Wall is a must-see for anyone visiting China. Built more than 2,000 years ago to guard against enemy tribes, the wall is a spectacular man-made achievement. Badaling, while crowded, is one of the most accessible places for visitors, while Mutianyu, a little farther from the city, is

Jakrit Jiraratwaro/www.shutterstock.com

less crowded and safer for children and seniors. Hikers may want to check out Simatai and Jimshanling (it's about a four-hour hike from one place to the other).

Beijing is also home to the massive and well-preserved Forbidden City, an imperial palace with 9,999 rooms (talk about playing hide and seek). Visitors to Beijing will also want to walk along the sprawling Tiananmen Square, which sits in the middle of the city surrounded by the Chinese Revolution History Museum, the Great Hall of the People, and the elegant and beautiful Tiananmen (Heavenly Peace Gate).

Ancient temples, such as the Temple of Heaven, the Yunju Temple, the White Cloud Taoist Temple, and the Confucius Temple are also among the exquisite stops in Beijing.

And then there's Shanghai, the largest city in the world, which is home to 16 million people. The modern architecture is a sight to behold as your tour group takes in the skyline while aboard a Huangpu River cruise, day or night. From colorful and exotic to modern style skyscrapers, the city is a diverse mix of old and new. The Bund, a popular waterfront enclave of buildings, is home to a wide range of architectural styles featuring Gothic, Baroque, Romanesque, and the Renaissance.

For culture and history, you can point travelers in the direction of Yuyuan Garden, a classical garden built in the Ming Dynasty on five acres, housing pavilions, halls, rockeries, ponds, and cloisters, and offering a scenic respite from the busy surrounding city. The Shanghai Museum in the People's Square is home to 4,000 collections, or more than 120,000 artifacts from ancient bronze and Ming Dynasty furnishings to modern works and photography.

For those who want the modern bustle of commerce and retail, a stroll along the nearly 3½-mile Nanjing Road should suffice. Some 600 stores and businesses line the streets and range from small specialty shops selling silk and embroidery to KFC and Pizza Hut. The road also has plenty of vendors and many non-Western restaurants and bars.

Similar to New York and London, Shanghai has a multitude of offerings, from the modern Shanghai Financial Center to the ancient Jade Buddha Temple. While you may want to maintain a "theme," this is a locale to include a bit of everything Shanghai style.

In the city of Dunhuang sit Buddhist treasures in the form of murals and sculptures in the Mogao Caves. Lunar Lake is another popular place for visitors. Huanglong, situated in the Sichuan Province, was established as a Chinese national scenic area in 1982 and is also a popular attraction.

It takes careful planning to keep your travelers to China in places where they will feel comfortable, as some of the lesser-traveled regions are not well prepared for tourists. Learn as much as you can about the areas in which you want to specialize and definitely make the trip.

The Caribbean and the Islands

There are many destinations for travelers in the Caribbean and the islands featuring lavish resorts and spectacular beaches. Of course, many of the cruise destination ports fall into this category as do ports in Mexico. You can also send your clients away (by air) for a relaxing week of lounging around the pool, or in the pool, with frozen margaritas or pina coladas in hand, or perhaps to play in the turquoise waters of the ocean. Boating, scuba diving, snorkeling, and other water activities can be part of the itinerary for your more active travelers.

The three Cayman Islands—Grand Cayman, Cayman Brac, and Little Cayman—are all breathtakingly beautiful. Snorkeling is a featured activity, and Seven Mile Beach is billed as perhaps the most beautiful beach on the islands, which is saying a lot.

The Bahamas consist of 29 islands. Paradise Island, with the world famous Atlantis, Cove Atlantis, and Reef Atlantis resorts, draws significant attention and, therefore, numerous travel agents are booking these majestic hotels. There are other options that are quite superb and that may provide better package deals, including the Paradise Island Resorts and Spa and the Harbour Resort. Andros, the largest of all Bahamian islands, is actually made up of three islands and features a famous barrier reef that is a must for scuba divers. This is also the location for those travelers who would prefer to avoid the crowds and to commune with nature. Some 2,000-plus varieties of colorful flora and fauna and plenty of marine wildlife should appeal to your ecotourists, not to mention the pink sand beaches. Activities including fishing and diving will appeal to those seeking a little more adventure.

Costa Rica, one of the most popular tourist destinations in the world, is located nearby in Central America. Set up a day or two in the itinerary for visiting Manuel Antonio National Park, which includes a rainforest, beaches, lagoons, and coral reefs. Snorkelers love this area as do bird watchers who can look for nearly 200 species.

In Arenal Volcano National Park visitors can take guided tours along hiking trails and see plenty of hardened lava at an active volcano. Talk about adventure.

Parks for hiking and communing with nature and observing wildlife, beaches for soaking up the sun, resorts for more lavish pleasures, or quiet bed and breakfasts for the more simple desires are all part of Costa Rica packages depending on the wishes of your travelers.

And then there's St. Maarten/St. Martin. Water sailing, windsurfing, and snorkeling will keep the more active set busy while great bargains and duty-free status on cosmetics, jewelry, liquors, cigars, electronics, and much more will delight shoppers. There is plenty of nightlife on both the French and Dutch sides of the island plus casino gaming and great dining in a number of gourmet restaurants. You can also set your destination package to include yacht trips, sailing, or island excursions to nearby St. Barts or Anguilla.

As for beaches, Orient Bay, or in French "Baie Orientale," is the most developed, the most popular, and the busiest beach on St. Maarten, featuring two miles of white powdered sand and clothing-optional bathers.

Sandals

The Sandals resorts in the Bahamas, Jamaica, Puerto Rico, Antigua, and elsewhere are all premiere vacation destinations complete with ocean front rooms, gourmet dining, and all the amenities your clients could ask for. These are high-end destinations, all very popular.

When planning your island destinations (and you can add Bermuda to the mix of fabulous locales), consider which places you've enjoyed the most—it's fun checking out the possibilities. Look to build interesting itineraries and/or find some off the beaten path possibilities since there is a lot of competition for these vacation havens.

Canada and Mexico

Our neighbors to the north and south offer some terrific, albeit quite different, travel options. Canada is often an afterthought for many American travelers, but there's plenty to see and you can use a variety of modes of transportation—air, sea, bus, or trolley—to show your visitors around. With a little promotion, you can sell some wonderful Canadian tours. Quebec is home to Montreal, a bilingual city featuring a delightfully quaint old section, a vibrant modern section, and plenty of activities. Offering everything from first-rate annual jazz and comedy festivals to numerous special events, Montreal is a cosmopolitan city with culture and flair. Visitors can look out at the city from atop Mount Royal, a 764-foot high mountain and popular recreation spot. The city's expansive botanical gardens and educational biodome are a must for ecotourists, with a rainforest, numerous varieties of plant life, and even penguins. Visitors to Montreal can tour 100-year-old cathedrals by day, enjoy fine dining in a number of choice locations in the evening, and take in all kinds of nightlife activities after dark.

Quebec City is a perfect location for a romantic getaway. Narrow cobblestone streets take you back more than 300 years and lead to elegant chateaus and five-star French restaurants in this charming old-world city. A Montreal, Quebec City package can be quite inviting. Perhaps sailing along the St. Lawrence River can be part of the journey.

Toronto is also a great city to visit and goes well after a couple of days at Niagara Falls. Visitors can stroll along the harbor front or the streets of fashionable Yorkville and get an overview of the city while dining high atop the CN Tower, the world's tallest building. A hockey theme can send fans to a Maple Leafs game and to the Hockey Hall of Fame, while film buffs may want to be in the city for the annual Toronto Film Festival.

You can also focus on Western Canada with excursions to Vancouver where visitors can take in the views of the harbor from Lions Gate Bridge, marvel at the amazing ecological balance of life while watching the Pacific salmon at the Capilano Fish Hatchery, or see grizzly bears and wildlife in their own habitat at Grouse Mountain.

Rock climbers will be drawn to the Canadian Rockies surrounding Banff National Park in Alberta. Explorers will be awed by the Athabasca Glacier, which is part of the Columbia Icefield, the greatest mass of ice outside the Arctic Circle.

Canada offers old-world charm, romance, active/adventure travels, sightseeing, and a number of specialty options, so be creative.

Unlike Canada, Mexico leaves a little less room to be overly creative. It's not the place to send vacationers out to explore lesser-known areas. It is, however, home to some remarkable beach resort areas, great cuisine, and cities rich in culture and history.

Mexico is quite large and diverse, stretching from the Pacific Ocean on its west coast to the Caribbean on the east coast. It is also approximately three times the size of Texas, an appropriate comparison, since Texas was at one time part of Mexico.

The main beach resort areas cover both the west coast, called the Mexican Riviera, and the east coast on what is called the Yucatan Peninsula. They also incorporate the Cabo San Lucas area on the southern Baja Peninsula, south of California.

Among the most popular Mexican resort destinations, you'll find Acapulco, on the country's Pacific coast in the state of Guerrero. The stunning beaches, first-class resorts, and electrifying nightlife make this a choice location, especially for the younger crowd on spring break.

Also on the west coast, north of Acapulco, is Ixtapa, with high-rise resorts, the latest in chic dance clubs, and plenty of golf for the non-spring-break crowd.

On the Yucatan Peninsula visitors can look out at beautiful turquoise blue waters while lounging on powder white sand beaches. The peninsula is made up of Merida, a beautiful colonial city with fantastic Spanish architecture and a unique culinary twist; Cancun; and the Rivera Maya, which stretches from Cancun in the north to the border of Belize to the south.

Cancun, the most popular Mexican travel destination, with more than 3 million visitors a year, offers fabulous resorts and spectacular beaches, plus a downtown that has a South Beach Miami feel and is just off a fantastic beach. Along with soaking in the sun, visitors can spend a day at the interactive aquarium or learn all about dolphins at the Delphinus inside the Dreams Cancun hotel. You can also book golf packages or set up tours to the heart of the Mayan culture with a number of well-known Mayan ruins open to the public.

If your clients prefer to experience a slightly slower pace, they may enjoy Riviera Maya. This area has more low-level resorts spread out over some acreage and on fantastic beaches. It is great for family vacations, honeymoons, and destination weddings.

Just off the east coast of Mexico sits the island of Cozumel, one of the top scuba diving areas in the world and a major cruise port.

The second largest city in Mexico is also drawing a lot of visitors. At 500-plus years old, Guadalajara has lots of history to offer in itsarchitecture, statues, monuments, and incredible museum collections. The city is also the home of tequila and mariachi music.

Mexico Safety Concerns

An April 2011 statement from the U.S. Department of State Bureau of Consular Affairs:

"Millions of U.S. citizens safely visit Mexico each year, including more than 150,000 who cross the border every day for study, tourism, or business. The Mexican government makes a considerable effort to protect U.S. citizens and other visitors to major tourist destinations. Resort areas and tourist destinations in Mexico generally do not see the levels of drug-related violence and crime reported in the border region and in areas along major trafficking routes." The statement went on to recommend visiting only legitimate business and tourist areas during daylight hours. Essentially, what this means is that if you are booking Mexico, you should be focusing on the major resort and tourist areas and not looking for out-of-the-way locations.

"While violence does exist in Mexico, it has very little impact on the major tourist areas," says Geoff Millar, who books Mexican vacations regularly for his company, Ultimate All-Inclusive Vacations. "The only tourist area with higher than normal violence is Acapulco. This can be attributed to the fact that Acapulco is a large industrial city of 2 million people and a major port city.

"The majority of violence in Mexico occurs on the border of Mexico and the U.S. in the towns of Juarez, Nogales, and Tijuana. These towns are at least 1,500 miles from the major tourist areas. If normal safety precautions are used, Mexico is as safe as any foreign destination and most U.S. destinations, and there have been no violent crimes committed against tourists in any of the major resort areas."

There is, however, more to Mexico than the beach resorts and Guadalajara. "Mexico is also a special place in the hearts of adventure and historical travelers," says Geoff Millar. "From the beautiful Copper Canyons of Mexico, near Chihuahua (which are larger than the Grand Canyon), to hiking in the Oaxaca cloud forests of southern Mexico, the country offers a wide variety of inland adventure experiences. With many older colonial cities, it is a haven for historians studying the beautiful Spanish architectural and culinary influences created during Spain's rule of Mexico."

▲

"The people of Mexico are a very warm people proud of their country and heritage," adds Millar. "They are very eager to show it off to the millions of tourists that visit their country each year. As they say, 'Experience the Mexico you never knew.'"

Staying Stateside

From campgrounds to luxury resorts and golf courses to extreme sports, you can find almost anything you are looking for in the United States. Choices abound, and it's hard to summarize them in a few short paragraphs.

Second only to France, the United States saw nearly 60 million visitors from outside its boundaries in 2010, not to mention the multitude of domestic travelers taking vacations within the 50 states, Washington, DC, and Puerto Rico and the Virgin Islands. New York City, Las Vegas, Disney World, the Grand Canyon, and Fisherman's Wharf are among the most popular perennial favorites. What this means is that you too can package these in-demand locations or seek some other popular, or soon-to-be popular, locations for U.S. tourists. Your destination choices will be

---

Top Ten U.S. Destination Travel Cities of 2010 According to *Forbes* Magazine

1. Orlando: 48 million visitors

2. New York City: 47 million visitors

3. Chicago: 45,580,000 visitors

4. Anaheim/Orange County: 42,700,000 visitors

5. Miami: 38,100,000 visitors

6. Las Vegas: 36,351,469 visitors

7. Atlanta: 35,400,000 visitors

8. Houston: 31,060,000 visitors

9. Philadelphia: 30,320,000 visitors

10. San Diego: 29,600,000 visitors

---

in response to what it is you want to offer, such as luxury, adventure, sightseeing, or golf. The key to stateside success is identifying your own niche market and providing options that differ from your competitors in some manner, be they more cost-effective choices, additional activities, or new accommodations.

Your tour considerations will need to factor in modes of transportation, such as walking around Manhattan on a shopping tour, boating around the island, or both. There are cycling tours, railway tours, and helicopter rides over the Grand Canyon. In Myrtle Beach you can even put your tourists on something called the Gator, which is essentially a bus that drives into the water and turns into a boat. Honest.

You'll also want to consider the type(s) of activities you are selling. Sure you can sell wine tasting in Napa Valley or skiing in Aspen, but you may be up against a wealth of competition. How about New England wine tours or perhaps wine tasting in the Hudson Valley in New York or even a wine-tasting package at the Regal Beaux-Arts Hotel in Washington, DC? How about skiing in Chicago, or down the slopes of Chestnut Mountain in nearby Galena? Mississippi River Boat Tours are becoming popular, so what about those on the Ohio River such as the BB Riverboats out of Newport, Kentucky?

The point is, you may have greater success with a popular favorite activity in a less crowded and less competitive up-and-coming location. Conversely, you may discover some lesser known haunts in major tried-and-true destinations.

The lack of language barriers and the slightly reduced security measures (compared with those in countries abroad) make domestic tour packages a little easier to build on your own. Networking and keeping your eyes and ears open for the latest accommodations and activities in your chosen destinations can give you a leg up on the competition. You also need to determine the economic impact on the domestic destinations you are booking. Neighborhoods change, accommodations change, popular eateries go out of business, and yesterday's family favorite water park is today's corporate park with no rides except elevators. Therefore, through your own repeat visits and feedback from your clients, as well as staying abreast of the areas you are planning to book (or are already booking), you'll be able to alter your packages accordingly. You must stay current, which includes knowing the latest activity craze and determining whether you believe it will last long enough to plan a destination tour around it.

If you're aggressive and creative, and have an eye for detail and a knack for networking, you should be able to create and sell your own U.S. niche tours to several destinations. Typically your host agency will have a list of suppliers with plenty of options for you to tap into.

In this chapter we featured just a few of a world of destinations. The idea is to get you salivating with ideas based on the places you love, your market research, and what you can put together through your suppliers, networking, and/or your host agency.

▲

Top Ten Winter Travel Destinations According to *U.S. News and World Report*

1. Puerto Vallarta (Mexico)

2. Playa del Carmen (Mexico)

3. Kauai (Hawaii)

4. Puerto Rico

5. St. Martin–St. Maarten

6. Key West

7. Miami Beach

8. Banff (Canadian Rockies)

9. Tulum (Mexico)

10. Disney World

As mentioned along the way, destinations change, so don't get too complacent. You'll want to stay abreast of various factors such as:

- The value of the dollar if you are booking overseas
- The political climate in other countries
- Travel advisories anywhere
- Seasonal weather patterns (such as hurricane season)

Once you find your favorite destinations to package and sell, let yourself fall in love with them, if you haven't already.

All About Cruises

Sailing, sailing . . . for millions of people, it's the only way to vacation. Cruises are indeed one of the hottest segments of the travel industry, growing steadily with a wide variety of new excursions departing from a range of ports. Among the reasons for the acceleration of cruise bookings is that travelers can enjoy a marvelous vacation in various destinations without having

Start Your Own Travel Business and More

R. Peterkin/www.shutterstock.com

to pack and unpack as they move from hotel room to hotel room—instead, the hotel, or in this case, the luxury cruise liner, moves along with them. In addition, delectable dining opportunities, attractive (if not spacious) suites, first rate entertainment, and typically gaming tables and slots, are all within a throw of the dice. In addition, there are cruises with various themes and amenities to fit every taste. From personal butlers to multiroom villas, health spas to rock climbing walls or simulated golf ranges, amenities abound. Plus, as an overall package, most cruises are not out of the realm of the average traveler's budget.

For the reasons listed above, among others, cruises were the vacation choice of more than 15 million people in 2010, with estimates that by the end of 2011, the number would be up to 16 million. To meet the increasing demand, more than 100 new ships will have been introduced since the year 2000. Yet almost 80 percent of the American public has yet to set sail on one of the numerous luxury liners, meaning there is plenty of room for you as the travel agent to entice these neophytes to hit the high seas.

Fun Fact

The median age of cruisers in 2011 was 48 and the median household income was $97,000. While you will find travelers from all 50 states most U.S. cruisers come from Florida, California, Texas, Massachusetts, New York, Pennsylvania, New Jersey, Illinois, Arizona, and Georgia.

Why You?

Question: There is a ton of information available about cruises on the internet, so why do travelers need you, as a travel agent, to book a cruise for them?

Answer: Because there is a ton of information available about cruises on the internet.

Azamara Club Cruises, Carnival Cruise Lines, Celebrity Cruises, Costa Cruises, Crystal Cruises, Cunard Line, Disney Cruise Line, Holland America Line, MSC Cruises, Norwegian Cruise Line, Oceania Cruises, Princess Cruises, Regent Seven Seas Cruises, Royal Caribbean International, Seabourn Cruise Line, Silverseal

---

Cruise Lines International Association (CLIA)

Formed in 1975, CLIA is the world's largest cruise association and is dedicated to the promotion and growth of the cruise industry. CLIA is composed of 21 of the major cruise lines serving North America and represents 97 percent of the cruise capacity marketed from North America. It is an organization that operates pursuant to an agreement filed with the Federal Maritime Commission under the Shipping Act of 1984.

In 2005, CLIA merged with the International Council of Cruise Lines (ICCL), a sister entity created in 1990 that is dedicated to participating in the regulatory and policy development process of the cruise industry. More than 16,000 travel agencies in North America are members of CLIA. The central offices are located in Fort Lauderdale, Florida, and Washington, DC. The CLIA website is www.cruising.org.

For travel agents, CLIA offers comprehensive training including a certification program, which requires agents to successfully complete a number of compulsory training courses and exams and do things such as attend cruise conferences in order to achieve one or more professional designations: accredited cruise counselor (ACC), master cruise counselor (MCC), elite cruise counselor (ECC), luxury cruise specialist, and others. CLIA's training programs are offered in classrooms, online, through touring seminars such as TrainingFest, in webinars, on DVD and CD, and at industry events such as cruise3sixty, the industry's annual conference and trade show. In addition, virtually all cruise lines offer their own training and certification programs.

▲

Cruises, and Windstar Cruises are some of the major players in the cruise business, but other lines offer niche or small ship cruising, including river cruises, one of the fastest growing segments of the market. These companies include Hurtigruten, SeaDream Yacht Cruises, AMA Waterways, Avalon Waterways, and Uniworld Boutique River Cruise Collection. Each of these companies has their own fleet with a number of cruises to choose from. These cruise companies have different styles, offer variations on a vacation at sea, and each offers ships with distinct personalities. They leave from a variety of U.S. ports and international ports and stop at an even wider variety of locations from Alaska to a host of tropical islands to dozens of ports in the Mediterranean, northern Europe, Asia, and the Middle East. Therefore, unless travelers are well-versed in the differences between these cruise lines, their styles, and offerings, they need you to help them make the right choice. Even those who have gone the cruise route before will benefit from the updated information a travel agent specializing in cruises can provide. There are constantly new amenities and new themes being offered.

Your job as a cruise booker is to become a cruise expert. This will come in part from hitting the seas yourself, in part from reading plenty of material from each cruise company, in part from joining CLIA and other industry groups, like the National Association of Cruise Oriented Agencies (NACOA), and in part from talking and networking with both people in the cruise industry, cruise line executives, other travel agents, and your customer, or clients, as they return from their cruises. There are also many host agency organizations or consortia that specialize in cruises, which can provide guidance. By utilizing all of these sources together, you should have no trouble becoming a cruise expert if you truly want a business that excels in this growing area.

Give the Cruisers What They Want

Before you can book a cruise, you will need to know what it is your clients are seeking and where it is they want to go. Some travelers will come in with specific destinations in mind, while others will know they want to go somewhere warm or cross the Atlantic to visit Europe.

You should be comfortable enough with your cruise knowledge to recommend various options for warm climates or European ports. Of course, there are a variety of considerations. For example, where do your travelers want to depart from? How long a cruise would they like to take? If, for example, they travel from a nearby port in New York City on a cruise headed to the Caribbean, then they will spend less time on the islands and more time at sea. However, if your clients want more port stops and fewer hours at sea, they might opt to fly to Florida and board in St. Petersburg. However, this means getting to and from the airport and making flight arrangements.

Personal preferences are all part of today's cruising options. These include activities, dining, stops along the way, cruise themes, and more.

The primary value of cruise-selling travel agents—to the cruise lines as well as to consumers—is their skill in matching a vacationer with the right cruise, and—in the case of first-time cruisers—identifying and convincing that customer to try cruising. With today's technology, travelers can find information and advice online through social media and any number of other sources, including cruise line websites. What travelers can't find is expert guidance in making the right selection; that's the role of the travel agent.

CLIA trains its member agents to be knowledgeable about the entire industry. Some may specialize in types of cruises—for example, adventure, luxury, small ship, or river cruising—but their real goal remains to match the customer to the right cruise. Part of that service should be the ability to offer clients the best value, but individual agents differ from large consortia, which may have preferred suppliers, and should be open to finding the right product for their customers wherever that may be found.

Providing Options for Your Customers

- *Cruise newbie or seasoned sailor.* People who have never cruised before may have little to no idea what to expect, what is available, or even what they want in a cruise ship, so you will need to be their guide. They will be most surprised by the extraordinary variety of cruise experiences, itineraries, destinations, shipboard lifestyles, and prices that makes up today's cruise industry.

   If clients have cruised before they may have fallen in love with that line and wed themselves to it, or they may be inspired to try a different line, perhaps in a different part of the world. Cruising enjoys the highest rate of repeat customers of any type of vacation, and typically, first-time cruisers start with a relatively short and inexpensive cruise and then move up to longer voyages, different destinations, or higher priced cruise lines. Even if they choose to stay with their favorite line, you can help bump them up to better accommodations, which today can even mean a luxury spa suite.

- *Shore excursions or deck-lolling.* Some voyagers want more time at sea, while others are more interested in cruises that offer shore time at intriguing ports of call. This is a personal preference. Get an idea of what your clients are looking to get from their vacation—if exploring new territories is part of their mission, plan for stopovers. If, however, the primary goal is the luxuries of the liner, then you might find a cruise with few or even no dockings. For those who may not have set sail before, you might recommend a cruise with a few stops to give your newcomers a feel for what it is to dock (get a break from the sea) and check out a couple of ports.

- *Learning or sunbathing.* Most cruises offer educational or cultural experiences such as shipboard lecturers, even celebrity experts, cooking classes, language classes, wine-tasting lessons, or educational programs for children. Many specialize in giving passengers a floating-resort experience featuring, in some cases, full-scale Broadway musicals, nightclub-type revues, comedy clubs, casinos, bars, and idyllic days of sunbathing with nothing to do but unwind. And today's larger cruise ships also feature luxury spas and fitness centers, sometimes operated by well-known land-based brands. Again, find out your client's preferences.

- *Time travel.* Unless you know the secrets of making time elastic, you can't send your clients on a round-the-world junket if they only have three days to spend (including travel to and from the cruise ship). Likewise, a client with two glorious weeks of vacation won't be happy with that two-day quickie to the Bahamas or an overnight cruise to nowhere. Most cruises are 3- to 7-day or 14-day voyages. Statistically, the most popular cruise has always been the one-week trip, but there are many time variations, so ask your clients how long they want to be out. Also determine how much time they have around their voyage to determine whether or not they have extra days to fly to the departure destination. In some locations (along the coasts) this won't be a problem—but for someone coming from Kansas, there is no local port that sets you off to the Bahamas. On the other hand, with more than 30 domestic ports of embarkation in America, roughly half the population is within driving distance of a cruise.

- *Party of five.* You'll need to know how many people will be going with the client. A retired couple out for a second honeymoon (or that first one they never took)

For Those Who Don't Like to Pack

Since 1991, Bare Necessities Tours & Travel has been offering clothing-optional cruises to Alaska on Holland America Cruise lines. Talk about finding your niche market.

would want an entirely different product than Grams and Gramps planning a fun cruise with the grandkids. People also often take cruises with a group of friends, from a trio of couples to a gang of twenty. In fact, two of the fastest growing passenger segments of cruising are families and extended or multigenerational families, and friends traveling together. As was the case with touring, get a spokesperson for the group so that they can filter the final group decisions to you and you can, therefore, avoid taking up a tremendous amount of time talking with all 20 members of the clan.

- *The cost factor.* Pitching a black-tie, champagne-and-caviar cruise to a client who has a beer-and-chips budget isn't going to do either of you any good. Neither is touting a four-day cruise to Nassau when your client is the type who likes Monaco and the Mediterranean with a suite and butler. You will need to determine the client's price range so you can more comfortably narrow down the possibilities.

- *Make a date.* One of the most important things you'll need to know is when your clients want to travel. Some people like to reserve cruises months in advance, which makes booking easier for you. Others decide at the last minute that they have to set sail.

  Timing will also factor into the decision-making process since certain cruises are less likely, if not impossible during certain times of year, based on weather factors.

- *Accommodations.* Some cruise customers prefer the posh treatment, which is usually an outside cabin with ocean view or a luxury suite. Others are perfectly happy with less expensive inside cabins. Different ships have different cabin configurations—double beds with a third berth disguised as a sofa, twin bed, or bunk bed. Especially when you have a group of travelers, you'll need to know who wants what configuration, and who sleeps with whom. Get an idea of how important the accommodations are to your client and what matters most to them—some people, for example want a balcony, while others will spend little time in the room and are not very concerned beyond a place to crash after dining, drinking, gambling, and partying.

- *Alternate dates or cabin preferences.* Like airline seats, cruise cabins are often sold out, or at least reserved, surprisingly far in advance. So you and your clients will need to brace for a bit of jockeying for dates and cabin categories. For example, say your client wants an A category cabin on a cruise that embarks April 6, but all the A cabins are already sold. The client, with your help, will have to decide if he or she would rather have a B cabin on April 6th, or go for an A cabin on May 6th. Flexibility is important when helping your clients narrow down the potential cruises. You may want to discuss scenarios

like this with your client ahead of time, or you can wait until you make the reservation and see what happens. As your business grows, you'll develop your own style and learn to read clients to determine whether they are the type that wants to tackle all the contingencies at once or be fed them in small doses. This is important, because it sets you apart from websites where most decisions need to be made all at once.

The tendency among major cruise lines is to market cruises independently of air travel. However, the cruise lines do make whatever air travel arrangements are required and requested, and there are occasions when an air-sea package is promoted. More important to note is the large number of cruises that sail from U.S. ports (more than 30) on the East, West and Gulf coasts. For millions of vacationers, this can mean a cruise without the cost of airfare.

> **Smart Tip** *Tip...*
>
> If your clients choose the cruise-only package, you'll need to make sure their route to the ship is accounted for. If the ship sails from Miami and they are from Baltimore, find out if they plan a leisurely drive down with stops to visit relatives along the way, or if they need some sort of transport from home to the embarkation port. It's very important that you help cover the client's plans to get to and from the cruise ship.

- *Dining decisions.* Today's cruise ship dining is defined by choice, flexibility, and variety. Some of the largest ships offer anywhere from a dozen to more than 20 restaurant options in which passengers may virtually eat when, where, and with whom they like—without having to "dress for dinner." Typically these ships will offer a choice of several dining rooms plus a variety of specialty restaurants— for example, French, Italian, Mexican, or Asian—that are available at a modest surcharge. Some ships even offer signature restaurants by celebrity chefs such as Todd English or Nobu. A few lines, most notably some of the smaller ships, have maintained the traditional dining room seatings with assigned tables, but even many small ship ultra-luxury lines have adopted a much more relaxed approach to dining.

In the case of groups, it is possible to arrange in advance for specific dining arrangements that suit the group's needs and interests.

Travelers booking on their own often don't know what to make of gratuities. With this in mind, many cruises will simply charge the additional 15 percent gratuity to the bill—make sure you review this with your clients. Travelers can also add to the tips for excellent service or discuss unsatisfactory service at the purser's desk.

CLIA's Cruise Counselor Certification

Lest you think going for CLIA certification is boring—it's not! Sure, you've got to do the studying and exam thing, which you can do online and on your own time if you choose or in a classroom structure, through manuals and DVDs, and at industry conferences and events. But to ensure that you have an up-close and personal knowledge of cruise products, CLIA requires that agents working toward certification also take cruises, and go on ship inspections. The number depends on the level of certification—accredited cruise counselor, master cruise counselor, elite cruise counselor, and so on. This is really tough duty!

There are four good reasons for spending the time and effort to get your CLIA certification:

1. The more you know, the better you will be as an agent, and the more sales you will make.

2. Certification makes you more reputable—and thus your products are a better buy—in the minds of prospective customers.

3. With CLIA certification, you don't need a host agency to sell CLIA-affiliated cruises.

4. CLIA certification gives you clout with hotels and suppliers.

Plus, you get goodies—a certificate to hang on your wall, a lapel pin, logos for your business cards and stationery, an ad and press release, and a listing on the association's website and in their direct mailings and "agency locator," and more.

Of course the quality of the food is something that you as a travel agent can get a gauge on from the feedback of your clients and from talking with other travel agents, host agents, and travel suppliers. Get to know the different types and levels of food and food service. Some people are very comfortable with more basic cuisine, while others are seeking the finest in dining choices.

One final dining note: many people today have special dietary requirements. While you're discussing food, find out if anyone in the party has special dietary needs (diabetic, kosher, vegetarian, etc.) or any disabilities that might require special attention.

- *Add-on attractions*. If the ship or cruise offers extra amenities, like revitalizing spa massages, beauty makeovers, or special shore excursions, find out which ones your clients want to spring for. As mentioned earlier, cruises today offer a lot of amenities, so get an idea of what type of "fun" extras your clients would enjoy and seek out some options.

Along with all of the other options, you will typically field questions, particularly from the newcomers, about seasickness. Most of today's large vessels are very stable at sea. The individual equilibrium of each of your travelers, however, will determine how comfortable, or not, they are while sailing.

Repositioning Cruises

Cruising in many parts of the world is seasonal. Alaska, Canada, and New England are summer or fall cruise destinations. Panama Canal voyages tend to be offered in the spring and fall. World cruises typically are offered during winter months and follow the sun around the globe. On the other hand, the Bahamas, the Caribbean, and Europe are now year-round cruise choices as well as seasonal.

The change in season and weather means that many cruise ships need to be shifted to another part of the globe on a seasonal basis. Cruise lines will therefore reposition their ships from Alaska to the warmer waters of the Caribbean in the fall, and then move them back to Alaska in the late spring. Many lines move ships based in the Caribbean during the winter to Europe for the summer and then back, usually to bases in Florida, for the next winter. Rather than sailing empty ships, the companies offer repositioning cruises often for exceptional value. Many are marketed as longer voyages with stops in the Caribbean or Europe along the way to final destinations. Nevertheless, repositioning cruises feature a lot of time at sea, a good opportunity for passengers to enjoy shipboard life, entertainment, the gaming tables, and shopping. These cruises can last for more than two weeks and provide a complete vacation without ever having to worry about getting back to the ship from a port.

The only catch is that clients must fly to and from the destinations since this is a one-way cruise. However, for someone who wants to see Alaska and the Caribbean, or the Caribbean and Europe, this might be a way to do it all in one trip. It's an interesting option.

What Is Seasickness and What Can You Recommend?

Fear of seasickness is one of the primary reasons why vacationers who love to travel do not opt for a cruise. Seasickness is the reaction of the body's inner ear balance system to the unfamiliar motion of the ship. The movement of the ship causes stress on the balancing portion of the brain. Objects that should not be moving appear to be moving, and often the person cannot feel the movement in his or her own body. Sometimes this is referred to as "not having your sea legs," as the objects feel like they won't function—but they will. In most cases this goes away once the person gets used to the ship. To avoid this possibility, people should drink plenty of water, make sure to keep something in their stomachs, and in many cases, lie down and "sleep it off." Being in the middle portion of the ship, particularly if the ship is on choppy waters, will help significantly, because the middle of the ship (often where the casino is) can be the least "rocky."

This being said, the percentage of vacationers who report seasickness is very small in contrast to the number of people who have loved cruising and never felt anything out of the ordinary.

Of course, it's fine to have some medication, such as Dramamine or Bonine, both of which are very popular for cruise-goers. Tell your clients to ask for the non-drowsy kind.

Preferred Suppliers

Jim and Nancy T., cruise-oriented travel agents in Dunkirk, Maryland, use preferred suppliers. "The cruising industry is growing by such leaps and bounds," Jim says, "that you'd drive yourself crazy trying to speak knowledgeably about every cruise line and every ship within it. Even though cruising is a segment of the travel industry, there's a lot to know within that segment. So we try to focus on our preferred suppliers," the former police captain explains. "We've culled out those in several different areas, be it your value market, your mass market, your premium, and then your luxury market. We can keep the variety there so we can accommodate any taste you may have or any budget you may bring to the table."

▲

Scopolamine patches, worn behind the ear, can also be an alternative. New wristbands are also available that offer a type of pressure above the wrist that helps alleviate seasickness.

Payment

You'll need to know whether your client will be paying by check or credit card. And in cases of group travel, you'll also need to know who's paying for what. Will each person or couple pay their own way, or will the group issue a single check?

Payment will be either directly from you to the cruise line, once you receive money from your clients, or it may be from your host agency to the cruise company. However payment will be made, you will first have to get all the prices and forward the information to your client. Try to find a couple of good options in the client's price range that meet his or her cruise wish list. Your clients will need to know exactly how much the cruise will cost, including port charges and any add-ons like shore excursions or those revitalizing spa sessions. Next you want to review the payment schedules with your clients. Cruise lines all have their own schedules for deposits and final payments, and these are tied to elements like the length of the cruise and how early or late the reservation is made. There can also be fees for making changes or (horrors!) cancellations. Although these rules are spelled out in the cruise lines' materials, it never hurts to go over them with the reservation agent. You, as a travel agent, will learn who has the best policies and what, if anything, can be done if there is a problem. Your relationship with the cruise line or with your host agency—who has a relationship with the cruise line's reservations department (possibly as a preferred supplier)—can be beneficial for getting the payment information as simplified as possible and ironing out any possible problems.

Stay Organized

While it's not quite the itinerary of a weeklong tour through five countries in Europe, a cruise does have a number of elements that you as a travel agent must be aware of. Here are a few tips to help you stay organized.

> **Smart Tip** *Tip...*
>
> Not an option! The date on which the deposit is due is called the option date, because up to that point your clients have the option of backing out of the cruise.

- *Write down confirmations.* Even if you have a group of 12, most cruise lines handle each cabin as a separate reservation with its own confirmation number. You'll use this number each time you call the line with any questions or changes, so be sure to copy it (or them) down correctly.

- *Find out cabin assignments.* Some cruise lines make their cabin assignments TBA (to be assigned at a later date), but others give you the cabin number when you make the reservation. Find out which is the modus operandi for the cruise line you'll use, and get your clients' cabin assignments in advance if available.

- *Park this.* If your clients are parking at the dock and boarding, make sure to give them the heads up on the parking situation since they want to leave their cars in a safe location for the time they are away.

- *Confirm ticket delivery.* Find out how the travel documents—air and cruise tickets and any vouchers for extra goodies—will be delivered. Today many, but not all, cruise lines handle reservations and ticketing electronically, much like current practices by the airlines.

- *Sign off.* Repeat your name and your travel agency name and give the reservation agent the CLIA number of your agency or your host's agency. It doesn't hurt to reiterate the part about the consortium-level commission, either. It's also a good idea to take down the name of the reservation agent so you have somebody to reference as the source for all the material you've just given and received.

Make the Sale

After you've booked that perfect cruise at a fabulous price, you still have to get your clients to pay for it. Some travel agents ask for the deposit when they make the booking. Others wait and present the booking and the brochure with the clients' cabin numbers enticingly circled on the deck plan before asking for that check or credit card number.

You'll also need to go over the following points with your clients:

- *Payment.* Review the payment procedures that are spelled out by each

Beware!
While you want to sell higher priced packages, be careful not to push your favorite cruise on your client—nobody wants to be pushed into something, especially if it gives you a higher commission. If word gets around that you are not listening to the specific wish lists of your clients, you can damage your reputation in a big way. Remember, travel agents rely heavily on word-of-mouth from satisfied customers.

cruise line. Be sure your clients know exactly when the final payment is due and how much it will cost them to change their minds in midstream.

- *Cancellation.* Make your clients aware of the penalties for canceling the cruise—not being made to walk the plank, but accepting the fact that there are situations when no money will be returned. Not to panic, though! Remind your clients that for a minimal charge they can purchase trip cancellation insurance.

- *Travel documents.* Let your clients know when they can expect to receive their necessary documents,

including airline and cruise tickets. Make sure they do receive them, and review the passports of everyone in the group to check that they're accessible and not hidden at the bottom of a drawer and that they are not expired or near expiration.

> **Tip...**
>
> **Smart Tip**
> Provide advice for travelers on the little things that cruisers need to know but may not find from searching through websites or brochures. For example, remind your clients to budget for their port visits, and to include shopping! Also remind them to pack accordingly, since leaving a cold port in New York and sailing south to the islands they will see a significant change in temperature. Toiletries, a camera and film, sunscreen, and sun block are among the items you'll want to remind them to bring along.

Cancellations!

It's important to discuss trip cancellation insurance with your clients, such as the "cancel for no reason" insurance mentioned earlier by Geoff Millar. They may not go for it, but as a travel agent you need to alert them to the dangers of not purchasing it. And since some lawsuit-happy types can get nasty and claim you didn't tell them they'd be liable for those stiff cancellation fees, you should also have them sign a disclosure or waiver if they refuse the insurance.

You can, and probably should, discuss other types of travel insurance with your clients, too. These include insurance for:

- Medical emergencies
- Baggage damage, loss, or delay
- Flight insurance
- Legal difficulties

Tour operators and cruise lines often offer travel insurance, especially trip cancellation coverage, for an additional fee.

You can also offer your clients travel insurance through various independent insurance companies, as Jim and Nancy T. do. "We sell insurance through both means," Jim says, "and we highly recommend that everyone take some form of insurance. We have every

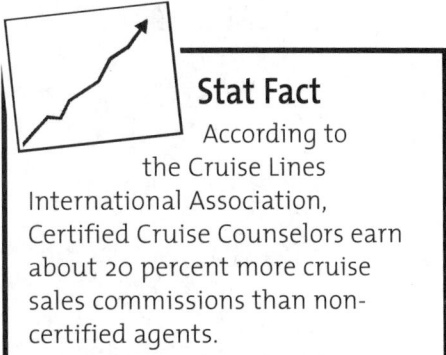

Stat Fact

According to the Cruise Lines International Association, Certified Cruise Counselors earn about 20 percent more cruise sales commissions than non-certified agents.

client sign a waiver form indicating we've discussed insurance with them and what their decision is—Decline, Cruise Line, or Independent. We always suggest that the independent is the best form of insurance because it will provide default protection against the cruise and airlines. Insurance from the cruise line will not." The best part of offering your clients travel insurance, besides peace of mind for both them and you, is that it's commissionable, which is pretty rewarding for you.

As a cruise "expert" your responsibilities should include:

- Studying the cruise industry and keeping up-to-date on the latest and most popular excursions.
- Evaluating what your client wants and how much he or she is willing to pay.
- Scouring the market and finding the best deals that fit within the client's criteria and budget.
- Presenting the cruise options and answering all of the client's questions—or finding answers promptly if you do not have them on hand.
- Having a very structured system of booking the cruises and explaining all payments to your clients. Being able to answer questions about the cruise lines' cancellation and payment policies.
- Handling and arranging for all additional needs including transport to and from the airport as well as any special needs, such as on-board child care, dietary restrictions, medical conditions, and disability needs.
- Handling payment and wishing them bon voyage.
- Getting feedback.

Referring to the last item on the above list, you want to know how the service and amenities were on the ship, as well as the accommodations, the food, and activities. Put together a short questionnaire and give it to all of your clients who have returned from cruises. This will help you with future bookings.

Get the Adrenaline Pumping!

It's Adventure Travel

For some, adventure means sailing over the jungle on a zip line, while for others it's white-water rafting or bungee jumping. Some prefer skiing or snorkeling, while others dare to venture into a crowded department store for a massive one-day-only sale. Adventure means different things to different people. It's all a matter of individual preference. It is estimated that more than 90 percent of American adults have indulged in some type of adventure trip in recent years, as the adventure travel market continues to climb. Camping and hiking, considered "tamer" adventure activities to some, are, nonetheless, the favorites, along with skiing. Water activities, including scuba diving, surfing, snorkeling, kayaking, and whitewater rafting, have also become popular favorites of the adventure crowd in recent years.

And then there are the extreme sports mentioned earlier. The definition varies depending on whom you ask. The preferred definition of an extreme sport is "an activity that gets the adrenaline pumping." Others define it as an activity in which you may be injured or killed. That, however, may not seem like as much fun to your more grounded clientele.

Andrey Bandurenko/www.shutterstock.com

In reality, extreme activities for the general public are monitored more closely than the activities of Evel Knievel were years ago. Insurance is simply too high for people to take great risks. Therefore, today's extreme activities focus on the adrenaline rush while not actually putting people in great danger —provided they follow the rules and regulations of such activities.

Extreme Examples

Mountain biking, mountain climbing, and riding along a zip line are examples of common extreme activities. There are also variations of other sports, such as skiing barefoot, which has become popular. And then there are completely new sports such as Zorbing, which means rolling down a hill in a giant (clear) inflatable globe called a Zorb®. It was invented in New Zealand, where it has become quite the rage. However, if your clients would prefer to go down a hill on a board, you can send them sand boarding on the dunes in Peru.

Sometimes it's not the activity as much as it is the location that draws people. Visiting the lion country on an African safari is enticing because it's real safari territory. If you're looking for good lion safari country, try Botswana. A shark expedition can be booked in Cape Town, South Africa, among other locales, and if it's gorillas in the mist you prefer, try a gorilla safari in Rwanda.

There are many extreme sport options, and new ones are always popping up as people discover more ways to find thrills.

Do You Have a Niche?

Adventure tours are a market within the larger travel industry, so it can be your niche. However, as the demand for such tours continues to grow, the increasingly more savvy travelers want someone with expertise in his or her area of adventure. While this doesn't mean you will book only white-water rafting trips, it may mean that you specialize in water-related adventures, including canoeing, kayaking, and whale or shark expeditions. The more "physical activity" involved in an adventure trip, the more it is considered "hard" adventure. For some travel agencies, certain regions provide a niche market, such as Adventure Tours of Africa, while for others it is more activity based, such as Great Mountain Biking Expeditions. Whatever route you decide to pursue, study and learn as much as possible. While you do not need to be an expert, or even an active participant, in the adventure activity, you need to know what your clients should expect every step of the way. Naturally it can be more fun for you if you are passionate about the tours you offer and take part in the activities. Travel agents who love to ski find it very rewarding to book clients on ski trips that they too have really enjoyed. There is a shared passion between such travel agents and their customers.

"I was an avid skier so I thought of trying to get a group to go skiing in Italy," says Toni Lanotte-Day, travel consultant for Toni Tours Inc. in Levittown, New York. The trip she organized was her first tour as a travel agent, and it worked out so well that every year since she has taken a group ranging from 10 to 40 people to Italy for some first-rate skiing plus fabulous Italian cuisine. "It's great fun and the suppliers have been very supportive," says Lanotte-Day.

Know Your Travel Suppliers

Unless you're planning to book your own adventure tours, which we will talk about shortly, you will need to establish connections with adventure tour suppliers or work with your host agency to put together your packages. If you are starting out with a host agency, see if they have suppliers that can handle the types of adventure tours you want to sell. If you are checking out suppliers, get references and find out as much as you can about their businesses. As adventure travel grows very quickly, so do a lot of would-be tour operators whose intentions may be good, but who cannot necessarily provide what they say they can.

In some cases you may need to add the adventure element to an otherwise packaged vacation. For example, you may have a package deal to Hawaii through your host agency or your own suppliers that includes air, accommodations, car rental, transport to and from the airport, etc. However, you can supply the adventure portion of the excursion by contacting the vendor separately. You could, for example, contact Paradise Helicopters and book a three-hour tour (sing: "a three-hour tour") over one of three active volcanoes. The tours have been popular for several years and can make an adventurous addition to a vacation. If you are booking Hawaii packages regularly, you can establish an ongoing relationship with this, or another, tour supplier and in time get better rates than your clients could get on their own. Thus you have made your own adventure travel excursion.

Of course, it all depends on the wishes of your clients and the direction you choose to take with your agency. Are you an adventure tour agency or an agency that can add adventure to your other bookings? Or, can you do both?

Know Your Clients

As is always the case when booking any type of trip, personal service, time savings, detailed knowledge, and attention to detail are your key selling points. After all, this is why your clients chose you, rather than booking over the internet.

Do your clients want to be physically active? Would they prefer an amazing guided journey? You need to figure out what the word "adventure" means to your chosen market.

For physical activities, you will also need to know the skill level of your participants. Are they first-time scuba enthusiasts or seasoned divers? Are they looking for "adventure" on the bunny slopes or did they just miss out on the Olympic time trials by fractions of a second? Often, you will find the need for varied activity levels, particularly with families, where the children may be learning while the parents can hit the big slopes. Many travel activities have various levels, but some may be beyond what younger children can comfortably handle. You will usually know from the supplier if there is a minimum age, and if not, ask them.

For the more strenuous adventure trips you also want to know that your future adventurers are not only excited about the possibilities, but also physically up to the challenge. Climbing one of the Alps in Switzerland or hiking through a rainforest requires your travelers to be up to the challenge. Very often, such trips look great and are very exciting for a day or two, but by day number three, the adventure traveler who is not accustomed to such a daily level of activity finds that he or she may be too sore and achy to keep on going. Backpacking throughout Europe, a lengthy bicycle excursion, or a horseback-riding trip all require great stamina. It is important that you, as the travel agent, review these factors with prospective clients so that they cannot say, "We didn't know it was going to be so exhausting." Sell the right trip to the right customers.

Even in more passive adventure trips, such as the helicopter ride mentioned earlier, hot-air ballooning, or a jeep tour through the rainforests, all of which are exciting, but do not require your clients to do anything more than sit and take it all in, you need to discuss fear of heights, motion sickness, or any medical condition that might not make this the right trip for them. Ultimately, they will sign a waiver, stating that the choice of vacation activity was theirs and not yours. However, it doesn't bode well for your reputation if your clients could not handle the elevation and blamed you, or even tried to sue you for booking them on such a trip. For this reason, make sure everything is in writing and signed by your clients. Lots of common sense, as well as caution, should be applied when booking people on hard adventure packages.

Priorities?

Some clients are looking to visit an exotic location and then take in some adventure, while others are seeking adventure first and will find it wherever you offer such activities. For this reason it is advantageous to have a little of both at the ready, including great locations such as Hawaii and the Caribbean that also offer adventure as well as adventure packages in locations that may not be as enticing. Of course, the best option is to find great adventure in great destinations. There is more competition to book these trips, so look carefully within the adventure niche and try to find something that makes your package unique. For example, include not only a lion safari in Africa, but also photos of your clients posing with the lions. OK, not a good plan, but you get the idea.

Accommodations will always factor into the planning—for campers, campgrounds and what they offer are part of the travel adventure, while for others accommodations will run the gamut. In between daily bungee jumps, do they want

Fun Fact

According to the Virtuoso® Luxe Report, an annual snapshot of travel trends and habits of affluent travelers, 40 percent of clients seek active vacations or active "add-ons."

to stay in a four-star hotel or would they prefer a quaint bed and breakfast? Even for skiers, there is a wide range of ski lodge and resort accommodations. Therefore, you also need to know the non-activity needs and wishes of your clientele and plan your packages at different price points.

You'll find that many younger adventurers and young families are not as concerned about luxury on an adventure outing, while the 40-and-over crowd may want to enjoy more luxurious spas in which to soak after a day of scaling mountains, swimming with sharks, or bringing in the herd on a cattle drive.

Do It Yourselfers

OK, so you've been sailing since you were seven and been whale watching since you were ten. You know the ins and outs of whale-watching excursions, and despite the fact that for you it's second nature, you are aware that for many people, going aboard a whale or dolphin-watching vessel off Cape Cod is somewhat of an adventure. In a situation where you can provide adventure, you may opt to start your own excursions. As with all tours, creativity, good marketing, and competitive pricing (for what you are offering) will be major factors in your success. As you probably guessed, for adventure travel, the more physical activity, the higher your insurance. Keep insurance and safety costs in mind while setting up your fees.

Four keys to good adventure tour planning:

1. *Tour guides.* Good guides can make or break your tours. On the island of Maui, I'll never forget how much fun our guide Randy made the trip around the "un-commercialized side" of the island—he knew the area like the back of his hand and was both informative and educational. Nearly 20 years later, my wife and I still fondly remember Randy, our tour guide. Choose your tour guides carefully, train them in how to interact with your esteemed customers, or better yet, find guides who have innate people skills, as this is difficult to teach. Have all your guides bonded. Provide your customers with the opportunity to supply you with feedback on your guides. This can be done through an opinion survey or well-designed questionnaire. Remember, word-of-mouth can make or break you.

   This has never been truer than now. In the technology age, you would rather have your client tell you about any problems, thus giving you the opportunity to correct the issue or compensate them. Otherwise, you risk them posting a negative review of your services on Tripadvisor.com or some other travel site.

2. *Deposits.* Unless you are a combination tour planner/travel agent, you will find yourself as a supplier, interacting with travel agents, hotels, and other suppliers, booking packages that include your own tours. Make sure you collect

deposits in advance. When it comes to deposits, Dan Austin of Austin Lehman Adventures says, "Establish 'your' policies and stick to them. Review what others in your niche do and mirror." Like you, your suppliers will have set policies about deposits and final payment. The requirements of your suppliers will largely dictate your own policies. You will want to, and likely be required to, pay your suppliers prior to leaving on any given tour. Neither you nor your suppliers can afford to operate on good faith—it doesn't pay the bills. Some of your expenses you should expect to pay upfront including your means of transportation, your contracted tour guides' pay, possibly refreshments, and certainly insurance.

3. *Know the selling points of your tour.* Are travelers joining your rainforest excursion to see the flora and fauna or for the exhilarating zip-line experience over the majestic trees? Perhaps your tour offers a cultural immersion feature in addition to bicycle touring through Italy; use this to differentiate your trip from tours offered by your competitor. Always focus on what the selling points are and market accordingly. If you're sending people over a waterfall in a barrel (and we hope that you aren't), then make sure it's in a top-of-the-line, reinforced barrel. Don't substitute a leaky 100-year-old whiskey barrel for the authenticity value and claim that you are "keeping it real." Silly example, but you get the point—be forthright and give the people what they want.

4. *Keeping it legal.* This is an area where many new business owners are tempted to take shortcuts in order to reduce costs. Don't! Before you embark on any type of tour it's essential that you know all licensing, permit, and insurance requirements and make certain that your guides hold the safety certifications that may be necessary. Additionally, you will want good legal counsel to prepare documents such as contracts and waivers.

Permit and licensing issues can range from how many people can ride in a jeep through the rainforest of Costa Rica to special licensing or certification requirements for a scuba diving excursion on the Red Sea. Know the rules and abide by them.

Regardless of what type of adventure you are providing, most likely it will involve some form of transportation. This may be

> **Bright Idea**
>
> For tours that involve hiking or even a substantial amount of walking, recommend clients purchase or put together a blister kit. Spenco sells a good kit and it can be purchased online through the company's website (www.spenco.com). Moleskin can protect against blisters and can be purchased at any pharmacy. Few things can ruin a hike, especially one that lasts several days, like blistered feet.

traveling by helicopter to some remote location or having participants take a four-wheel drive into the jungle. Either way, know what licenses are required. If your tour requires participants to operate a vehicle, it would be prudent to know whether an international driver's license or one issued by the country you are exploring is required. If your group is made up of mostly Americans, who probably don't have a driver's license valid outside of the United States, you may need to consider a different form of transportation or hire additional guides as drivers.

Insurance and licensing requirements can vary dramatically from country to country and based on the activities carried out on a particular excursion. Because so many variables come into play, many in the business recommend having someone in the country where you operate handle these matters or at least assist.

When you start exploring a foreign country as a potential destination, you'll have to determine what services are available. You might be able to find domestic contacts who can refer you to terrific sources before you arrive in-country. Domestic tourism bureaus of foreign countries may also be helpful, along with publications and associations pertinent to your area of interest.

In order to make your tours work, you may need additional guides, or other employees. Tour operators—especially those with more than one tour going at a time—often take on guides in the form of independent contractors hired on location. These professionals are a boon for the new travel businessperson who might not have enough scheduled trips or startup capital to hire permanent, full-time guides. You can still meet your needs by working with expert freelance guides that you hire at your destination, or by hiring a ground service operator to supply you with escorts and other support personnel (as well as any transportation you need).

If you visit different countries at different times of the year, you may want to continue this type of arrangement as your business grows, working with operators you know and trust. However, if you operate a year-round tour to a particular foreign destination and find some sterling freelance guides, you may want to offer them permanent positions.

Of course, for adventure guides, you need to know that they are experienced and even licensed (depending on the activity) to serve as a guide. Before you send a group of your clients out on a tour with an unfamiliar adventure tour operator or guide, take a tour with him yourself. This is the only sure-fire way to determine his particular charms and capabilities. This is crucial to the success of your operation. A guide should have a thorough knowledge of the region and be skilled in the activities included on your tour. He or she should also be able to educate the participants in an exciting and entertaining fashion, and ensure that everyone on the trip has fun, without ever compromising safety.

"The guide must be experienced—and able to handle the logistics of a group and compassionate to group dynamics," says Andy Crisconi of One World Trekking. You might speak to a potential guide by telephone and he might have stellar customer service skills and brim with personality in this situation. However, the same individual may not be able to handle the group dynamic, which is quite different. We've all heard it said, "One bad apple can spoil the bunch." This is rather accurate. Negativity tends to be contagious. You want your guide to take control of a situation before it affects the whole group.

Medic, Please

As a travel agent, it is important that you provide adventure travelers with the basic information regarding nearby doctors and hospitals. This requires only a few phone calls, and can be easily covered by the ground travel supplier with whom you are working. An adventure travel tour company should be able to provide you with the security that they are cognizant of what to do in the event of an emergency—make sure to ask.

The International Society of Travel Medicine (www.istm.org) has information about clinics in nearly 50 countries around the world. The American Society of Tropical Medicine and Hygiene (www.astmh.org) also has a list of clinics.

If you are putting together the tours, add information about doctors and clinics to your research. While you will have your own medical kit on hand, as will all your tour operators, you need to know what to do for anything from a bee sting to a more serious accident, whether it is a fall on the slopes or someone being tossed from a horse. Tour operators need to know how to handle emergencies, and for that reason, there are emergency medical training courses widely available. An online search of "wilderness first responder training" will provide you with many options. Some organizations even specialize in emergencies that are unique to a specific region, such as Africa. Be prepared or have someone on staff that is equipped to handle these special circumstances.

Travelers can also purchase additional insurance that will provide for airlifts and

> **Tip...**
>
> ### Smart Tip
> Let people know that it's a good idea to bring along the basics for handling cuts and injuries. Starting with some bandages, they should make up a handy emergency kit for adventure travel—depending on the nature of the travel activities, this could include something to put on rashes, such as those caused by poison oak or poison ivy. Also include Bayer® Aspirin, which can be helpful for potential heart attacks.

The Adventure Travel Trade Association

The Adventure Travel Trade Association (ATTA), formed in 1990, is a member-based international organization that works with travel agents, suppliers, and marketers to promote new adventure travel opportunities. Along with providing professional support, the ATTA works to help members serve their clients with cost-effective resources. The ATTA also encourages sustainable and environmentally and culturally sensitive adventure travel practices. Find more about ATTA at www.adventuretravel.biz.

a medical interpreter through On-Call International or Chartis. You may choose to work with one of these insurance providers, but if not be sure to have a list of companies that offer the kind of additional coverage that a client may request.

Hiking with the Boss

For team building, retreats, or incentives featuring adventure travel for the corporate set were once big business. But cutbacks and fiscal scrutiny have reduced the demand for this type of excursion. Because tour providers are seeing less corporate adventure travel, many have all but abandoned the market. Yet despite their newfound frugality, corporations do still participate in such activities. While it may be on a smaller scale and trips may be less frequent, this market should not be ruled out as viable.

This could be an opportunity to position your business as a corporate specialist. Of course, you won't want to focus all your efforts in this area, but if you are prepared to offer packages to the corporate client that other travel agents cannot, then you can create a niche within the niche. Additionally, you will be ahead of the pack when the economy turns around and corporate adventure travel makes a comeback.

For you, this is an opportunity to book 10, 15, or even 50 people on a journey with the corporation picking up the tab. Whether you are providing an opportunity for team building while setting up tents in a national park or a stay at an authentic dude ranch, the idea is that new surroundings encourage out-of-the-box ideas and stimulate employees who fall into the doldrums while in their cubicles—or their corner offices—on a daily basis.

Keep in mind that you will need to make all the arrangements you would for any other group of travelers on a multiday excursion including meals and on-site support. You can then set up an evening debriefing, where the participants review what they did during the day and evaluate ways in which their adventures can be utilized in their business endeavors.

Don't be too quick to go with prepackaged suppliers when booking adventure travel for corporations. Many companies want to put their own stamp on their outings. Therefore, you will need to offer flexibility and creativity—or add the adventure elements to the trip yourself. This gives you room to be creative and provide that special touch for your corporate client.

Corporate clients can be a marvelous source of repeat business if the adventure proved successful and met their goals, whether serving as a team building experience or a retreat from the daily grind. Get corporate feedback, analyze what they did and did not like, and then, in a few months, let them know you have some great plans for their next corporate outing.

Family Adventures

Unlike Billy Crystal and his pals in the 1991 movie *City Slickers* or John Travolta and his buddies in *Hog Wild*, going out on an adventure is not necessarily for adults only. Today, more than ever, ski trips, kayaking, biking, hiking, and many adventure vacations are geared for families. You need to find out what is available for families and then brief them on how to best select and prepare for an adventure excursion. You should recommend that parents let the children in on the decision-making process after the adults have narrowed down the choices. If the kids have some ownership in the vacation, it can be more pleasant for all concerned. Of course as an agent the best

Women Adventure Seekers

In recent years a new segment of the adventure travel market has emerged—trips for women. This can be in the form of girlfriend getaways or excursions for the solo female traveler. The majority of female adventure travelers are between the ages of 35 and 65; some are married and traveling without their spouses, while others are single. Like other adventure tours, these women-only trips run the gamut from the tamer hiking or kayaking to gorilla safaris. With women adventure-seekers being one of the fastest growing segments of this niche market, you may want to seriously consider catering to this group when setting up shop.

you can do is suggest it. Also, you will need to know what level of activities the kids can comfortably handle.

Double-check that packages are kid friendly and if there are minimum age requirements for any activity. Have these details ahead of time, so you can pass along the information.

If you are planning adventure tours, consider families, as this is a potentially large market. Sure, you can gear some activities that are for the more "expert" climbers, skiers, or bikers, but also consider various activity levels to include younger members—it broadens your market.

Seniors on the Move

Much of the baby-boomer generation is now past 50; in fact, the first of the boomers turned 65 on January 1, 2011, and they are not slowing down in the least. Today, one of the largest segments of the travel population is the "senior" set. While the 50-something crowd may be somewhat insulted, being included in the senior category, they undoubtedly won't mind if

▲

travel discounts come their way. After all, who doesn't like a discount no matter how it comes? Many travel suppliers recognize that this is such a large demographic group, with 10,000 baby boomers hitting the big 5-0 daily, that they are willing to cut some prices to grab a share of the market. To ignore this segment of the population would be foolish.

As a travel agent, there is, potentially, a windfall in profits if you can provide specific travel packages and personalized service for this large target market.

Keep in mind that many seniors today are sitting on substantial savings from 401(k) plans and good advice from financial planners. While the young "seniors" may still be working and saving for retirement, many have accrued lengthy vacation time. Then there are the retirees, who have plenty of time to travel. Both accumulated time off and retirement afford this group the opportunity to take trips of longer duration, often for two, three, and even four weeks at a time.

As life expectancy continues to increase, a more health-conscious and health-savvy population of seniors age more gracefully than ever before. Therefore, offering many more travel options, including active travel, to this demographic group is a good idea. Also, with greater life expectancy you have the potential to provide services to this segment of the population well into the future.

Catering to the Market

If you are going to sell travel to seniors, you need to know what is popular in their circles. Cruises are very big with the 50-plus market because it is a self-contained vacation without a lot of packing and unpacking. In fact, within the cruise market, many smaller ships are catering largely to this demographic group. They offer a homier atmosphere at sea (or on river) with only 250 or 300 passengers, thus providing an attractive alternative to the bigger ships. These smaller ships also require less walking than people must do on the mega-ships. Seniors do not want to be exhausted just getting to dinner. Additionally, because these smaller ships can more easily navigate rivers and smaller ports-of-call, tour planners are able to broaden their already extensive list of destinations.

Seniors also enjoy activities and in many cases, adventure tours. It's important not to pigeonhole your business by putting seniors into one grouping. You'll need to find out the age, activity level, and interests of your clients—many of whom are in very good shape today, still engaging in sporting activities well into their '60s, and in some cases, their '70s. Therefore, you need to start with no preconceptions and find out what your clients want. Then you can start looking for the appropriate packages and the "senior" discounts that often accompany them.

Smaller Is Better

Grand Circle Cruise Line is an example of a company that has featured smaller ships for the past 15 years. In fact, the small ship business now accounts for more than 80 percent of the company's business. Very popular with the 50-plus set, Grand Circle saw more than 160,000 Americans aged 50 and older take one of their 100 overseas vacations in 2008. Itineraries include tours such as The Great Rivers of Europe, a 16-day river cruise along the Rhine, Main, and Danube Rivers, as well as Holland & Belgium in Bloom, a 12-day river cruise along the Rhine River. For the past six years, Grand Circle has been included on *Conde Nast Traveler's* Gold List, and in its 2011 Readers' Poll, the magazine named seven Grand Circle vessels among the "Top 20 World's Best." It is just one of several cruise lines opting for smaller ships and catering to the senior crowd.

As you work with the more traditional seniors, those in the "65 and over" grouping, you will find that many are more than happy to let you handle the details rather than deal with the internet. Growing up in the pre-computer generation, this is a demographic group that should be cherished for still appreciating human interaction—something that much of the youthful culture today has lost via emails, text messaging, social networking, and smartphones. You do not have to sell seniors on what humans can provide that computers cannot. Instead, you can focus on what is of importance.

A sense of security and comfort are the two prime concerns of the over-65 senior market. Security in this case encompasses health and safety. Available, competent medical personnel on a cruise ship or a tour overseas as well as the ability to be in touch with family members all fall into the security category, since health and family are commonly major concerns. Comfort, meanwhile, encompasses not only the accommodations, but ease of travel—meaning that they can move through the various stages of a trip comfortably without hassles. While multiple layovers may seem like a good idea if they save 30 or 50 bucks, ultimately such stops add stress to the trip.

To meet these needs, you must put your attention to detail (the mark of a good travel agent) and focus on tour suppliers that go the extra few yards by providing what this demographic audience is most concerned about. It also means doing the little things that go a long way, which can be anything from calling ahead to make sure they know where a wheelchair access ramp is located to simple reminders about packing medication to take, important phone numbers, and a list of medications,

Meal Management

Many seniors are on restricted diets. You therefore need to research the dining options more carefully when planning senior trips. Travel suppliers that frequently cater to the senior traveler are usually aware of this. Nonetheless, some may still provide limited choices. If there are no meals included in the package, or you are creating the package, then you can look closely for area restaurants that you think might have more health-conscious cuisine. For many people of all ages, dining is an important part of their travel experience. If options are limited, find out how limited ahead of time. This is a great reason for networking with other travel agents and going on travel agent chat rooms or discussion boards to talk about dining in specific regions. Visiting your travel locations is also always recommended.

In certain areas where you may be sending many potential senior travelers, you might even talk to the management of a restaurant and let them know that a couple of additional menu items or alternatives such as low-sodium or heart-healthy meals could bring them a lot more business. Always build up your relationships.

the dosages, and the conditions they treat. A majority of people in their '60s have spent years providing for and looking after their families. While they do not want to relinquish their independence, they certainly don't mind being pampered a little. You will have to judge from the phone conversation, or even an in-person meeting, whether you are dealing with someone who wants to be on their own or wants more handholding. Providing the right degree of pampering and care is very important to the relationship. If you get it right, you can have steady business year after year. People from the baby-boomer generation, and before, have a strong sense of loyalty, so even if the first trip does not provide you with ample commission, think of this as the first of many journeys in the years ahead.

Tip...

Smart Tip

As a booking incentive or as a token of appreciation, offer a free folding medication card that fits into a wallet. Purchase it and have it imprinted with your logo through a promotional item company such as www.qualitylogoproducts.com or www.USimprints.com. It is a small gesture, but it gives seniors a handy place to keep a record of their medications, and because it is imprinted with your information, it keeps your business in the front of clients' minds.

Intergenerational Travel

A 2006 University of Florida survey found that 80 percent of grandparents were very positive about the idea of traveling with their grandchildren. These intergenerational trips are becoming increasingly popular, spiraling upward by 60 percent over the past 15 years. Due to such popularity, the grandparent and grandchild travel combination has been given its own name—grand travel. A few companies have emerged that specialize in these trips. Elderhostel Inc., the creator of Road Scholar educational programs, offers a number of intergenerational trips both in North America and abroad. Its trips provide an educational component while being fun for both young and old(er). The Sierra Club also offers multigenerational travel but seems to have fewer selections. Depending on the ages of both grandchild and grandparents, some of the club's family trips may fit the bill. Considering the research and the increasing number of baby-boomer grandparents, you might want to focus your attention on this group. It could set you apart from the pack.

So, how do you book intergenerational travel? Well, first, you'll want to know when and where the grandparents want to go, since they typically make the destination decision. Naturally, a child-friendly location will be on tap for young children, such as a theme park. However, tours all around the world have attracted these relatively new traveling tandems. Cultural centers draw a lot of attention, including New York City, Washington, DC, and Boston. For teens, a lengthier trip to Paris may be appropriate.

While grandparents generally choose the location (and foot the bill), the kids often pick the restaurants and some of the activities. The key is to find common interests that both generations can share together. One tour company sets up tours where grandparents and their grandchildren attend baseball games at Yankee Stadium, Fenway Park, tour the ballparks, and visit the Baseball Hall of Fame in between. For the baseball lovers, this is a terrific excursion.

One reason these trips have blossomed is because the kids get to travel without mom and dad, and grandparents are usually ready to spoil their grandchildren.

As a travel agent, you'll need to work with travel suppliers, tour operators, or your host agency, or proceed on your own to meet the needs of both parties. And as a selling bonus, you can work both senior and children's discounts into the packages.

Depending on the ages, the levels of chosen activities may be very similar or quite diverse—find out where they meet on the activity continuum and see if you can work within that framework. Cruises offer everything from bingo to surf pools and rock climbing walls, and this diversity makes them a popular choice for grand travelers.

You will also want to make recommendations on how this pairing can best travel together. Suggest packing light bags, since neither the younger nor the older members of the traveling set may be able to lift heavy luggage. If driving is involved, try to avoid destinations or lodging that will require night driving, as many seniors are not comfortable under these conditions, and the grandchildren, well, you get it.

Groups and Single Seniors

Many seniors enjoy traveling with friends. This could be two couples or a club with 15 members who all want to take a cruise together. Marketing your travel offerings to senior groups or having plenty of packages available that are geared for group travel is a way of building a lucrative niche within a niche. From there, you can personalize the tour to fit the group. A one-day botanical garden excursion might be the crown jewel in your New York-bound adventure for a Midwest-based senior gardening club.

Of course you need to ascertain what the goal is for your group. If the package is air and hotel, you can turn it into a Broadway trip with group sales to two of the hit shows. Know the interests of the group and seek out and/or build the trip that suits them. Make sure to include the little things, like dinner at Sardi's, the popular Broadway theater crowd favorite.

There comes a point when many seniors become widowed but they may still have the desire to travel. Get to know the client. Listen to what she is saying and sometimes not saying. As Sue Bonchi of Odysseys Unlimited says, "Someone newly widowed might have real fears about traveling alone, but it comes out as 'What if I don't like the people?'"

Older singles may be looking for someone with whom they can travel. This is an opportunity to matchmake, not romantically—although that does happen—but by pairing individuals with similar interests to tour together. By considering ages, interests, and physical conditions you can successfully group people. Again, you can find a niche within a niche if you can come up with the best travel buddy program for single seniors.

Playing It Safe

The extensive variety of tours for seniors is quite diverse, and not unlike booking any tour or cruise packages (or combinations of both), you will take into account the wants and needs of your clients while trying to find the best fit among the many possibilities.

One key aspect of booking seniors (or any demographic for that matter) is being able to provide travel tips that fit the specific group. For seniors, medical and safety concerns are a high priority. While trying to plan a trip that is stress free and safe, you can also offer suggestions, perhaps on a printed sheet. It's a nice touch that your travelers will appreciate and serves to differentiate you as an agent who provides a personal touch.

Suggestions from orthopedic surgeons and chiropractors to avoid luggage and travel-related injuries include:

Stat Fact

According to the U.S. Consumer Product Safety Commission, more than 50,000 luggage-related injuries were treated at hospital emergency rooms, doctors' offices, and clinics in 2007. Seniors accounted for a high percentage of these injuries.

- When lifting luggage, stand beside your bag, bend at the knees, and stand using the leg muscles, not the waist and back.

- Avoid twisting the body when picking up luggage. Lift with the case next to you and your feet pointed forward in the direction you will be walking so you do not have to swing the back around.

- Lift then walk; don't try doing both in one motion.

- Purchase lightweight luggage, preferably with wheels, and consider two smaller suitcases instead of one large suitcase. Avoid luggage that is heavy or bulky when empty.

- Look for luggage with a handle that is easy to attach and pull.

- When carrying or pulling a suitcase on wheels, alternate arms often.

- On airliners, when lifting carry-on luggage into overhead compartments, lift evenly to the back of the seat first. Then lift from the back of the seat to the luggage compartment, putting the bottom, or wheel end, in first and sliding the luggage back.

- Check all bags that are more than 15 percent of your weight—therefore, if you weigh 140 pounds, the bag you carry onboard should not exceed 21 pounds.

- Make sure all backpacks have two adjustable shoulder straps that are padded and keep the weight evenly distributed.

- Carry rolling luggage up stairs and on escalators.

- Ask for help if you cannot lift something easily.

- Don't sit for extremely long periods of time. Pull the car over and take a walk, stand up on the plane and walk to and from the lavatory, whether you need to use the facilities or not.

- Change seated positions periodically to shift your weight and maintain good circulation.

- Sitting in a stiff position can cause aches and pains. Roll your shoulders gently on occasion and move your neck to relax those muscles.

You can provide these types of travel tips for any number of situations, and include cruise safety, public transportation safety tips, or suggestions for carrying medications.

▲

This is a population that reads and is often more amenable and appreciative of your suggestions than the younger clientele who are simply anxious to follow Nike's slogan and "Just do it."

Travel Insurance for Seniors

Yes, it may cost more, but if you seek, you shall find. While some travel insurers will have age limits, others will provide coverage and you will need to discern which you might want to recommend to your client. This will depend on the age, health, and travel plans of the individual(s) in question.

With this subgroup many of the same rules apply as with the adventure travelers. You may consider looking for a medical assistance program to recommend to your clients. Such programs can help your clients locate hospitals, doctors, and appropriate medical attention in foreign countries, conduct telephone consultations with doctors while abroad, arrange interpreters in the event of a medical emergency, and arrange and cover the cost of escorted medical evacuations. Such assistance programs are not particularly expensive and can be invaluable, especially for travelers headed overseas.

For travel insurance suppliers, medical assistance companies, and a wealth of information in general for travelers leaving the United States, you should be aware of the U.S. Department of State's Bureau of Consular Affairs website at http://travel.state.gov/travel/tips/health/health_4971.html. Within the United States, you can provide some medical information numbers through a quick web search and provide your clients with whatever it is that will make them feel more comfortable and secure while traveling.

Bright Idea

If your clients have not had a medical checkup in a while, recommend that they have a pre-travel physical. This is especially important if they are planning a more active or long trip. Too many people (not just seniors) have the idea that they are infallible on vacation. That isn't the case. If traveling overseas, remind them that the foods will be prepared differently and that they should discuss dietary changes with their physicians. Additionally, they should be made aware of any necessary vaccinations prior to traveling to certain regions. They should be immunized long enough ahead of time to see if there are any adverse reactions. They should also consider that some inoculations require more than one dose of the antibody, administered over several months.

Advertising and Promotion

In this chapter we explore one of the most fun, creative, and demanding parts of the travel business—advertising, marketing, and promotion. After all, no matter how exciting, relaxing, informative, or entertaining your travel packages are, nobody's going to know about them unless you spread the word. As a travel professional, you should put a great deal of effort into designing and implementing your marketing plan to take your sales to the limit and beyond.

Much like most industries today, the travel industry is embracing new technology. Using everything from websites to handheld devices and the social media, travel agents are posting new offers on their Facebook pages and sending e-newsletters, while also blogging and tweeting away. They have also found that the travel CD has not quite replaced a beautiful brochure, but has indeed become another major tool in the travel agent marketing kit.

In this section, we'll take a look at all the newer options for marketing your business as well as some of the longtime favorites, such as direct mail and print ads.

Marketing Plan

While you may not want to write out a formal marketing plan, you should determine your basic marketing strategy.

This strategy will focus on your niche, your market, how to define yourself in that market, and finally how you will reach your target market. What this means is that once you have determined the type of products you will be selling (your tour packages) and who your potential buyers are, you will need to position yourself so people can find out all about you through your marketing materials, especially your website. Your goal is then to be able to develop and build relationships with customers.

Your Website

A homebased travel business relies heavily on a good website. Since there is no storefront, and you don't want people dropping by your house at all hours, this is your window to the world. Make sure your website has a professional look and that the pages featuring your tours:

- Look great (photos from suppliers and/or professional photographers are important)
- Are easy to navigate
- Explain the details of your tour packages
- Are written in an enticing, easy-to-read manner
- Are concise, with good content in readable chunks (long, wordy web pages do not work well)

Your website should also have an "About Us" page that lets readers know who you are and what your business is all about.

Tip...

Smart Tip

The "About Us" page should give a brief story about how you got started and sing some of your praises—but don't overdo it. You want it to be professional.

Forget the bells and whistles or long lead-ins. You will lose the multitude of people who want information fast and don't have the patience to sit through your intro. Also, make sure your website matches the tone and style of your vacations. Elegant vacations? Have an elegant looking site, with less on the page and a more eloquent writing style. Tours for families with young children? Make it colorful, with family photos and things that kids will enjoy.

Photos are terrific for a travel agency. Just make sure they load quickly. The slower the site, the more lost customers.

In terms of sales and marketing, your website can be a place for people to gather as much information as you would like them to have before booking a trip. Unlike the online booking sites, you'll want to provide some personal attention, which you can do through the website. Be interactive—have prospective customers communicate with you via email, a link to your Facebook page, Twitter, or text or phone.

Some people put everything on their web pages, while others entice potential travelers to contact them so they can provide more details and personalized service. Remember, there are plenty of budget travel websites out there. One of your selling points is personalized service, so be ready to follow up with such service.

Also, remember that sometimes less can be much more on a website. The sites packed to the brim with deals and offers look like bargain-basement advertising with signs everywhere. That can detract from your goal of creating a relationship with your clients.

Finally, remember to keep your website updated regularly. Dated material is the sign of a business that is not being well run.

In Savannah, Georgia, Karen A. believes her company website is one of her most cost-effective advertising venues. "We have spent a total of about $3,000 on this in two years, including photography, software, and our internet service provider—excluding our labor," she says. "We run it in-house, and it has undergone many revisions. The site has generated most of our corporate business (corporations holding meetings in Savannah who want leisure-time activities for attendees), and some Girl Scout and school business, to the tune of around $20,000 in revenues."

While the modern-day website can cost much more, it doesn't have to if you find someone who can build a basic site at a reasonable ($1,500 to $3,000) cost. Of course it helps if you look at other websites to help you find a look that you might also like. Don't steal, but generate ideas for the site layout from sites you like.

Many people spend more money on their initial website because they are constantly redoing the look of the site. It's too expensive to do trial and error as you pay for the web designer's time. Grab a pad and pen or pencil and draw some site pages you like or show the web designer similar pages online that you'd like to model yours after.

> ## Bright Idea
>
> Join the wide world of blogging. Thousands, if not millions, of people are writing daily or weekly blogs. Why not write something new about travel for a weekly or even twice-weekly blog? Talk about the places you have traveled, or provide travel tips or entertaining anecdotes. You can build a following by writing short 250- to 400-word blogs regularly about travel. We'll offer more on blogs later in the chapter.

You can also enhance your marketing by adding messages that readers will want to "forward to a friend" such as great travel discounts, travel tips, even a joke or a recipe for your next camping trip. People enjoy sharing tidbits of information with others. You can help by providing such tidbits with a nearby forward-to-a-friend, on one easy click. Have the name of your company on there as well. The more your web visitors send your name around, the more marketing you will get without having to pay extra for it. This is called viral marketing.

To maintain your relationships with your growing public, respond to emails or postings on your Facebook pages within a reasonable amount of time—certainly within 12 hours.

Clearly, vacations are big purchases and large commitments. For this reason, your personal attention is best given via phone, or even in person if you have a nearby Starbucks at which to meet, or a similar locale. You might even make some house calls.

No Spamming

People who shop for travel or anything else the e-commerce way don't care for excessive hype. They expect to be informed and entertained, but they don't want to be electronically shouted at, patronized, or pandered to (which you shouldn't do to your customers at any time). Sending requested email updates is good business, but "spamming," or sending e-junk mail, is definitely poor Netiquette and will not win friends and influence customers. Spam is actually illegal, although the FCC and other web policing organizations are far behind at ever catching many spammers. More significantly, what spam will do is ruin your reputation. This is very much a word-of-mouth business, and if you are known as someone who sends junk emails constantly, that does not bode well for your business. What will? The same elements that win you paper customers—honesty, integrity, fairness, service, and respect. Show your web customers they are important by how you treat them. Offer discounts, freebies, and any other perks you can think up.

Try these tips for winning and keeping internet customers:

- *Give your customers easy access to you.* Don't force them to wade through page after page before finding your email address and phone number.

- *Check and answer your emails on a daily basis.* Don't let virtual customers languish any more than you would phone or mail customers.

- *Update your site frequently.* If a cruise or tour is sold out, let people know. This way they don't get frustrated drooling over something that's not available, and it shows them that your products are popular and that they have to move on these things!

- *Add new information frequently.* This helps you market new products as soon as you have them available and also keeps e-travelers coming back for more. If your site stagnates with the same material week after week and month after month, clients will get bored and stop visiting.

- *Don't frustrate customers with a site that's slow or difficult to figure out.* You'll quickly lose people this way.

- *Offer customers some quality content.* Use elements that will draw them in, hold their attention, and make them feel you're a part of their world and they're a part of yours. Post an article on the best vacation spots for the season, or ten tips for traveling with kids.

The Social Media

Facebook and Twitter, as well as LinkedIn, have all become part of the latest in marketing tools by which travel agents communicate with their clients.

The objective of using the social media is to have more direct communication with clients that goes beyond just having them visit your website. You can sign up on Facebook.com for a free account by clicking on "Sign Up." A form will appear for you as a business to fill out. Then, following some standard security checkpoints, you'll get a confirmation email from the folks at Facebook and you'll be all set. You'll then want to set up a profile of your business complete with photos of great destinations.

"Give people a reason to respond. Ask open-ended questions; remember to keep it interactive," says Kris Ruby, who specializes in media marketing as president of Ruby Media Group LLC in Westchester, New York. "Facebook pages have worked very

▲

well for businesses," adds Ruby, who also points out the importance of updating your page often.

Twitter is a free social networking and micro-blogging site that has become a favorite of many business owners. By going to Twitter.com and setting up an account you can get started. You should use your business name when creating the account. Then, by clicking on "Join the Conversation," you can begin sending tweets, which are 140-character messages, or updates. You can also read tweets from followers as you build them up on Twitter. The best part about Twitter is that it is an interactive media tool that keeps you updated in the moment. It allows you to converse in brief tweets to let people know what is going on. While it's difficult to respond to every tweet, you'll want to interact with clients and potential clients in travel-related conversations.

LinkedIn, which you can also join for free at LinkedIn.com, is designed to link professionals. The best way to use LinkedIn is to join groups and talk about travel topics.

The social media sites are the places to be these days and with a strong presence, you can increase your marketing success significantly.

Of course, with all your other responsibilities, you may not have a lot of time to spend on social media sites.

"There are companies out there that you can hire to set up and handle all of your social media needs," says Geoff Millar with Ultimate All-Inclusive Vacations in Arizona. "They charged us about $1,000 to set us up and now charge about $100 a month to do nothing but brainstorm ideas of things to post on our Twitter account and how to post them. They can also help you come up with something to give away, such as $50 off your next vacation." This is what the new age of social media experts are doing to help travel agents market themselves. "We sent them photos and they set up a slot machine on our Facebook page that visitors could play," says Millar. "If they got three of the same photos in a row they would get $50 off the next trip they booked with us."

"I started with everything and then narrowed it down to what was most effective, which was Facebook," says Toni Lanotte-Day of Toni Tours Inc. "It connected me with people from my past who would ask me if I was still in the travel business. Some of these are people I hadn't talked to in 20 years," adds Lanotte-Day, about connecting with and getting business from people who know you but might otherwise not be in touch. "I also write blogs since people search blog sites. This way if they like something you write about a destination, they may contact you. Sometimes it results in booking a trip. However, very often people are looking for free information," says Lanotte-Day, who has learned to tell when a connection is going no place fast. "I know when they're not really interested but just trying to pick my brain," says Lanotte-Day, who has learned from experience to politely limit such conversations.

Blogs: Reading and Writing Them

Blogs can serve both as a means of educating yourself about the travel industry today and as a great way to market your business.

For many in the travel industry, blogging has become a necessary marketing tool. Whether you incorporate a blog into your website or have a stand-alone blog, you should consider adding one to your marketing cache. Blogs are a journal or diary of sorts with recurring entries. They may include commentary in an article-like format as

Getting Your Blog Up and Running

If you are building your blog into your website, then whoever does your web programming should take care of setting it up. It should be user-friendly enough that you can easily update and post new information. If you decide to go with a stand-alone blog, some popular do-it-yourself services include wordpress.com, blogspot.com, tumblr.com, and typepad.com. Each service has its pros and cons, but with any one of them you can set up your blog with little or no programming knowledge. You will need to do your research and decide which service works best for you.

Below are some URLs for travel industry blogs as well as some notations on what makes them noteworthy. Reading blogs can also be a great way to learn more about the business, while responding to blogs gets your name out to the public along with your opinions.

❍ *http://blog.bikehike.com*. This blog uses written content, photos, and video. It is appropriate to the business and informative.

❍ *http://mymelange.net/blog*. This is a beautiful blog. It is visually appealing and transitions from blog to website almost seamlessly. It offers information and services beyond travel arrangements.

❍ *www.tranquilobay.com/blog/index.php*. This has a clean, crisp design. It is easily navigated and has interactive components. It is updated often and is also educational.

❍ *www.ietravel.com/blog*. This offers easy navigation between the website and blog. It has a clean design and is informative and visually appealing. It has frequent updates and guest bloggers.

well as photos and video. As a travel professional your blog should include well-written, informative, and interesting content. If you choose a stand-alone blog it should link back to your website and vice versa. The link should be easy to find; otherwise you are defeating the purpose.

Blogs aren't necessarily intended to sell as much as to inform. This might make you wonder why they are important. The simple answers are:

1. They keep people coming back to your business's online presence.
2. They illustrate your knowledge of, and commitment to, the travel business.

Blogging gives you opportunities to provide clients (past and future) with information and photos, as well as special offers on travel destinations, in a way that is more like education and entertainment than sales.

There is no set rule as to how often a blog should be updated, but blogs that have a set schedule for posting tend to garner more traffic. If you post every Tuesday and Friday, for instance, people come to expect it and will return to your blog to see what's new. Chuck Flagg of the Flagg Agency, which specializes in cruises, typically updates his blog weekly except when he is out on a cruise or doing a resort stay. Then he blogs "live" from that location. What he is doing is trying to convey to readers the experience. This is what all travel blogs should do, whether it is through narrative, photos, video, or any combination of the three. The goal is to entice people and ultimately translate that into sales.

Old School

Yes, the wonderful world of print remains. Brochures are still in style as are write-ups in magazines. Other means of print marketing, however, such as direct mail, are slowly falling by the wayside.

Direct Mail

What exactly is direct mail? It's a means of mailing marketing material directly to your target audience. It can take the form of fliers, brochures, postcards, or any other printed material you send winging into the mailboxes of previous and potential clients.

Direct-mail advertising was once extremely effective, but it could not compete with email and the social media. By the time you pay for the paper, envelopes, printing, and postage for a major campaign, you've spent thousands of dollars. Even if you use desktop printing, it will cost you a lot of money in paper and mailing, not to mention a lot of time, which in business, translates into money. So before you decide to do a mailing to every potential traveler on the Eastern Seaboard, make sure you've thoroughly considered what your niche market wants and how your products will meet that desire or need.

The biggest problem with direct mailing is that too many people simply toss unrequested mail as quickly as they delete unwanted emails. The difference is the cost is much more for direct mailings than it is for an email.

Nonetheless, you may have a niche market such as seniors who appreciate your low-tech approach.

The Wow! Brochure

Brochures are still around, although websites and DVDs have cut significantly into their popularity. There is so much more you can present on your website. Nonetheless, as an independent travel agent, you may want to put together some brochures highlighting your destinations.

What should your brochure look like? That depends on your products and what will appeal to your target market. If your tours are aimed at the upper-crust set and feature European five-star hotels and tea with a Lord and Lady, your brochure, like your website, will need to reflect this ambience. You would use high-quality paper, photographs, and perhaps castles, crests, and heraldry sprinkled about on the pages. If your tours are targeted toward budget travelers, you could emphasize your cost-effective approach with a simpler design. If you are doing city walking tours or other day tours, you can get creative with a simple pamphlet that recreates the image you're selling. Digital cameras make it very easy to get the photos you want and download them for safekeeping and/or desktop publishing.

Even though most people think high gloss when they think brochure, you don't have to go with an expensive four-color masterpiece, especially not when you're starting out with just a few tour offerings and trying not to do further damage to the environment. Use your imagination liberally, instead of your wallet. Choose a light-colored card stock and one or two

Smart Tip *Tip...*

Have a trusted friend or family member proofread your brochure very carefully. Sometimes it's almost impossible to detect minor typos in your own work; and while computer programs that check spelling and grammar are helpful, they can sometimes miss the spelling of names, such as those of cities or even countries.

▲

bold, professional colors for your text. With the bounty of desktop publishing software out there, you can choose from a dazzling array of fonts, borders, and line art to jazz up your text. But don't sacrifice clarity for flashiness. A few graphics go a long way.

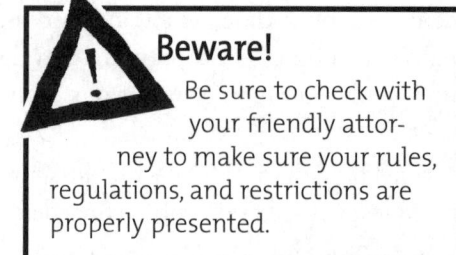

Beware!
Be sure to check with your friendly attorney to make sure your rules, regulations, and restrictions are properly presented.

- *Tempt with teasers.* Tease your potential customers with highlights of your tour's content, like this:
  - Take a ghostly walk through the most haunted hotel in Chicago.
  - Stroll our crystal shores and discover for yourself why Panama City Beach's Emerald Coast is called one of America's unsung scenic treasures.
  - Dine in candlelit splendor at a midnight supper with the master of the castle.
  - Relax, refresh, and revitalize your energies on our forest hikes for frazzled workaholics.
  - Think like you're writing a movie trailer or the blurb on the back of a best-selling book. Leave your client eager to experience the details, which he can only do by booking a tour!
  - Details, details. Don't forget the details! Make sure you explain where and when your tours take place and how they're priced.
- *Discounts and freebies.* Tempt them further with discounts for seniors, spouses, students, or groups; or with freebies like special tour tote bags, T-shirts, mementos, or some other giveaway.
- *Contact.* Put your address and phone number, along with your website and email address, on every page.
- *Drum roll to enroll.* Include your reservation form—the really important part!
- *Road rules.* Add in any regulations, restrictions, and information about insurance, refunds, exchanges, single supplements, and other rules of the road.

Advertising

Thanks to the advent of social media and more ways to present yourself on the internet (i.e., responding to blogs and talking about travel in forums and discussion groups), you can save some of the advertising dollars you may have once spent to grow your business. Additionally, travel is a word-of-mouth industry, meaning if someone enjoys their vacation, they will tell their friends and family.

Many travel businesses today do limited advertising. In fact, many travel agents do little more than place an annual ad in the local Yellow Pages. Nonetheless, you should have an idea of what the advertising process is all about, so you can selectively plan any ads you may be placing in the print media, on websites, or on the radio (TV is generally too costly).

The first thing to do when you start your advertising campaign is to take a figurative step back. Revisit your market research. You need to determine:

- Who are my potential customers? Do they travel for business or pleasure? Are they hard or soft adventurers? Physically challenged? Are they looking to sightsee or simply relax? Are they students, families, or seniors?
- How many are there?
- Where are they located?
- What are their priorities? Fine dining? Sticking to a tight budget?
- Where else might they find the travel products I want to provide?
- What can I offer that they're not already getting from other sources, such as the internet?
- How can I persuade them to purchase travel products from me or go on my tours?

Look over the answers to these questions—then ask yourself:

- What knowledge and skills do I offer?
- What image do I want to project?
- How do I compare with my competition and how can I be better?

Feature your benefits as often as you can; use different descriptions so they stick in your customer's mind. If you have testimonials, use them too. They lend credibility to your tours and your company, and they add another dimension to your copy by showing that it's not just you who thinks your products are great—it's other people, just like your prospects.

Whether you are hyping your services in your brochure, in a print ad, or on the internet, make sure your phone number and email address are clear and legible. If you've included a discount with a time element or a freebie, this is also the place to mention it.

The Personal Touch

When preparing a brochure or your web ads, try to incorporate these sales tips:

- Grab that prospect's attention. Remember to relate your content to your tours and packages and include how your business stands out from the crowd.

- Use time-proven winning words like "secret" and "free." Everybody wants to know a secret and everybody wants something for free! Like what? How about something like: "Discover the secret life of New York, the city that never sleeps!" or "Free fat-burning calculator when you enroll in our high-energy, low-fat cookery tour!"

> ### Bright Idea
> Try putting in a time element like "Order by June 14th to receive your 20 percent discount off the normal tour price of $999," or "Order by June 14th to receive your free companion guidebook." This lights a fire under your customer. She won't want to put off ordering because she'll lose out on the discount or freebie.

- Don't write for thousands of prospective clients. Write to just one, as though you're speaking to him or her personally.

- Save the flowery prose for that poetry contest. Instead, use everyday language for the average person.

- Focus on both the features and the benefits of your tours.

- Keep your materials clean and free of grammar and style errors. Have someone you trust as a spelling, punctuation, and grammar star check your work before you commit to a print run.

- Be concise—long-winded copy is no longer read. People are in a hurry today so make sure everything is easy to read and digest quickly.

A few other tricks of the trade include:

- *Time-dating your offers.* Say something like "If you respond within 30 days, you'll receive a free _____," or "This offer is good only through _____." This encourages your customers to book now instead of in the nebulous future.

- *Write riveting headlines.* Your brochure, web ad, or print ad must compete with all the others. Penning your headline before your text will help you focus on what basic need or desire your product satisfies.

- *Accent with artwork.* Illustrations and photos attract attention. If you use a caption under a picture, make sure it has sales value. People will read captions even when they don't have time to read the rest of the piece.

- *Help customers respond quickly.* Accept credit cards and toll-free calls. It's much easier for your customer to pay by credit card.

Mailing Lists

If you are going to do a direct mailing, remember, a mailing list can make or break a direct-mail campaign, and a good list can be very worthwhile. You can target your audience very effectively with a mailing list.

When you rent a mailing list, you want to have your audience targeted to a T. Therefore, you must select very carefully from whom you are renting. There are many legitimate mailing house providers along with many mailing houses that will sell dated lists or any lists they have available, whether they really fit your demographics or not. Get referrals from other businesses that have successfully conducted direct-mail campaigns.

You can specifically seek out the targeted group you would like . . . such as for those hiking and biking tours, you can choose Midwestern families who subscribe to health and fitness, or outdoor magazines. Or for those Maine sailing expeditions, you can get a listing of men in the New England area who buy marine equipment and earn over $50,000 per year.

Common Threads

In the mailing list world, there are two types of lists: the compiled list and the buyer or response list. A compiled list is made up of people with the common thread of belonging to a specific group or organization. For example, these could be members of alumnae organizations or car clubs; members of professional organizations from doctors to contractors; or even people who have attended different types of vacations, tours, seminars, or workshops. A compiled list can also be made up of people with certain demographic characteristics in common: those who are currently living in Manhattan, making more than $50,000 a year, and are between the ages of 45 and 60. You get the picture. The main point to remember with compiled lists is that unless you rent a list comprised of previous tour participants, you can't know that those doctors, contractors, or car aficionados have booked a tour or are likely to do so.

The other type of list—the buyer list—is the one you want to shoot for. Why? Because

> **Beware!**
> If you use testimonials, they must be from real people who have given their permission. Likewise, if you use other people's photos, make sure the photographer grants his or her OK to have them on your marketing materials. Also, make sure any people in your photos grant you the OK to use their images or you could get sued.

Finding Your Mailing List

Where exactly do you get your mailing lists?

○ Rent them from any number of list brokers, which you'll find in your local Yellow Pages under "Advertising—Direct Mail," within the pages of direct-marketing magazines like *Catalog Age* and *Target Marketing*, or from the internet. (We've provided the names of a few list brokers in the Appendix to get you started.)

○ Rent directly from associations whose members fit your target market.

○ Buy lists from a competitor who's gone out of business. This doesn't happen too often, but it is worth keeping an eye out for.

○ Build up your own list through extensive marketing.

---

the people on it are already known tour participants. They might be buyers of gourmet cooking tours, Amazon adventures, or Disney-mania programs. The main idea here is that since they've already booked a tour similar to yours, they're more likely to book yours, which may not be the case with people on compiled lists. This doesn't mean you should never use compiled lists. It does mean, though, that you should use them carefully. List brokers are experienced at this sort of thing, so let them advise you on what's best for your particular situation.

Salting the List

Notice we've referred to renting your lists, not buying them. This is how it's done in the direct-mail world. Unless you're swapping or purchasing outright, as we described above, you rent a one-time use of the list from the list broker. You're free to take any names that respond to your mailing and incorporate them into your very own house list, which you can use anytime you like. However, you can't use the rented list more than once, unless you rent it again.

How does the list broker or owner know if you decide to cheat? They salt in bogus names (for instance, their mother, brother, or dog) and addresses. Then, if Mom, Bubba, or Fido receives your mailing, you're caught. So don't try it.

The one-time rental fee for most lists runs from $100 to $150 per thousand names, and most list brokers insist you rent a minimum of 5,000 names. You'll also be charged

$5 to $10 extra for each selected, or special qualifier, that you choose (age, income, geographic region, etc.).

Remember, there are good list brokers and bogus ones. Don't assume everyone is on the level with current names and addresses—you'd be surprised at how many mailing lists were compiled ten years ago and are still for sale. Talk to other people who have used the mailing house.

The Golden Word

Most independent travel agents will agree that word-of-mouth is their absolute best advertising source. Of course, this doesn't just happen by chance. What does happen is that as a travel agent, you will need to get out and let people know about your business. For Jim and Nancy T., their business just sort of snowballed on its own. "One of the people we'd been cruising with became our first client, and it grew from there," Jim says. "Since both of us had worked in government agencies before, we had access to a large number of people."

Spreading the word means going to places where your demographic audience can be found and handing out fliers, sponsoring a local event, or setting up a booth at a local street fair. It means being visible with some literature about your tours, your cruises, and what it is that makes your travel agency worthy of their attention.

It also means establishing an ongoing rapport with your clients, which takes us back to the social media, where you can stay in touch on Facebook or with the occasional tweet. Don't forget to send birthday or anniversary wishes as well.

Print Ads

Along with spreading the word through networking, electronically, and by establishing a presence in your community, you can run print ads in local publications. Outside of the top major markets, newspaper advertising is typically within reason. Place ads during the times preceding peak travel months so that you can reach your target market when they are planning vacations. Also, look for the section in the newspaper, or a local magazine, where your ads will attract your target audience.

If, for example, you or your suppliers have a baseball stadium tour, start advertising prior to the April start of the major league season and place your ads in sports sections. If, however, your cruises serve a large family population, look for sections that appeal more to families. The right magazines can also be an excellent place to advertise.

▲

Barry S., the car race tour operator, found that advertising in magazines targeted to car and fishing buffs, respectively, works. Most industry insiders agree, however, that advertising in general consumer publications does not work. Why? Because, once again, you are not targeting your market.

You'll probably want to go with a display ad, the kind that usually features some sort of graphics combined with the printed word and is found throughout a publication— as opposed to classifieds which consist solely of the printed word and are found only in the classified section. Display ads in magazines can be very expensive and generally don't pull a significant response until they've run for several consecutive months.

Think carefully before you buy print ad space, and do your homework first. Get circulation numbers. Remember, a lot of newspapers and magazines are losing readers to the internet, so try to get bargain rates. Also, if the magazine or newspaper has a web presence, and most do these days, look to double up by advertising in print and on the publication's website.

Local Listings

Local giveaways, such as penny savers and community papers, are inexpensive means of advertising and getting your name out there. Look for papers that have columns listing travel options.

"People will save those papers for months, weeks, and even years," says Phil, the maven of walking guides. So readers who might not show up for tomorrow's tour may become die-hard groupies at a later date.

Phil advises compiling a slate of your local papers, then finding out who the editor is and submitting a listing every month. Make sure you check ahead to find out when they need the listing; it may be as much as two or three weeks before the date you want your material published. For instance, if you're doing special Halloween ghost walks, you may need to get your information in by early October.

And don't forget about those target markets.

Convention and visitors bureaus can be great places with which to establish relationships. If they can list your business or refer business to you, that is a big plus.

> **Smart Tip** Tip...
>
> Conventions and seminars can be very fruitful places to network. While travel conventions and seminars will provide you with information, other such gatherings typically have people standing around, with nametags, looking to strike up a conversation. If you can meet other new entrepreneurs, such as yourself, you can impress upon them that their growing companies will likely need someone to handle their travel needs.

Current Customers

To quote the title of a Simon & Garfunkel song, "Keep the Customer Satisfied." Most businesses, including travel agencies like yours, will do the majority of their business with existing customers. It is estimated that 80 percent of business (in general) will be from repeat customers. If people have a great vacation thanks to your efforts, they will come back again. In addition, they will tell friends and family, since travel choices are often based on the word-of-mouth recommendations of others. Therefore, your happy customers are your best sales force.

It also helps to create an incentive for your customers to refer a friend and watch your business grow. For example, you might offer a frequent traveler program with points not only accrued for travel purchased but also for referring business to you. Gift cards are very popular today, so you might offer them to such places as Barnes and Noble or Starbucks. Giving a $20 gift card to the referring customer is always a nice touch and something that everyone can enjoy. It is not as if you are buying referrals, but instead you are thanking your existing customers for their business and support for your business.

> ## Bright Idea
>
> Add in a coupon to be redeemed for a discount. It's a cool way to keep your clients reading through your newsletter and eagerly anticipating the next one.

Email Newsletters

Printed newsletters have all but vanished these days, with the exception of those for longtime membership groups with a relatively small circulation. Print newsletters are easy to make on your own computer, but are not necessarily cost effective to mail out. For that reason, and to get them in the hands of your clients quickly, you may elect to send email newsletters.

An email newsletter takes on the same general premise as a traditional newsletter—providing information that your clients want to read about, or "content" as it's called. This can come in the form of one or two short articles, perhaps a couple of paragraphs each. You do not need to fill nearly as much space with an e-newsletter as you would with a printed one. The idea is to grab the reader's attention with a headline and provide content about travel—not just a list of promotions, but some quality content. You can then put all of your ads and promotions around the travel-related articles. There's plenty of material to choose from. If, for example, you primarily book travel cruises, you could offer: "Ten Packing Tips for a Caribbean Cruise" or "The Latest in Cruise Dining Options, Which Is Right For You?" As long as you give them some interesting content to look at, they won't delete your email and will instead read the content and see your promotions all around it. Of course you need to keep in mind that people won't scroll down endlessly, so don't overdo it.

It's a good idea to stockpile story ideas as you go through your daily business routine. Set up an envelope, and every time you see something that might be the germ of an idea for a short newsletter story, write it down and put it in the envelope or save it on your computer.

> **Bright Idea**
>
> Can't afford that magazine advertising? Try a trade-out. Offer that publication a free product in exchange for advertising; for example, a three-day cruise or tour they can use as an incentive.

Final note, make sure your newsletter is permission based, meaning that people say "yes" they want to receive it after seeing the offer on your website or your Facebook page. Don't trick people into receiving it; instead get their email in some legitimate manner for permission-based emails. Also, in the "From" line, make sure it consistently says the name of your business. People tend to delete emails very quickly from places they do not know.

Reasons for sending an e-newsletter include:

1. Keeping your name and the delights of travel in your clients' minds.
2. Keeping your clients up-to-date on your latest products and tempting them with specials or discounts.
3. Making your clients feel special! You've remembered them and added them onto your "exclusive" list.

And since your email newsletter is about travel, by all means include photos—just make sure you have permission from the supplier or photographer to do so, unless you took them yourself.

Listings and Free Advertising

There's an old cliché: "There's no such thing as a free lunch." However, there are some terrific things you can do to get free advertising. Naturally, you have to put forth effort, intelligence, and creativity; so it's not "free" as in easy—but the rewards are worth it.

So what are these free advertising opportunities? One is word-of-mouth, which we have already mentioned on several occasions. You can enhance word-of-mouth by letting your satisfied customers advertise for you by providing T-shirts, caps, and other accoutrements with your business name.

You can also take advantage of the thousands of available magazines, journals, and websites by writing articles or blogs. People do not always give ads a second glance,

See and Be Seen

The place to be seen for specialty tours is *Specialty Travel Index*, a biannual magazine that, in addition to editorial features, allots space for more than 500 adventure and special interest tour operators to strut their stuff.

The magazine also offers travel stories, travel links, a newsletter, and more. You can try it out at www.specialtytravel.com to see if it can benefit you.

but they do read articles and blogs. Many small publications and/or websites are in constant need of content, and if you're willing to write articles about travel, or offer some tips for travelers, such publications are often happy to use them. Once you start getting published, your credibility as a travel expert will soar along with the desirability of your products. Remember to make what you write read like an article and not like hype, which will look like an ad—and people will stop reading. A good article will get torn out by readers and passed along to friends or a good blog might be forwarded to friends. Ads don't have the same pass-along (or viral) marketing possibilities.

You can volunteer to write a travel column for little or even no pay for a local magazine or newspaper. You can also put your name and bio in front of any travel show producers on radio, internet radio, or TV. Get your name out and about as an expert in your area of travel. Many local YMCAs as well as schools have evening seminars. Offer to teach one on how to travel for less or how to get the most out of a cruise or anything you do that puts you in front of an audience that includes your target market group. Travel websites and those associated with travel organizations and associations also offer webinars—again, offer to run one.

The best thing to do is look at the magazines and websites that fit your niche market. Then contact the editor by email (preferred these days) and find out if they would be interested in an article on whatever it is you want to talk about. Send them a short "pitch" telling them in a paragraph or two what you want to write about and who you are. Explain why you are an expert in this area.

If you elicit interest, if they are not sure, but interested in the topic, send a one-page query letter enticing them with the key points that you will include in such a story or

> **Tip...**
>
> **Smart Tip**
> Make it easy for anyone who reads your article or blog to contact you. Most publications will let you add an endnote that says: "For more information or for a free tip sheet, call, or email so and so."

a blog. Keep it brief and to the point—also sell them on why it's a great idea for THEIR readers. While you want to get business from the story, you have to remember that the web or publication editor has to please their audience. If they are interested in the article, then ask about the word count and due date and write the story. There's your free advertising. As a bonus, they may pay you for your piece. So not only is the advertising free, but they're paying you for the privilege!

Smart Tip **Tip...**

You can also write articles for the in-house publications or newsletters of client corporations and associations. You may or may not get paid, but you will keep your name uppermost in their minds.

Travel Writers

Another terrific way to get your name out there in print at no cost is through journalists and bloggers who are looking for quotes for stories they may be working on. Network and find writers (travel or other journalists) with whom you can leave your card and remind them periodically with an email that you are still out there for the next time they are working on travel stories. You may also sign up with places such as Help a Reporter Out (HARO) at Helpareporter.com or ReporterConnection.com, both of which send out emails three times a day with listings of reporters, bloggers, and other writers looking for people with specific expertise that they can interview. Therefore, if someone is looking to interview an expert on travel to Japan and you book trips there on a regular basis, you should respond and let the person know you'd be delighted to be quoted in their story or on their blog.

You should also check out what the North American Travel Journalists Association (www.natja.org) has to offer. A convention or seminar might be a great place to meet travel writers. Additionally, you can gather information on what is hot and being covered by the leading travel writers.

Be leery of people looking to strike deals with you for freebies. Most legitimate journalists want to remain objective and can't do so if you are bartering with them.

Public Relations

In the travel industry, public relations is an important component of doing business successfully. Good public relations can accomplish two things:

1. It can put your company name out to people who may not otherwise have heard of you.

2. It can keep people who are already your customers thinking fondly of you and thus create repeat bookings.

In other words, PR is another potentially terrific source of free advertising. There are all sorts of low-cost techniques you can use. Try some of the following:

- *Find a local group looking for guest speakers.* Offer yourself on a free, or pro bono, basis to local associations or clubs that match your target audience. If you are selling local walking tours, you can talk to women's groups, men's clubs, business groups from the Jaycees to the chamber of commerce to various networking clubs, and even kids' clubs. Just be sure to tailor your topic to your particular audience.

- *Join any organizations that match your target audience.* Volunteer for things that will get you and your company recognized and well thought of. Most people respect volunteers within an organization and consider them experts in the organization's area of interest, which heightens your credibility.

- *Go on the radio, or even on TV.* Volunteer yourself for a local radio station's chat show. You can discuss your niche, be it local walking tours, fun for the business traveler, or the new face of soft-adventure travel or cruising. Listeners can call in with questions. When they talk to you—on the air!—they'll be interested in booking your products. They may also ell their friends and relatives, which means more word-of-mouth advertising for you. Internet radio is growing in popularity, so look for internet radio stations that have shows on travel.

Walking Ads

Those T-shirts or hats imprinted with your company logo can also be a good source of advertising, especially if you're offering products like half-day tours in a tourist-heavy area. Potential customers will see other people walking around wearing your ads, and if they look trendy enough, some will simply want to wear one as well. All this advertising will result in calls to inquire about your tours.

Before trying this one on for size, make sure you can buy the T-shirts inexpensively enough and—at least for starters—in small enough quantities that they don't break your piggybank. Dr. Phil S., in New York City, sells T-shirts for $6 each to go along with his Brooklyn Bridge walk. Since he pays $2.50 for them, it's a good deal—for his tourists and for him.

As always, do your homework. Take your own walk around town and scout out how many "walking ads" you see. Analyze what makes them work and what doesn't.

▲

- *Go on web chats and discussion boards and talk about travel.* Then let it be known that you have a travel business.

Press Releases

Once you have done some research and located the travel editors and travel writers in your area, you can then update them periodically on news from your company. This need not be earthshaking, but simply something that might grab their attention and keep your name in front of the media.

Press releases should be no more than one page, featuring an attention-grabbing title, a paragraph or two that sparks the attention of the reader and provides the who, what, where, and when of your news story with some pertinent details. Another paragraph should be a "boilerplate," which is a short paragraph that you can re-use often describing your business, including when it was formed, your specialty or niche, and a few key facts or accomplishments. If you send press releases out to your press contact list once a month, you can keep your name in their minds. Look for interesting angles and lead into your first paragraph with your "hook." For example: Headline:

Rolando's Wine Presents Tours of the Hidden Valley Vineyards

First sentence:

Wine enthusiasts are invited to take a special afternoon tour of the Hidden Valley's unique vineyards, followed by a rare look inside Da' Macios Winery.

You would then describe the tour, the vineyards, and the winery in a few brief, inspiring sentences followed by the paragraph on your business. Finally, you include your business and contact information.

Press releases are often tossed, or deleted, by editors and producers, but the more you send with interesting potential stories, the better chance you have of them writing about your latest news in one of their columns.

Hint: Find out the person who might be most receptive to your press release at a publication or website, so you don't waste anyone else's time. Get their email address—then email your press release. Don't be discouraged, since many people will simply delete such press releases unless your timing is good and they are looking for a story or unless your headline and news item really strike them. Sometimes tying into something going on in the news can be helpful, so pay attention to current events and popular trends. Also, make the story something that is newsworthy to the publication's readers—self-indulgence, such as posts by people on Facebook about what they had for lunch that day—does not work for promoting a business. So think about what will benefit the readers.

Controlling Your Finances

Maintaining control of your finances and staying up-to-date on your numbers is essential to running any successful business. Financial awareness will let you know whether you can afford to buy new office equipment or you should make do with your current printer for a few more months. It will give you an idea of how much is coming in and where you need to cut back if necessary.

"Crunch those numbers," urges Karen A. in Savannah, Georgia. "We do spreadsheets at the end of every month. You need to analyze everything to find out where you're making money, where you're losing it, and to answer questions [like]: What will your revenues be next year? Is this type of tour more profitable than that one? What will happen to cash flow in February if ski season is slow? What proportion of proposals actually converts into tours?"

These are among the many questions you'll want to figure out from your financials. To make your life easier, there are a variety of software programs that can tell you where the numbers should go and help you calculate all kinds of totals. But only you can make decisions based on the numbers. And having an accountant or someone with expertise in the area of finance is important in any type of business.

Making a Statement

An income statement, also called a profit-and-loss statement, charts the revenues and operating costs of your business over a specific period of time, usually a month.

You'll want to tailor your income statement to your particular business. Remember that to make the statement work for you, you'll need to pro-rate items that are paid annually, such as business licenses, and pop those figures into your monthly statement. For example, if you pay annual insurance premiums of $600, divide this figure by 12 and add the resulting $50 to your monthly insurance expense, even if you're not paying it on a monthly basis. Knowing the monthly costs helps you balance your budget.

Figuring Out Profits

Let's look at how much you can expect to make, which means figuring out how to price your services. Warning: This section contains actual math problems.

Travel Agency Pricing

As a specialty travel agent, you have three basic ways to earn revenue:

1. Sell products for which the supplier has already set a price and for which you will receive commissions from suppliers or from your host agency.
2. Buy packaged tours at wholesale prices and then mark them up.

3. Create your own packages and price them with enough markup to make money, but not to the point where your packages will not be competitive.

Put Yourself into Commission

The first method—selling prepriced products for a commission—requires the least computing and is pretty simple. Say you sell a "Mayan Magic" Mexican tour that's priced at $1,500 double occupancy and carries a 10 percent commission. Tours and cruises base their fees on double occupancy rates, which is another way of saying "times two." If the brochure says $1,500 per person, look for the small print that also says "double occupancy" and multiply that price by two. If your client is traveling alone, he or she must pay a single supplement, usually up to another 50 percent of the "per person" rate.

The price for your clients that bought the "Mayan Magic" tour is $3,000, and the tour operator pays a $300 commission (10 percent of the $3,000 price tag). As discussed earlier, if you have a direct relationship with the tour supplier, you will typically get a 10 percent commission.

If, however, you are working with a host agency, they will likely get a 15 percent commission as a preferred supplier. Host agencies then typically give you from 70 to 90 percent commission. Therefore, the 15 percent commission of $3,000 is $450. Let's say your deal is an 80/20 split with the host agency. Now, you get 80 percent of the $450 or $360, or $60 more than you would likely get on your own. For this reason, as discussed way back in the early part of the book, host agencies (even after they take their cut) can very often get you more money than working directly with travel suppliers. However, once you establish yourself, that will typically change as your volume of bookings and commissions goes up. If this is confusing, re-read; we'll wait.

To determine what your annual income will be, you need to look at how much inventory you can move in a year. Inventory essentially refers to hotel, cruise, and/or resort accommodations. In nontravel lingo, that means the number of tours, cruises and/or other travel products you can sell. As a newbie, this can be difficult. If you've never sold even one product, how can you know how many you'll do over the course of a year?

The answer lies in your market research. You go by what your homework has shown your prospective clients will be willing to purchase, and by what others with similar businesses are doing. You'll also need to base your figures on how hard you plan to work. The travel specialist who knocks herself out to identify clients, make sales, and satisfy her clients' needs is going to earn a lot more in revenues than the one who dabbles.

Your Monthly Income Statement

For the month of _____

Monthly Income

    Gross Monthly Income $_____

Monthly Expenses

    Rent $_____

    Phone/utilities   _____

    Employees   _____

    Postage   _____

    Licenses   _____

    Legal services   _____

    Advertising/promotions   _____

    Accounting services   _____

    Office supplies   _____

    Transportation & travel   _____

    Insurance   _____

    Subscriptions/dues   _____

    Loan repayment   _____

    Miscellaneous   _____

    Total Monthly Expenses $_____

Net Monthly Profit $_____

Be conservative in your estimates at first, and don't fret. New businesses can easily take one to three years to make any significant profits. Also, remember, the more satisfied clients you have, the less you will need to depend heavily on marketing to new customers. One of the reasons social marketing has taken off and is such a boon for the homebased entrepreneur is that along with your website, it can save you a lot of money when trying to reach out to your potential market. The cost of brochures and mailings is far less than it was even a few years ago thanks to the internet and the ability to use Facebook, tweets, texts, and emails to connect and interact with your clients.

> **Bright Idea**
>
> Some travel agents supplement their earnings by selling travel-related products and services, from luggage and luggage tags to house-sitting services, travel guidebooks, and other merchandise. Don't forget that you will typically have to pay sales tax in most states, but it is another way to build an income stream.

Figure out which methods of marketing are most effective and stick with them.

Connie G., who specializes in travel for Christians and the physically challenged, personally makes about 100 bookings (or reservations) per year. A booking is not necessarily per person—one booking can encompass a single traveler, a party of two, a party of five, or the entire cast and crew of a Broadway road show. When Connie adds in the bookings sold by her outside agents, she averages about 150 per year.

Let's say that, over the course of a year, you'll sell 150 "Mayan Magic" tours and on the average there are two people per tour (some singles and some families, but primarily couples). Now, you have put 300 people on the tour at $3,000 per person, or booked $900,000 in Mayan Magic tours. The commission, as a preferred supplier through the host agency, is 15 percent, so they receive $135,000 in commissions. If your cut is 70 percent then you've made $94,500. Of course you will need to subtract your business expenses before you determine your profit, but you get the idea.

Get It for Them Wholesale

The second method of earning revenue as a travel agent is to buy products from wholesalers and then sell them to your clients at a markup. When you sell a pre-priced, commissionable product, such as a tour, you send the client's payment directly to the supplier. Aside from expenses like advertising, it doesn't cost you anything to sell the product. But when you sell a wholesale product, you must first purchase the product yourself, then turn around and resell it to the client. Obviously, you'll need more money in the bank for this type of booking. The problem with this type of booking today is that your discounted travel product may be equally attractive online.

▲

Therefore, it's hard to mark up something that travelers know they can find for less. To do this successfully, you need to get discounts on travel products not readily found on the myriad of internet discount travel sites, or compete with a site of your own, offering something more for the extra money. Of course volume also works, but it takes time to build up. If you booked all of those Mayan tours mentioned earlier directly through your own relationship with the travel supplier, he or she will likely land you a wholesale discount and even make you a preferred customer the following year. Buying wholesale and selling typically takes establishing yourself in the business, knowing where to find great deals, and having positive cash flow.

When Jennifer Doncsecz of VIP Vacations Inc. books destination weddings at fabulous resorts, the resort owners know her, know she's booking a sizable number of guests, and give her great deals. "We try to impress upon couples that they're not paying for our services; the resort or tour operators give us the commissions. Because of our deals with the resorts we can offer them (our clients) so much more. If, for example, they look at a resort for $400 a night and then at our resorts for $400, they're getting so much more for the same price," explains Doncsecz of how building a relationship with a supplier can benefit you as a travel specialist.

Something Fishy in Scotland

Let's say you've found a "Go Fish! Scotland" package that sounds like just the ticket for your clients, the fly-fishing fiends. You can purchase it from the wholesaler for $980.

Now, here's how you figure out how much to mark it up. First, do a bit of reverse engineering and decide how much you need to make. At the very least, you've got to have $980 to pay yourself back for the price of the product. Then decide what other costs you'll incur. If you do a special giveaway on your Facebook page that

Lower Costs

Not long ago, direct mailings, print ads, and flashy brochures forced agents to mark up their products because of the added expense. Today, thanks to technology, you can spend almost nothing, beyond your monthly web costs (which are minimal), to spread the word about your new tours. While you can't be sure how much income a tour will bring, it's much easier to run new products up the flagpole and see if there is interest without incurring expenses.

Estimating Your Annual Gross Revenue

Use this worksheet to help you calculate your annual gross revenue for pre-priced commissionable products.

1. Choose a product you think you'll sell fairly often.

    $_____ Fill in the sales price of the product.

    _____ x 2 Multiply by two for double occupancy

    $_____ This is the price your client will pay for this product.

2. Now take the client's price tag and multiply it by 10 percent, which is what most tour and cruise suppliers pay as a commission.

    $_____ Price to your client

    _____ x 10%

    $_____ This is the total commission on this product.

3. Determine what your commission split will be with your host agency. Most outside agents start off with a 70/30 percent or 80/20 percent split.

    $_____ Fill in the total commission on this product.

    _____ x ( )% Multiply by the split you expect to receive from your host agency.

    $_____ This is your commission on this product.

4. Estimate how many products of this type you'll sell in a year.

    $_____ Fill in your commission for this product.

    _____ x ___ Multiply by the number of like products you expect to sell in a year.

    $_____ This is your annual gross revenue.

costs you $500, you'll need to consider how much that will add to each sale. Now add in a 50 percent markup (another $490), and you'll charge your client $1,470, $490 of which is a profit. If you sell 20 packages at this price, you'll earn actual profits of $9,800 ($490 times 20) less the $500 for your online giveaway, which leaves you with $9,300. Or you can lower your markup to 25 percent ($245) and sell each product for $1,225, which will earn you $4,900 in profit ($245 times 20) less $500 or $4,400.

Before marketing such a deal, however, you need to know the going rate for such a trip. Therefore, you need to look at what your competitors are charging. If other travel agents are selling the same, or an equivalent trip, for $1,400, your $1,470 deal will fall flat—unless you can offer something more without raising your cost very much. Think of intangibles, of services you can provide and freebies you can throw in that can make your package worth another $70. Customized/personal service and attention is often worth more to discerning clients, but sometimes it's not so obvious—meaning you need to sell your abilities or lower your prices. Remember, pricing is always in line with what the market rate is for goods and services. Therefore, you need to constantly monitor other prices and see if you are in the ballpark. You also need to monitor how well sales of a tour to a specific destination, or of a specific niche, are going.

> **Smart Tip** Tip...
>
> Get your clients a better room rate by asking about discounts off the rack rate. Hotels often give discounts for corporate or other business travelers, seniors, military personnel, members of the Automobile Association of America, and even members of discount clubs like Sam's Club or Costco. But they won't offer the discount unless you ask!

Sell the Big-Ticket Items!

To make more money, what's a savvy travel agent to do? Sell those higher-ticket, higher-income products. It may take a bit more time and effort to send your clients off on a $10,000 tour of Tuscany, but once you get the hang of it, the difference in time and effort isn't all that great. So as long as you're putting forth the effort, you might as well work smart instead of just hard, and go for the gold. That being said, don't completely overlook the "discount customers" that come to you looking for a good deal.

The More the Merrier

Booking groups on tours and cruises makes your income merrier. You could send one couple on a Tahitian holiday cruise or do the same amount of research, set up a tour package, and promote it to groups. The more cabins on a cruise or rooms at a resort you can book the more money you will make and the more you will establish a relationship with the supplier(s). VIP Vacations Inc., for example, makes more money booking destination weddings, with a number of rooms booked in one shot, than it would just booking honeymoons, which it also handles.

There are, however, all sorts of permutations here. If everybody decides to go for the least expensive cabin category and the early booking fare, your per-couple price will drop considerably. Of course, you need to figure in markup and make sure that however you do it, the package is worth your time and effort.

So encourage those group bookings. Ask your clients if they have friends or relatives who might like to go along. Group bookings can focus on families or they can encompass any size group from three couples to clubs of 50 individuals or more. "We do a lot of group business that are repeat groups," says Jim T., the cruise specialist. "Each time we do one, we build a little more business for the next time."

Try it yourself. Actively solicit groups of all kinds—mystery or romance writers, bridge clubs, garden clubs, RV clubs, networking groups, singles groups, and various associations. Use your imagination and get those groups fired up!

Commission Time

The other commission payment question, besides "How much," is "When?" What's the timetable for getting all those lovely, fat commission checks? Again, it depends on your host agency, on the suppliers, and on how much effort you put into the mix. Today, as Tom Ogg points out earlier in the book, electronic deposits and services such as Paypal make it much easier to handle settlements, or payments.

Of course, you need to understand that you won't get that check the second you give the supplier your client's credit card number. So if you're sending someone on a FIT (foreign independent tour) of France three months from now, and you've booked her five nights at a hotel room in Nice where she'll arrive in three months, you won't enter the hotel commission picture until then, since she can cancel. Tours and cruises don't generally pay commissions on bookings until after the final payment is received and the tour or cruise has been taken.

This may sound strange, but if you think about it, it makes sense. In the same way that a real estate agent doesn't get his commission until after the house has closed escrow and all monies have changed hands between buyer and seller, a travel agent doesn't get paid until the travel is a done deal. Otherwise, if the client backs out of the deal and the agent has already been paid, the supplier is going to have a hard time getting its money back. So they withhold it until they're assured they've been paid.

Greater Rewards

It's nice to sell your clients the highest-priced package on a tour or cruise—you reap higher revenues. But saving your clients money on a package can ultimately lead to far greater rewards.

"When a client does a booking," Jim T. says, "we don't forget about them until it's time for final payment. We continue to monitor all our bookings. If there's an unannounced special or a price reduction in some way, the client may never know, but we look for it and then pass it on. We had a client who went on an Alaskan cruise. We found a special that ended up saving them $1,350 over what they thought they were going to pay. We didn't have to tell them, but we did, and it turned into a number of referrals from that client."

What more could a travel agent ask? When you pass along "windfall" cost savings, that original client is likely to be yours for life—and so are all those referrals.

If you'll be acting as a tour operator, take heed! Make sure your travelers have followed through before you pay travel agents. But don't drag your feet, either.

Slow to Pay

Some suppliers are very slow payers. The hotel industry, in fact, has had a notorious reputation for "losing" commissions. That, however, has changed in recent years. Nonetheless, read travel agent-oriented websites, e-newsletters, and magazines, and you will see lots of hotel ads that proudly proclaim, "Agents paid promptly."

You may also find articles and/or blogs about suppliers that are slow to pay.

Tour operators who are living on the financial edge may also have a difficult time coughing up the commissions. Sometimes, perfectly respectable suppliers honestly lose commissions in their computer systems, or in the mail. Talk with or email other travel agents and get the lowdown on suppliers and hotels.

Tour operators, take heed again. If you drag out paying travel agents, sooner or later they'll stop sending business your way. Develop and maintain a reputation of paying commissions as promptly as possible, and they'll reward you with increased sales.

Spiffy Promotions

The travel world operates under the same laws of human behavior as the rest of the known universe. One of those laws is that people perform better when given incentives. Understanding this, travel suppliers frequently offer bonuses, freebies, prizes, contests, sweepstakes, and whatever other perks they can dream up.

Just how spiffy are these spiffs, as they are often called? They can be mildly enticing or terrifically motivating, depending on the supplier, the promotion, and what you think is worth working for. Sometimes suppliers will offer a specific monetary bonus—say $10 or $50—for every booking made within a certain time period. Sometimes the spiff is an off-the-chart commission rate during a specific time period. Or, instead of monetary awards, a promotion might offer vouchers that you redeem for your own free travel.

Selling a certain number of hotel bookings might entitle you to a drawing for a free week at the chain's Cancun property. All six members of the VIP Vacations Inc. staff now drive around in brand-new cars thanks to the folks at Sandals and Beaches who sent the cars (with Sandals wraps) as a way to say thank you for so many bookings.

Of course, a down economy may limit the incentives that some businesses can offer—but the hope is that what goes down will go up again and the economy will eventually turn back around.

Tour Operator Pricing

As a specialty tour operator, you'll be looking at pricing from a different perspective by creating your own packages, which is the third of the three ways of earning revenue. One major factor in setting prices is just what sort of tour you'll offer. A half-day walking tour of your hometown is much easier to price than an all-inclusive motor coach and museum extravaganza in a foreign country.

Pirates for Lunch

Let's start with the easy one and say you're doing a half-day tour of Panama City Beach, Florida, that you'll call "The Pirate Walk." It begins with an Alligator Breakfast in St. Andrews State Park, takes participants on a two-hour nature walk along the crystal sands, and concludes with a boat trip to Shell Island for a Pirate's Picnic Lunch. Take a look at "How to Price a Half-Day Tour" on page 240 for an idea of how to price your tour and how much you can expect to make.

Keep in mind that the $79,200 you see at the bottom as annual revenue for "The Pirate Walk" represents an estimate. You are planning on 20 participants as your ideal number per tour. If you only get 10 people on some of your tours—or only five!—your bottom line will sink like Blackbeard stepping into quicksand.

You will also have to account for operating expenses, such as advertising and insurance. What about special equipment like a chest for the pirate's treasure, and food coolers and warmers? Since you'll buy those only once (or at least only once every few years), those go into your startup costs. Keep in mind, too, that you may want to do more than "The Pirate's Walk." If you're a major go-getter, you might opt for an evening tour in season, something like a "Crystal Sands Sunset Walk and Fish Fry." This will add additional revenue to your annual income.

Antarctic to Zimbabwe

If you do decide to go for the 14-day motor coach extravaganza—say, a safari in Zimbabwe, or a tour of the Falklands and the Antarctic, for example—your pricing strategy will be the same. Make sure you factor in every detail and get good solid price estimates. Small elements as well as large ones can throw off your profit margin if you ignore, or forget about, them.

Lots of Possibilities

You may include some, or most, of the following items in your pricing, depending on the type of tours you will be offering to your customers:

- *Transportation on the tour*. Have all your transportation worked out in advance, as part of your package. Be flexible, as you may need to increase the number of vehicles or make changes depending on the number of travelers you can book. You may also have to make changes based on other factors, such as the weather.

- *Parking fees or tolls*. Factor these into your rate.

- *Hotel rooms*. Add accommodation costs for participants—don't forget to divide by two for double occupancy! You'll also need to figure in the cost of having rooms for your driver(s) and tour conductor(s).

- *Luggage handling*. Find out what it will cost to transport your clients' personal belongings and your tour equipment, and factor this cost into your price.

- *Meals*. If you have planned meal packages, factor this into your rates and don't forget to include feeding your driver and tour conductor.

- *Parties*. Also account for the cost of hosting a welcome/reception party, or a farewell party for your participants.

- *Admission*. Be sure to include any admission fees (per person) for attractions that your tour may include.

- *Salary*. Figure in salaries for your driver and tour conductor—unless, of course, it's you.
- *Tack on 10 percent assuming that something will come up*. This may be something that you have not factored in, a rate that may have gone up, or any such extra cost. Therefore, if your costs for the entire package come to $3,000, make it $3,300 before you decide to hike it up to $4,500 or $5,000 so you can make a profit. Again, a lot will depend on how competitive your price is in the market.

The Tax Man Cometh

When you earn money from your wisely planned and brilliantly executed travel sales and products, someone will be queuing up for a piece of the action: That someone is Uncle Sam. Therefore, you should also have an accountant factored into your budget. You won't need him or her for your daily or monthly concerns, but it is worth the expense to have someone in the know at the reins when it comes to April 15, or for those panicking questions that come up now and again. Of course, as someone who is running your own business, you can spread out your estimated tax payments to minimize a large one-time payment.

Your tax deductions should be about the same as those for any other small or homebased business. You can deduct a percentage of your home office, as noted earlier, as long as you are using it solely as an office. These deductions include all normal office expenses, plus interest, taxes, insurance, and depreciation (this is where the accountant comes in handy). The IRS has added in all sorts of permutations such as: The total amount of the deduction is limited by the gross income you derive from the business activity, minus all your other business expenses (apart from those related to the home office).

Basically, the IRS doesn't want you to come up with so many home office deductions that you end up paying no tax at all.

Also make it clear that those you hire to run your tours, as tour guides, bus drivers, or people who do any other jobs, are freelancers or independent contractors and not full-time employees. If, however, you hire full-timers to work for you as staffers, then let that be known as well. The IRS is strict about whom you consider an employee and whom you hire as a freelancer

Dollar Stretcher

You may be able to get meals for your driver and tour conductor comped, which means the restaurant or hotel will feed them for free as a way to say thank you for the tour business you bring in.

How to Price a Half-Day Tour

Take a look at the following calculation of the price to charge for a half-day tour and the projected gross annual revenue that will be earned.

1. Park entrance fee per person $6.00

2. Breakfast per person (provided by local restaurant) $5.00

3. Walk led by you $0.00

4. Boat trip per person (chartered by local outfitter) $8.00

5. Picnic lunch per person (provided by local restaurant) $8.00

6. Pirate's treasure (candy and trinkets) per person $5.00

    Total tour expenses per person $32.00

7. Add 50 percent markup $16.00

    Your price per person $48.00

8. Multiply your price per person by the number of expected participants.

   $48.00 x 20 = $960.00 (your gross earnings each time you run your tour)

9. Multiply your expenses per person by the number of expected participants.

   $30.00 x 20 = $600.00 (your costs each time you run your tour)

10. Subtract your costs from your gross earnings.

    $960.00 – $600.00 = $360.00 (your earnings per tour)

11. Multiply your earnings per tour by the number of days you expect to run it per week.

    $360.00 x 10 (two tours, five days a week = $3,600 per week)

12. Multiply your earnings by the number of weeks you expect to run the tour per year.

    $3,600 x 22 (you're accounting for the seasonal nature of beach visitors, May-September)= $79,200 (your gross annual revenue from this tour)

How to Price a Half-Day Tour, continued

You may need to factor in extra costs for rainy days or other expenses that may cut into your profit and assume that you will probably end up with $75,000.

While this is a half-day tour sample, full-day tours or weeklong tours operate under the same principles. Gather all your costs first, get a total, and determine your markup to get your price. Then look to see if your price is competitive within the marketplace—if it is, start marketing; if not, see where you can cut costs by getting better deals or altering the package.

to do a job for your business. For example, are you providing the sole income of the employee? Do you mandate his or her schedule? Does he or she have several other employers? The IRS website at www.irs.gov will help you with tax questions and designations of employees so you do not get into hot water.

What else can you deduct?

- Business-related phone calls
- Business equipment and supplies (again, as long as you are truly using them solely for your business)
- Subscriptions to professional and trade journals
- Auto expenses, when you drive your trusty vehicle in the course of doing business or seeking business

In other words, you are chalking up deductible mileage every time you motor out to meet with clients, deliver tickets, give a travel talk or seminar, visit printers, or take a spin upstate to check out suppliers' products.

It's wise to keep a log of your business miles. You can buy one of several varieties at your local office supply or stationers, or you can make one yourself. Keep track as you go. It's no fun to have to backtrack at tax time and guesstimate how many miles you drove to which clients and when.

You also can deduct entertainment expenses, such as wining and dining a client during the course of a meeting, or hosting potential clients at a coffee hour. Keep a log of all these expenses as well, especially if they come to under $75 a pop since you don't technically need to keep receipts for these. If you're entertaining at home, have your clients or customers sign a guest book.

▲

You must have a business-related purpose for entertaining, such as a sales presentation. General goodwill toward your potential customers or suppliers doesn't cut it, so be sure your log contains the reason for the partying.

When you travel for business purposes, you can deduct airfares, train tickets, rental car mileage, and the like. You can also deduct hotels and meals, and, under certain circumstances, you can even deduct recreational side trips you take with your family while you're traveling on business. Since the IRS allows deductions for any such trip you take to expand your awareness and expertise in your field of business, it makes sense to also take advantage of any conferences or seminars that you can attend.

In the end, when it comes to taking deductions, use common sense.

15

Flying High or Bailing Out

Most people succeed in the travel business by combining the tried-and-true business methods of persistence and plain old-fashioned hard work with a healthy dose of optimism. If we've illustrated anything in this book, we hope that it is this: Becoming a successful travel professional involves lots of effort. It can be very rewarding and sometimes a lot of fun.

We also hope we've managed to convey that becoming a travel professional is not the same as becoming an overnight success. It takes careful market research, a lot of planning, and the ability to network, meet people, and build relationships with a host agency, suppliers, and your clients. Remember, 80 percent of your business will come from repeat clients and/or their family and friends.

Love and Homework

When the travel professionals interviewed for this book were asked for some words of advice for beginners, they gave—not surprisingly—some very thoughtful responses. "Do your homework," says Jim T., the Maryland-based cruise specialist. "Set yourself up to be knowledgeable before you talk to your first client. Don't think you're going to start out, open your door, call yourself a travel agency, and then wait for people to come to you." Roberta E., the Georgia-based cruise specialist, echoed this sentiment. "If you're going to have a host agency," she says, "research, research, and just keep learning and attending seminars. Keep up-to-date on everything that goes on in this particular industry. The more you know, the more it's going to help you."

Margie Jordan, who runs JETS & ASAP travel, is a big believer in doing research. "If someone emails or tweets me, I go to my information about them, and if I've worked with them before I can see if they recently had an anniversary so I can wish them a happy anniversary when I get on the phone with them," Jordan says. "I can also see if they opened an email I sent them about visiting on Africa and we can talk about the possible tours."

"Find business advisors whether you have any previous business experience or not," says Karen, the expert on Savannah, Georgia. "You can always go to the SBA or get a SCORE advisor. [SCORE is composed of retired business professionals who volunteer to assist new business owners in their quest for success.] Join the Chamber of Commerce, or better yet, the Small Business Chamber, the Women's Business Group, or some other organization that will help you find people to advise you."

"Be creative," advises Connie G., the specialist in travel for the physically challenged. "Develop specialties. Take a look at what you're interested in and make a niche out of it."

"Get good advice on writing a business plan and figuring your taxes," counsels Judy, the cooking school rep. She also thinks it's

> **Beware!**
> The fear of failure prevents more would-be business owners from succeeding than just about any other factor. Some are so scared of failing that they never start. Don't let this happen to you!

crucial to screen "the people [cooking schools, in Judy's case] you'll be representing very carefully to make sure they're good."

As for customer relations, "Use technology to the fullest but treat the customer as if he or she is sitting across the desk from you," says Geoff Millar of Ultimate All-Inclusive Vacations in Arizona.

Barry S., the racecar enthusiast based in Newport Beach, says, "Do something you love. If the profits aren't excessive, or [are] nonexistent to start with, you'll still want to continue."

And in Seattle, walking tour and event expert Terry S. advises, "Do it because 1) you think you can do it well, and 2) you really would enjoy it. Don't do it to make big money. If it happens, great, but don't count on it. Be prepared to work hard and long at it to be successful in the sense of 'I'm glad I'm doing this!'"

Yin and Yang

If you're the type of person who can handle the ups and downs of entrepreneurship in general, and the yin and yang of creativity and the number crunching that makes up the specialty travel world, you'll probably thrive. If not, you may discover during your company's first year of life, or beyond, that the business isn't for you. You may feel that instead of flying high, you're contemplating bailing out.

You Need Not Do It All Yourself

Business experts tend to agree that a team can be the best solution most of the time. Since most people do not excel at everything such as providing a product or service, marketing that product or service, handling financial matters, and being the tech expert, don't be scared to ask for help in areas in which you need it. You may not have the funds to pay, but you can usually find help from family, friends, neighbors, and students looking to learn about the business. Plus, you may be able to pay off your helpers with some great travel deals. The point is, nearly every major success story in the business world has involved some helpers in key areas. Don't try doing everything yourself. Remember Mark Zukerberg of Facebook fame had Dustin Moskovitz. Sears had Roebuck, Ben had Jerry, and numerous entrepreneurs have had a partner who excelled in areas in which they did not, or in which they had no interest or passion.

Whether or not you're earning money, the success of your business is contingent on a happiness factor. Since running a business takes a lot of work and a lot of responsibility, you may discover that you'd be just as happy or more so working for someone else—and that's OK. With everything you will have learned from trying to be an entrepreneur, you'll be a great job candidate.

However, none of the entrepreneurs interviewed for this book, from a relative newcomer to a veteran with 30-plus years seems to have any intention of packing it in. Rather, they seem to have a sense of delight in doing what they enjoy.

Bumps on the Road

Is it all sunshine and roses? Nope. Even the most successful travel specialists hit some bumps on the road to success. For some it is a tour that just doesn't catch on or one that has caught on for so many competitors that the specialist is squeezed out of the region. In other cases Mother Nature can wreak havoc and leave travelers stranded, disappointed, and in need of rescue—and refunds. Modern technology has been a blessing but also a culprit, with glitches and malfunctions that have resulted in lost information or bookings going awry. In some cases, it is simply a combination of more expenses than profits or poor marketing that causes a bad year. Most successful travel agents will tell their stories of starting out with some ups and downs before they began to see the profits they had worked so hard to attain.

Some Kind of Wonderful

Lest you decide to turn tail and run after some bad experiences or down years, Karen A. points out that the road to success is paved with far more good experiences than bad.

A good experience for Karen has been realizing what competent employees she has, employees who can handle even the toughest situations on their own. Karen remembers, "There was the time Beth and I had gone to visit a barrier island—out of mobile phone range. Janis was in Savannah with a Girl Scout troop scheduled for outdoor activities, in what turned out to be ten inches of rain in seven hours." The group was scheduled for visits to "the Railroad Roundhouse (which was flooded); a walking tour; a program at the [Juliette Gordon Low] Birthplace, which [had] a flooded entrance and backed-up sewer; a picnic in Pulaski Square; and dinner at the Pirates House, which by midday [had] a ceiling from which tiles [were] falling."

Karen explains that her employee, Janis, was able to reschedule the events and bring the Scouts safely back to their hotel. Janis then arranged for their picnic supplier to bring the picnic to the hotel, which graciously offered the use of a breakfast room

Wheel and Deal

As an up-and-coming travel professional, you need to keep your costs pared to the bone to make a profit. So whether you're inquiring about special software, print advertising space, printing services, or suppliers' products, the key word is to negotiate. Don't accept the first price anybody quotes you. Ask for a better deal, and surprisingly enough, you'll often get it.

Besides bargaining, shop around. Get quotes from several suppliers. Talk to suppliers about discounts. Don't be afraid to ask questions. Nobody expects you to be an expert on everything, especially not in the early stages of your business. Remember, if you don't ask, you don't learn.

for the Scouts' meal. Karen recounts that dinner also had to be rerouted. Janis called a local café, covered the meal with her own credit card, and "subsequently [pointed] out to me that all this proved cheaper than several of the restaurants we regularly use," says Karen.

What Will It Be Like For You?

It's hard to look at the success and failures of past travel agents and get a good idea of how it will work out for you once you embark on your own business. For one thing, the business has changed tremendously in the past few years and continues to change. Technology was once a tool that travel agents used and their customers knew very little about. Today, the internet has created a glut of savvy travelers, many of whom book their own trips through Orbitz, Travelocity, or one of the other popular discount travel sites. These are not really your competitors because as a travel agent, you are offering more than just quick budget fares. There is room for online travel booking and travel agents, only you need to be savvier than your clients and know that much more. Therefore, as mentioned earlier, you have to stay one step ahead of the learning curve by being privy to information from travel organizations, trade magazines, online travel agent discussion groups, and anything else that separates you from the glut of online sites.

As one host agency owner noted, "We need a better name for homebased agents." While he may be right, it is a changing world, and unlike ten years ago, people are not taken aback by someone working from home—in fact, today, thanks to communications technology, millions of people are running homebased businesses, and many of those who are not are bugging their superiors about the option of telecommuting. The technology of today is available for everyone, but you can use it to your advantage by being creative, shrewd, and ready to take on the travel industry with an "I can do this" attitude.

If you go into this business with the right stuff—the willingness to work hard and to learn everything you can, the confidence to market yourself and your business, and the drive to succeed—chances are you will!

Appendix
Travel Resources

They say you can never be rich enough or young enough. While this could be argued, we say, "You can never have enough resources." Therefore, we present a wealth of sources for you to check out.

These sources are tidbits, ideas to get you started on your research. They are by no means the only sources out there. We've done our research, but businesses—like people—do tend to move, change, fold, and expand. As we have repeatedly stressed, do your homework. Get out and start investigating and you will find numerous travel resources.

Associations

Adventure Travel Trade Association (ATTA), 601 Union Street, 42nd Floor, Seattle, WA 98101, (360) 805-3131, www.adventuretravel.biz

Air Transport Association of America (ATA), 1301 Pennsylvania Ave. NW, #1100, Washington, DC 20004-1707, (202) 626-4000, www.air-transport.org

Airlines Reporting Corporation, ARC Corporate Communications, 1530 Wilson Blvd., #800, Arlington, VA 22209-2448, (703) 816-8525, www.arccorp.com

American Society of Travel Agents (ASTA), 1101 King St., #200, Alexandria, VA 22314, (800) 275-2782, www.astanet.com

Cruise Lines International Association (CLIA), Florida Headquarters (Marketing, public relations, membership, agent training, and support), 910 SE 17th Street, Suite 400, Fort Lauderdale, FL 33316, (754) 224-2200, www.cruising.org

The International Air Transport Association (IATA), Montreal, (514) 874-0202, www.IATA.org

International Airlines Travel Agency Network (IATAN),703 Waterford Way, Suite 300, Miami, FL 33126, (877) 734-2826, www.iatan.org

International Ecotourism Society (TIES), P.O. Box 96503, #34145, Washington, DC 20090-6503, (202) 506-5033, www.ecotourism.org

National Association of Career Travel Agents (NACTA), 1101 King Street, Suite 200, Alexandria, VA 22314, (703) 739-6826, www.nacta.com

National Association of Cruise Oriented Agencies (NACOA), www.nocoaonline.com

North American Travel Journalists Association (NATJA), 150 S. Arroyo Parkway, 2nd Floor, Pasadena, CA 91107, (626) 376-9754, www.natja.org

Outside Sales Support Network (OSSN) (supports homebased travel agents), 22410 68th Ave. East, Bradenton, FL 34211, (941) 322-9700, www.ossn.com

United States Tour Operators Association (USTOA), 275 Madison Ave., #2014, New York, NY 10016, (212) 599-6599, www.ustoa.com

Books

Home Based Travel Affiliate, Tom Ogg, Tom Ogg and Associates, 2007

How to Start a Home Based Travel Agency, Tom and Joanie Ogg, Tom Ogg and Associates, 2001

The Travel Agent's Complete Desk Reference, Kelly Monaghn, The Intrepid Traveler, 5th Edition, 2009

Travel Perspectives: A Guide to Becoming a Travel Professional, Ginger Gorham and Susan Rice, Delmar Cengage Learning, 4th edition, 2006

Consortia

Cruise Shoppes America Ltd., 2690 Weston Road, #200 Weston, FL 33331, (954) 888-9779, www.cruiseshoppes.com

Vacation.com, 1650 King Street, Suite 450, Alexandria, VA 22314, (800) 843-0733, www.vacation.com

The Nest, 43 South Street, Oyster Bay, NY 11771, (888) 245-6378, ext. 3002, (516) 624-6024, www.jointhenest.com

Helpful Government Agencies

Bureau of the Census, www.census.gov

Internal Revenue Service, www.irs.gov

U.S. Postal Service, (800) ASK-USPS (275-8777), www.usps.com

United States Small Business Administration, (800) 827-5722, www.sba.gov

Magazines and Publications

Cruise Travel **magazine**, published by World Publishing Company, 990 Grove Street, Evanston, IL 60201-4370, (847) 491-6440, www.cruisetravelmag.com

FAMfacts, GTC FAMfacts, 717 St. Joseph Dr., St. Joseph, MI 49085, (650) 380-4888, www.famfacts.com

Hotel & Travel Index, Northstar Travel Media, LLC, 500 Plaza Drive, Secaucus, NJ 07094, (877) 410-1484, (201) 902-2000, www.hotelandtravelindex.com

JAX FAX Travel Marketing, 52 West Main Street, Milford, CT 06460, (203) 301-0255, www.jaxfax.com

Meetings & Conventions, Northstar Travel Media, LLC, 500 Plaza Drive, Secaucus, NJ 07094-3626, (201) 902-2000, www.meetings-conventions.com

Specialty Travel Index, #313, PO Box 458, San Anselmo, CA 94979, (415) 455-1643, (888) 624-4030, (415) 455-1643, www.specialtytravel.com

Travel Agent, www.travelagentcentral.com

Travel Pulse, published by Travelliance Inc . 593 Rancocas Road, Westampton NJ 08060, (856) 505-1400, www.travelpulse.com

Travel Trade, www.traveltrademagazine.com

Travel Weekly, (303) 470-4445, www.travelweekly.com

TravelWireNews, eTurboNews Inc., www.travelwirenews.com

Weissmann Travel Reports, Northstar Travel Media, LLC, 500 Plaza Drive, Secaucus, NJ 07094-3626, (800) 776-0720 or (336) 714-3328, www.weissmann.com

These are just some of the many travel magazines and publications available, both trade and commercial. Few industries have as many magazines and newsletters as the travel industry, even with the multitude of websites. *Note*: Most magazines will send a sample issue free of charge if you call and ask. So be sure to!

Mailing Lists

Allmedia International, AllMedia Inc., 5601 Democracy Dr., Plano, TX 75024, (469) 467-9100, (800) 466-4061, www.allmediainc.com

American List Counsel, American List Counsel Inc., 4300 Route 1, CN-5219, Princeton, NJ 08543, (609) 580-2800, www.alcdata.com

Travel-Specific Software

The three companies listed below are the leaders in software and solutions for the travel industry, offering a number of products.

Amadeus, 9250 N.W. 36th St., Miami, FL 33178, (1-888-Amadeus)

Amadeus North America's Canadian office, 14 Duncan Street, Suite 301, Toronto, Ontario, Canada, M5H 3G8, (888) 611-5554

Galileo by Travelport, Morris Corporate Center III, 400 Interpace Pkwy., Parsippany, NJ 07054, (973) 939-1000, www.travelport.com

ITAMS Ltd., 1339 Twp. Rd. 653, Ashland, OH 44805, (419) 282-6484, www.itams.com (makers of ClientEase)

Sabre Travel Network, Sabre Holdings Corporation, 3150 Sabre Drive, Southlake, TX 76092, (682) 605-1000, www.sabretravelnetwork.com (makers of ClientBase)

Travel Websites

Aardvark Travel, www.aardvarktravel.net

All-Hotels, www.all-hotels.com

Home Based Travel Agent, www.homebasedtravelagent.com

International Airlines Travel Network, www.iatan.org

itravelnet Travel Directory, www.itravelnet.com

Life & Travel Hotel & Resort Guide, www.lifentravel.com

My Travel Agents.com, www.mytravelagents.com

Ready American, www.ready.gov

Travel Agent Sites, www.travelagentsites.com

Travel Institute, www.thetravelinstitute.com

Travel Now, www.travelnow.com

Tripadvisor.com, www.tripadvisor.com

Vax Vacation Access (web-based bookings for travel agents), www.vaxvacationaccess.com

Video Globetrotter, www.videoglobetrotter (travel videos), YtbTravel, www.ytbtravel.com

Some Leading Host Travel Agencies

Archer Travel, 4148 Ocean View Blvd., Montrose, CA 91020, (818) 236-4250, www.archertravel.com

American Discount Cruises & Travel, 376 Rte. 9 North Englishtown, NJ 07726, (866) 214-7447, www.sellcruisesfromhome.com

Authorized Agents, 30230 Rancho Viejo Rd., # 108, San Juan Capistrano, CA 92675, (800) 684-3260 ext. 205, www.authorizedagents.com

Carlson Wagonlit Travel, All About Travel Inc., Robert J. van Bloemendaal, CTC, owner, 1901 Northwest Hwy, Ste. 104, Garland, TX 75041-4850, (800) 856-3228, www.carlsonwagonlit.com

Coral Sands Travel, 1165 Riverbend Dr., LaBelle, FL 33935, (863) 675-9900, www.coralsandstravel.com

Cruise Planners/American Express, 3300 N. University Dr., Coral Springs, FL 33065, (888) 582-2150, www.cruiseplannersfranchise.com

Montrose Travel, 2349 Honolulu Ave., Montrose, CA 91020-1821, (800) 870-5799, www.MTravel.com

Travel Quest, 6597 Laketowne Place, Ste. A, Albertville, MN 55301, (800) 392-6484, www.TQagents.com

For a list of travel host agencies you can also visit www.nacta.com/nacta_hosts.aspx or www.homebasedtravelagent.com/hosts.htm

Some Successful Travel Agents and Tour Operators

AAT Kings Tours, (Tour Operators) Jeff Adam, vice president of sales and marketing, 801 East Katella Ave., 3rd Floor, Anaheim, CA 92805, (866) 240-1659, www.aatkings.com

Austin Lehman Adventures, Dan Austin, founder and director, PO Box 81025, Billings, MT 59108-1025, (800) 575-1540, www.austinlehman.com

Connie George Travel Associates, Connie G., owner, PO Box 312, Glenolden, PA 19036, (888) 532-0989, (610) 532-0989, www.cgta.com

Cruise and Land Affairs, Jim and Nancy Terracciano, owners, (410) 257-4300 or (800) 860-8802, www.facebook.com/CruiseandLandAffairs

Cuisine International, Judy Ebrey, owner, PO Box 25228, Dallas, TX 75225, (214) 373-1161, www.cuisineinternational.com

The Flagg Agency, Chuck Flagg, owner, a Cruise Holidays franchise, (770) 355-9569, http://cflagg.cruiseholidays.com

Grand Prix Tours, Barry Simpson, president, 26 Corporate Plaza, #l50, Newport Beach, CA 92660, (800) 400-1998, www.gptours.com

J&L Travel, Jesse M. MacKay, owner, 4 Woodlee Ct. North, Homosassa, FL, (352) 382-7708 or (866) 257-3466, www.jandltravel.com

Jordan Associate Travel Service (JETS & ASAP Travel), Margie Jordan, CEO, PO Box 551235, Jacksonville, FL 32255-1235, (888) 745-2727 ext. 702, www.margiejordan.com

KS Travel and Tours LLC, Kerrie Strumolo owner, 24 Patton Court, Wayne, NJ 07470, email:kextravel@yahoo.com

New York Talks and Walks, Dr. Phil Schoenberg, founder and owner, 65-45 Parsons Blvd., Flushing, NY 11365, (888) 377-4455, www.newyorktalksandwalks.com

Odysseys Unlimited, Sue Bonchi, vice president of marketing, 2 Newton Place, 255 Washington Street, #240, Newton, MA 02458, (617) 454-9105, www.odysseys-unlimited.com

One World Trekking, Andy Crisconi, founding director, PO Box 3084, Aspen, CO 81612, (970) 945-2601, www.oneworldtrekking.com

Rod and Reel Adventures, Dale Williams owner, 32617 Skyhawk Way, Eugene, OR 97405, (541) 349-0777, www.rodreeladventures.com

Seattle Walking Tours & Events, Terry S., 11980 SE 87th Ct., Newcastle, WA 98056-1743, (425) 226-7641, www.see-seattle.com

Joselyn Tepper & Associates Inc., Dr. Robert W. Jocelyn, Bruce B. Tepper and Maxi S. Joselyn, principals, 8075 E. Morgan Trail, #1, Scottsdale, AZ 85258, (480) 443-0098, www.joselyntepper.com

Toni Tours Inc., Toni Lanotte-Day, owner, Levittown, NY 11756, (516) 369-5738, www.tonitours.net

Tootsy Tours Inc., PO Box 30279, Savannah, GA 31410, (888) 736-3828, www.tootsytours.com

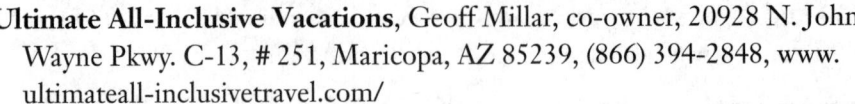

Ultimate All-Inclusive Vacations, Geoff Millar, co-owner, 20928 N. John Wayne Pkwy. C-13, # 251, Maricopa, AZ 85239, (866) 394-2848, www.ultimateall-inclusivetravel.com/

VIP Vacations Inc., Jennifer Doncsecz, president, 3108 Sodl Lane, Whitehall, PA 18052, (800) 678-2274, www.travelbyvip.com

Glossary

Accredited Cruise Counselor (ACC): CLIA certification to sell its members' cruises.

Adventure travel: leisure vacations typically focusing on outdoor activities or cultural exploration.

Adventure Travel Society (ATS): professional association of adventure travel tour operators.

Affinity group: tour group with a particular interest, such as genealogy or gardening.

Air-inclusive: tour package that includes airfare to the tour's origination city in the price.

Airlines Reporting Corporation (ARC): Company that handles airline ticket distribution, control, and settlement. They also control ticket stock and accreditation of travel agencies that issue airline tickets.

Air Transport Association of America (ATA): an industry group made up of the major domestic airlines.

American Society of Travel Agents (ASTA): professional association of travel agents.

Appointment: designation to write airline or other travel product tickets.

Base fare: air, cruise, or other fare excluding taxes and other fees.

Booking: a travel reservation.

Certified Travel Agent (CTA): certification available from the Institute of Certified Travel Agents.

Comp: abbreviation for complimentary; in this context, a hotel room, meal, or other product given for free.

Computerized Reservation System (CRS): online system for booking airline and other travel product reservations; also known as Global Distribution System (GDS).

Concierge: guest assistant that is part of a hotel staff.

Consolidator: a company that buys bulk airline tickets and resells them at discounted rates.

Consortium: a group of suppliers—like tour operators and cruise lines that enter into a shared association. As a result, they can provide higher commissions to travel agents in exchange for doing a specific volume of business with them.

Cruise Lines International Association (CLIA): a marketing association made up of international cruise lines that accredits travel agents to sell cruises.

Deadheading: driving an empty bus from a passenger drop-off point back to a home base.

Double occupancy: travel term meaning that the price must be multiplied by two because it assumes two people will occupy a cabin or room.

Ecotour: tour focusing on ecologically or environmentally sensitive areas and practices, aka Green Tour.

e-Ticket: electronic ticket issued by airlines instead of a paper ticket and boarding pass.

Fam trip: abbreviation for familiarization trip, which is a product offered by suppliers to travel sellers at a reduced price to acquaint them with travel opportunities.

Focus group: a small group gathered for the purpose of conducting market research.

Foreign independent tour (FIT): a tour, generally of a foreign destination, in which the client explores on his or her own instead of with a group.

General seating: cruise dining room plan in which passengers do not occupy the same table each night.

Guaranteed group rates (GG rates): term meaning a supplier guarantees a booking agent will match any lower price quoted on the same product to a different agent.

Hard-adventure tours: high-energy tour including athletic-oriented activities like white-water rafting or mountain biking. (*See X-tours.*)

Homebased travel agent: The rapidly growing segment of professional travel agents booking trips, including cruises and worldwide tours, from a home location.

Host agency: travel agency (with appointments to write airfare, cruise, or other travel products) through which travel suppliers sell to homebased agents. Host agencies typically offer homebased agents a higher commission and easier access to numerous travel suppliers.

Hub-and-spoke concept: tour practice of lodging clients at a centrally located hotel and taking day trips to outlying areas.

Inbound operator: tour operator that brings in clients from abroad and takes them around the operator's home region.

Independent travel agent: a travel agent who works alone or with a few associates or employees and is usually homebased.

International Airlines Travel Agent Network (IATAN): industry association that accredits travel agents to sell tickets for international air carriers.

International Air Transport Association (IATA): industry association of international airlines.

Inventory: Rooms or cabins available to be booked.

Land-only: tour package that does not include airfare to the tour's origination city in the price.

Master Cruise Counsellor (MCC): Higher-level CLIA certification to sell its members' cruises.

Meet-and-greet guide: a tour representative who meets clients at the airport and escorts them to their hotel.

Modified American Plan (MAP): tour configuration in which clients are fed two out of three meals a day, usually breakfast and dinner, as part of the tour price.

Motor coach: tour bus.

National Association of Career Travel Agents (NACTA): a professional organization for independent travel agents.

National Association of Cruise Oriented Agencies (NACOA): professional association of travel agencies that specializes in selling cruises.

Option date: the date on which a tour or cruise deposit is due.

Outbound operator: tour operator that takes local clients abroad.

Outfitter: tour operator who provides trip-oriented gear like river rafts or bicycles.

▲

Override: higher-than-average commission awarded by suppliers to highly productive sellers.

Preferred supplier: travel product supplier that rewards highly productive sellers with higher-than-average commissions.

Products: tours, cruises, hotels, and other elements sold by travel agents and tour operators.

Rack rate: the regular rate hotels charge for rooms.

Seller of travel laws: state laws governing travel agents and tour operators.

Single supplement: extra price charged to tour or cruise clients who do not want to share a double-occupancy room or cabin.

Soft-adventure tours: culturally oriented activities like antiquing or gardening.

Spiff: an incentive offered by a supplier such as a bonus, an extremely high commission, or a free product.

Split itinerary: tour configuration in which clients are given a choice of activities on the same day.

Step-on guide: a local guide who steps onto the motor coach to show clients a particular city or area.

Ticketless travel: see e-ticket.

Tour director: tour operator representative who leads clients throughout tour; also called tour manager, tour escort, tour leader, or tour host or hostess.

Tour operator: a company that designs, markets, and runs tours.

Traffic documents: airline tickets.

Travel Industry Association of America: an organization that works to meld the various elements of the U.S. travel industry into a cohesive group.

Travel supplier: companies such as air and cruise lines, tour operators, and hotels that provide travel products.

Trip cancellation insurance: insurance available to clients to protect against losing deposits or payments in the event of trip cancellation.

United States Tour Operators Association (USTOA): professional association of tour operators.

X-tours: Extreme adventure/action tours featuring adrenaline pumping activities.

Index